MANAGERS MUST LEAD!

*A Supervisor's
Roadmap to Advancement*

By Ray A. Killian

If a company is to stay profitable, the ability to lead people and direct their energies toward desirable goals must be developed in all managers at all levels. MANAGERS MUST LEAD! is directed to those supervisors who are intent on progressing to higher managerial positions. It explains, in the language of supervisors, sound and up-to-date management techniques that can be applied to daily on-the-job activities.

Here is a book that will be extremely helpful for beginners as well as for experienced first-line supervisors and higher-level managers. It is a practical guide that discusses frankly the human aspects of management, including these major subjects:

- ★ The fundamentals of leadership
- ★ The development of responsible work attitudes
- ★ The techniques of motivating employees to achieve maximum job contribution
- ★ The delegation of responsibility and the proper uses of authority
- ★ The methods for handling complaints and the effects of changes.

With this AMA publication you will learn the newest training and interviewing techniques, the best procedures for counseling and rating subordinates, and proven ways to achieve goals through two-way communication.

Ray A. Killian is vice president and director of personnel and public relations for the 400 Belk Department Stores. Mr. Killian is the author of numerous articles and has been chapter president and national director of the Society for Advancement of Management, president of the Personnel Directors Association, and has served on the Board of Directors for the National Retail Merchants Association.

AMERICAN MANAGEMENT ASSOCIATION

Managers Must Lead!

Managers Must Lead!

A Supervisor's Roadmap to Advancement

By Ray A. Killian

Illustrated by Alnos Hall

AMERICAN MANAGEMENT ASSOCIATION, INC.

To
Betty, Ray, Jr., and Ann
whose cooperation and understanding
made possible the writing of this book
and
John M. Belk and associates, whose
contributions and activities are reflected in these pages

Preface

THIS BOOK has been written expressly for the ambitious supervisor who is seriously dedicated to climbing the ladder of management success. It deals specifically with those keys to management growth that are based on results through people.

The book will be of greatest benefit to the man or woman who is willing to agree that management leadership consists of certain identifiable tools and techniques, and that these can be mastered through intelligently applied effort. It has in mind the rising executive who is seeking practical guides for effective human achievement. Its premise is that leadership abilities will render a genuine service to the employee and the enterprise—that the supervisor then deserves to increase his span of influence, his leadership role, his achievement, and his job-related personal compensations.

The rule-of-thumb, hit-or-miss method of supervisory leadership is outmoded; neither management nor employee will tolerate its haphazard handling of people or its uncertain results. Rather, the demand today is for leadership that is skillful in applying tested techniques that insure complete utilization of every resource at its command— recognizing that if the employee fails to make a contribution equal to his fullest potential, a share of the blame belongs to leadership. Why? Because it has failed to meet its responsibility for providing sufficient knowledge, skills, and motivation.

Leaders are busy people. They want to get right down to realistic facts—facts proved by successful experience. These pages offer specific guides and principles, supported by illustrative examples, for dealing with the very real drama of everyday human problems. The book is based on many years of firing-line experiences in handling all types of situations involving all levels of employees and management in a variety of types and sizes of companies, as well as a great many leadership and supervisory training sessions.

Appropriate consideration is given to the traditional concepts of human relations, but equal attention is paid to firm, unvarying adherence to reasonable standards of job performance. Although the responsibility of leadership is significant, management has not surrendered its traditional prerogatives; it cannot rely solely on voluntary performance. The employee has an obligation—of which he must be made fully aware—to respond substantially to sound leadership as it relates to job performance.

The principles of human relations and the achievement of results through people are universal. Thus the guides in this book apply with equal force to all leaders whose accomplishments hinge on motivating people effectively. Whether the reader is a beginner or is an experienced first-line supervisor, he should find here recommendations that are both realistic and practical. They should even benefit higher-level managers, up to and including the top executive himself, as well as civic and church leaders.

The book should provide an excellent self-training program. It is also suitable as a textbook for college and company courses, each chapter supplying the subject matter for one or more sessions. It should, in brief, serve as a realistic reference for supervisors and would-be supervisors who are concerned with goal achievement—both for themselves and for their people—right now.

Mastery of this material will not guarantee management growth. The book does, however, represent a map of the road traveled successfully by many who are top executives today. It can therefore open the opportunity doorway. But the degree to which the individual applies himself and succeeds in increasing his managerial ability will of course determine the degree to which he is able to take advantage of that opportunity and hence his ultimate role in management.

The supervisor's future, in other words, is in his own hands. It is possible to learn to manage effectively; the genius of leadership is effort applied intelligently and persistently in building according to a master blueprint.

Ray A. Killian

Contents

1. Keys to Getting Results Through People.   13
   Human Behavior Is Predictable—The Human Factors in
   Achievement—The Humanizing Revolution—The Fine Art
   of Working with People—Supervisory Guides to Effective
   Human Relations—Results Depend on Adherence to Guides

2. Leadership for Goal Achievement.   22
   Leadership Can Be Exciting—Recognizing Leadership—The
   Many Forms of Leadership—The Primary Functions of
   Leadership—Profile of the Effective Leader—Guides to the
   Practice of Leadership—Keys to Improved Leadership—Lead-
   ership and Executive Growth

3. Mastering the Skills of Managing People.   37
   A Craftsman Needs Tools—Key Human Factors in Super-
   vision—Tools and Techniques for Handling Human Problems
   —The Leader and His Tools

4. Understanding Human Behavior.   51
   Man's Behavior Can Be Understood—Sources of Job-Related
   Satisfaction—Laws of Human Association

5. Creating Positive Job Attitudes.   64
   Understanding Attitudes—Significant Facts Concerning Attitudes—Responsibility for Attitude Development—Guides for
   Changing Attitudes—The Supervisor's Own Attitude Development

6. The Key to Controlling and Changing Behavior.   73
   Why People Behave the Way They Do—Environmental and
   Cultural Influences—Changing Behavior by Changing Causes
   —Causation and Its Effect on Supervision

7. Minimizing Frustration for Improved Results..........   82
    Sources of Frustration—Symptoms of Frustration—Four Pat-
    terns of Frustrated Behavior—Preventing and Remedying
    Frustration—When the Employee Reaches His Ceiling, Then
    What?

8. Motivation for Maximum Job Contribution............   92
    The Fine Art of Motivation—How People Can Be Motivated
    —Factors Which Determine Response to Motivation—Guides
    for Effective Use of Motivation—Putting Motivation into
    Practice—Motivating Employee Cooperation—Job Interest
    and Motivation—Motivation and Efficiency—Self-Motivation

9. Correction: The Unique Opportunity................   113
    Correction Demands Top Skills—The Unique Service of
    Correction—The Appropriate Approach to Correction—The
    Correction Procedure—Conducting the Correction Interview
    —Guides in the Effective Use of Correction—Tips on Main-
    taining Good Discipline and a Productive Environment—The
    Supervisor's Own Attitude and Correction

10. Guides for Handling Complaints and Changes..........   128
    Two Types of Employee Complaints—Possible Approaches
    to Handling Grievances—A Four-Step Guide to Handling
    Grievances—Skillful Handling of Change—Types of Job-
    Related Changes—Reasons for Resistance to Change—Guides
    for Reducing Resistance to Change

11. Techniques of Learning............................   139
    The Learning Machinery—Basic Laws of Learning—Methods
    of Learning—Determinants of Learning—Methods of Gaining
    Attention—Steps in the Learning Process—Influences on
    Learning Achievement—Changing Incorrect Learning—
    Learning and Supervision

12. Improving Knowledge and Skills Through Training......   153
    Objectives of Training—Effective Training Techniques—Im-
    portant Training Guides—Selecting and Training an Assistant
    Supervisor

13. Improving Memory and Retention.................... 165

Reasons for Poor Memory—How Ideas and Events Can Be
Recalled—Techniques for Remembering Names—Supervision
and Memory

14. Harmonious Results in Working with Women.......... 173

Placement of Women—Assisting the New Employee—Criticizing and Counseling Women—Identifiable Female Types—
Some Common Misconceptions—Evaluating Women as Supervisors—Opportunities for Women as Supervisors—Special
Note

15. Counseling: Helpful Understanding................... 186

The Goal of Counseling—The Counseling Technique—Areas
of Employee Counseling—Developing Counseling Skills

16. Evaluating and Improving Job Performance............ 195

Purpose of a Rating Program—Advantages to the Company
and the Department—Methods of Rating—Successful Performance Appraisal—The Supervisor's Role—Training of
Raters—Common Rating Errors—Characteristics of a Good
Rater—The Rating Procedure—The Evaluation Interview—
Conducting the Interview—Concluding the Interview—Utilization of Evaluation Results—Follow-up

17. Technique for Improved Work Methods.............. 210

Approaches to Methods Improvement—Analysis of Work
Methods—Guides for Improving Work Procedures

18. Effective Delegation of Responsibility................ 219

How Well Do You Delegate?—The Need to Delegate—Selective Delegation of Authority—Mastering the Skill of Delegating

19. Goal Achievement Through Two-Way Communication... 228

Underlying Concepts—The Supervisor's Communication Role
—What to Communicate—Communications Media—Improv-

ing the Downward Flow of Information—Increasing the Upward Flow—Suggestion Systems—Developing the Skill of Listening—Guides to More Effective Communication

20. Creativity: Pearl of Great Price..................... 240
Ideas Don't Just Happen—Brainstorming: Group Ideation—Selling Ideas—Fly High on Jet-Propelled Ideas

21. Guides to Favorable Public Relations................ 248
Creating a Favorable Corporate Image—Go the Extra Mile

22. Moving up the Executive Ladder.................... 255
Keys to Executive Progress—Resources for Self-Development—Executive Development: Whose Responsibility?

23. A Program for Executive Growth.................... 265
Building Blocks for Executive Growth—Move Forward and Upward

24. Conclusions Worth Applying....................... 277
The Moral Responsibilities of Leadership—The Goal of Involvement and Participation—Unlocking the Doors to Future Growth—Building the Steps to Success

About the Author...................................... 285

The art of developing effective relationships is the best known and the most inefficiently practiced of all human activities.

1. Keys to Getting Results Through People

EXECUTIVE VICE PRESIDENT JOHN BARBOUR: I'm in favor of giving the promotion to Fred Morton. He knows how to get others to work and how to build a team.

GENERAL MANAGER DAVID HELMS: I agree that Fred is a good man, but he hasn't been with us nearly as long as several of the others who are expecting this promotion.

MR. BARBOUR: David, you're probably right. But let me ask you, what do we spend the most money for around here? Payroll—that's what takes the largest share of the expense dollar. Now, which one of the supervisors out there is getting the best return for those payroll dollars? Fred Morton, that's who. Fred has demonstrated during the past two years that he knows how to get along with people. He keeps his people satisfied; and what's more important, he has the top production department. His people are well trained; he has practically no turnover; he's firm, but they still think he's a great guy; he knows everyone in the department; he always seems to know how his people will react and exactly what they can be expected to do.

MR. HELMS: Yes, when you put it that way, I begin to see what you mean.

MR. BARBOUR: What's more, a man who has done that kind of job is needed in a bigger job. He develops people and makes money for the company. We want more of both. David, you talk with Fred Morton and tell him that as of the first of the month he will be plant superintendent. Any man who can handle people the way he does

The ability to predict what people will do and how they will react has tremendous potential.

deserves a bigger job. In the meantime we'll have the necessary meetings to make the announcement.

It was in this manner, and for these reasons, that Fred Morton became plant superintendent of the Marion Manufacturing Company. He had been a foreman for only two years and was promoted over three senior foremen, *because he knew how to get results through people*.

Yes, leaders can predict with a practical degree of accuracy the reaction, job performance, and total contribution of other people. A leader's actual success depends on his ability to anticipate those responses and to exert those influences which will result in the reactions and job performance that will contribute most to the desired goals. This book is concerned primarily with the implementation of this fundamental as applied to human achievement.

HUMAN BEHAVIOR IS PREDICTABLE

It *is* possible to predict human behavior. The industrial firm and the gasoline company predict percentages of honesty before extending credit. The bank teller greets customers graciously, thanks them for their business, and invites them back because this procedure will result in a more favorable customer reaction. The bank recognizes that a favorable reaction is desirable and has learned how to bring it about.

Being able to anticipate and predict what people will do and how they can be expected to react has tremendous potential. It means that, on the basis of his knowledge of human behavior and of his own group, the supervisor is able to forecast job activity, attitudes, reactions—and results. This ability should lead him to exert that type of influence which will bring about the desired job performance and encourage him to enlarge on the favorable influences and minimize the negative ones.

The executive must also recognize that in order to achieve certain established goals, specific things must happen. He knows the reactions and job performance he needs. It follows, then, that his knowledge of people should give him the keys to insure that these reactions and this performance will occur. He is in essence predicting human behavior and then bringing to bear those influences which will lead to desirable activity.

Because experience has proved that certain procedures are most effective in achieving a favorable response, definite fundamental rules have emerged that can be used as guides. Disregard of these rules will lead to poor results. The quest for satisfactory results, through people, must begin with an understanding of goals and then go logically through a series of steps, as follows:

1. It begins with an identification of the exact results desired, including production goals, economical use of resources, and the maintenance of favorable working relationships. Once this picture has been clarified, then the process involves determining what activity must occur before these results can be achieved.

2. Accomplishment is based on the occurrence of certain job activity. Something has to happen: Things have to be done; jobs must be performed; energy must be brought to bear on the problem. The supervisor determines what must be done to accomplish the results desired and how people must be influenced to apply themselves in the most efficient manner.

3. The greatest area of opportunity for leadership lies in influencing performance. Here the supervisor applies his knowledge of people and human skills to exert the appropriate influence that will bring about the specific activity which will lead to the desired results.

4. The supervisor now moves to the individual and group resources available to him. Because he must build on and operate through the strengths and weaknesses of individuals, he tries to employ only the best-qualified people available. He determines the most effective way to work with each member of the group and seeks to utilize each one's potential to a maximum degree. Then he sets into motion as part of the continuing job environment those factors which are most effective in causing the individual and the team to engage in the appropriate activity to a sufficient degree to achieve the goal.

Once this process is understood and applied, the supervisor should achieve maximum results through people. However, the degree of success depends on the leader's skill in influencing appropriate job performance. This influence, in turn, depends on a thorough understanding of people and their basic behavior patterns, together with the leader's ability to bring them to bear effectively on the problems at hand.

THE HUMAN FACTORS IN ACHIEVEMENT

It is a modern-day paradox that, in spite of automation, executives are becoming increasingly aware of the critical need for people who willingly and skillfully apply themselves to job requirements. The problem is one not of machines but of people. When a machine is needed for a particular job, one can be bought or designed. If it does not function properly, a skilled mechanic can repair it without delay or difficulty. The power of the machine can be stepped up, or it can be rewired to change its output. However complicated the machine, it is still relatively simple as compared with the challenges of altering the input-output of the human component in production. Yet this is precisely the responsibility of the supervisor, and one that he can handle with skill only if he recognizes and follows the rules of the "human game."

THE HUMANIZING REVOLUTION

Today approximately 90 percent of human failures on the job are the result of a breakdown in human relations. The individual fails to make the proper adjustments in his association with others and thus decreases his effectiveness in the group, develops a negative attitude toward his job, loses confidence in himself, and nullifies his job contribution.

A recognition of this problem has led management to seek solutions to it. It was discovered early that slave labor and brute force are too costly and inefficient. In 1776 Adam Smith offered a key in *An Inquiry into the Nature and Causes of the Wealth of Nations.* His theory was that management should treat its employees with consideration and understanding. This approach, he reasoned, would in turn cause the employee to give the job his maximum effort. The theory was fine, but managers did not consider it necessary to cultivate the goodwill of employees because, in the early years of the Industrial Revolution, the workers available far outnumbered the jobs to be filled.

During the early 1920's industrial engineers began to look in earnest for the most effective methods of managing employees. They had only limited success because there was still a surplus of labor. Then, during World War II, almost 25 percent of the workforce was taken into the armed services; and the manager who was tempted to discharge a slow, insufficiently trained, or inadequately motivated employee had to stop and realize that if this were done, chances were that there would be no one to take his place.

Now the search for the most effective way to get people to produce had to be pursued in earnest.

The procedure that was eventually developed was actually a restatement of the human relations concepts taught in the New Testament. It hinged on the importance of every human life, the need for human dignity, consideration for the individual, and an attempt to conduct the total enterprise in such a manner as to merit each person's maximum contribution.

Clarence Francis, while chairman of General Foods, best expressed this new philosophy with these words:

> You can buy a man's time, you can buy a man's physical presence at a given place, you can even buy a measured number of skilled muscular motions per hour or day. But you cannot buy enthusiasm, you cannot buy initiative, you cannot buy loyalty, you cannot buy the devotion of hearts, minds, and souls. You have to earn these things. . . . It is ironical that Americans—the most advanced people technically, mechanically, and industrially—should have waited until a comparatively recent period to inquire into the most promising source of productivity; namely, the human will to work. It is hopeful, on the other hand, that this search is now under way.

It was this search for the key to "the human will to work" that caused the humanizing revolution in the relationship of manager and managed in the industrial world. It led to programs of training in human relations for all levels of management. It led to a revamping of employee benefits and of the entire structure of the business organization. In fact, the pendulum swung so far that supervisors were concentrating more on understanding people than on meeting production schedules. This caused Malcolm McNair, Harvard Business School professor, to state:

> The world's work has to be done, and people have to take responsibility for their own work and own lives. Too much emphasis on

human relations encourages people to feel sorry for themselves. It makes it easier for them to slough off responsibility, to find excuses for failure, and to act like children. When somebody falls down on a job, but does not behave in accordance with codes, we look into his psychological background for factors that may be used as excuses. Undue preoccupation with human relations saps individual responsibility, leads us not to think about the job any more and about getting it done, but only about people and their relations.*

Emphasis on a benevolent managerial philosophy is no panacea; it has significant value and must be a part of the process of getting results through people, but it is not an excuse for accepting less than every man's best. A proper balance must be maintained and should include fairness, firmness, and a consideration for the individual's feelings. However, it should be clear at all times that a man is being paid to get a job done and that the expectation of certain results is not unreasonable. It is also good human relations not to retain a man on the job if he fails to live up to his responsibilities after management has made every reasonable effort to provide the necessary job ingredients.

The supervisor, then, has the challenge of bringing into proper relationship a consideration for the individual and maintenance of a high standard of production. This requires skillful leadership and appropriate consideration for the human aspects.

THE FINE ART OF WORKING WITH PEOPLE

Modern management seeks to practice the art of working with people in such a way as to bring about the desired behavior or job performance. This recognizes that the employee is free to apply or not to apply himself fully to the task. It requires effort to harness the human will to get a job done in the prescribed manner. This means that the company must engage in those activities and practices which offer the best chance for achieving maximum results through people.

In applying this philosophy, management accepts the responsibility for providing job knowledge and incentive through training. It accepts the challenge of motivating through fair pay, forms of com-

---

* Personnel Service, NRMA, July-August 1957.

petition, and enlightened leadership. It seeks to provide a favorable job environment, machines, and a functional organization which offer the employee the most productive medium in which to exert his effort.

According to this philosophy, if production schedules fall behind or sales quotas are not met, it does not necessarily follow that the employee is at fault. Management must accept its rightful share of the responsibility for the failure and must make an objective evaluation of the situation and change what must be changed.

SUPERVISORY GUIDES TO EFFECTIVE HUMAN RELATIONS

Perhaps no activity has a more significant common denominator than the basic needs and feelings of people. The prudent supervisor builds his house upon this foundation, but at the same time he makes individual adjustments to suit individual needs. The human leadership program should have these two cornerstones:

1. *Operate from a base of honesty and sincerity.* There is no place in long-range, positive human relationships for the slick operator or the fast talker, for sleight of hand or for fakery. The supervisor must at all times be honest and forthright, and he must deal fairly with his employees.

2. *Job-related activities should be mutually beneficial.* The concept of getting work done through others presupposes that one person will control and direct the activity of other people, not because one person is better than another but simply to assure that assigned responsibilities achieve desired results.

This attempt to influence or persuade should bring about results which will be mutually beneficial. The supervisor should not seek to satisfy his own needs at the expense of others. The practice of effective long-range human relations is built on the premise that positive job performance is beneficial to the employee as well as to the company.

RESULTS DEPEND ON ADHERENCE TO GUIDES

Achievement is dependent on leadership; leadership, on the capacity to influence behavior. Both the leader and the follower require identifiable patterns within which to function—frameworks in which to operate.

The supervisor who expects to get results through people must give attention to effective human relations, a broad understanding of human nature, the practice of certain supervisory rules, and a deliberate course of action. George Halsey summed up the idea best in *Supervising People* when he stated, "It has been demonstrated time and time again that almost any person of normal intelligence and sincere desire to be of service to people can acquire considerable skill in the art of supervising people if he will study its principles and methods and apply them thoughtfully, conscientiously, and persistently."

* * *

Appropriate supervision brings about the best results when it is an intelligent, thoughtful, planned, deliberate, and continuing process. Just as the athlete practices long hours and concentrates on every phase of the game, so must the supervisor. People are complex, their reactions are often puzzling, and their relationships are confusing. The supervisor's capacity for predicting behavior and anticipating job performance can be his most valuable asset as he moves toward goal achievement. The facts, the guides, and the information are available; it is up to the supervisor to assume the initiative in identifying and utilizing them to carry out his duties and responsibilities.

The responsibility for controlling and directing human lives is the most sacred trust of leadership.

2. Leadership for Goal Achievement

THE ABILITY TO LEAD PEOPLE and direct their energies toward desirable goal achievement is the most significant factor in the success of men and enterprises. The speed of growth and the eventual height reached by the man who expects to move upward in accomplishment and monetary reward will be determined by his effectiveness in leading others toward established goals. No business will progress without leadership.

In the final analysis the only real advantage one organization has over another in a competitive economy where each can buy essentially the same products and machinery is the quality of management. Leadership decisions determine who are employed, how they are trained, what supervision they are given, and even how they perform on the job. Leadership decisions determine whether the company grows, what products or services it offers, what direction it takes. In truth, the most vital factor in every business and industrial enterprise is the caliber of its management leadership.

LEADERSHIP CAN BE EXCITING

Although leadership carries a heavy burden of responsibility, it can be an exciting game. It has in it the stimulation of command, organization, and accomplishment, the sense of game participation, and the satisfaction of winning that some people realize through sports. The more a man enjoys it, the more time, attention, and resourcefulness he devotes to it; a keen anticipation of excitement, opportunity, and all of the human compensations which come with quarterbacking the team increase immeasurably his chances of becoming a real "pro" in the big leagues of management.

Leadership can be a completely stimulating activity. For example, take the young man in his late thirties who was one of the principal heirs to a multimillion dollar business. From a financial standpoint, it was not necessary that he work; however, he enjoyed the stimulation of decision making and needed the satisfaction of accomplishment. His associates marveled at his devotion to the almost endless business and civic projects to which he successfully applied his seemingly limitless resources of time and energy. He was a successful leader by every criterion, and much of his accomplishment was attributable to his enthusiastic attitude toward every activity in which he was engaged.

What is leadership and how can it be developed? Shakespeare said in *Twelfth Night* that "some are born great, some achieve greatness, and some have greatness thrust upon them." Since the odds that greatness will be thrust upon most of us are remote, those who seek to achieve greatness—or leadership—must identify the qualities of leadership and devote maximum attention to improving the skills necessary for their application.

Leadership is largely a rational process which becomes the foundation for subsequent action. Popularity is not its chief end. Rather, leadership concentrates on effective relationships with others, maintains respect, but at all times is oriented toward forward movement and achievement.

RECOGNIZING LEADERSHIP

Leadership can be measured by the amount of influence which one individual has over the behavior or job performance of others. If this influence is significant, the leadership is effective. If the influence is slight, then there is almost no leadership—the supervisor has failed to influence others sufficiently. On the other hand, the leader who moves forward is able to bring sufficient influence to bear on the activities of others to orient them toward the desired results.

It is obvious that the supervisor or business leader cannot hope to become successful without the qualities of leadership. The individual

Leadership can be exciting.

who emerges from the group to a position as first-line supervisor, and continues up the ladder to top executive responsibility, is the one who has learned the art of effective leadership and has learned to extend this influence in an ever-widening circle.

THE MANY FORMS OF LEADERSHIP

Concepts of successful leadership have undergone rapid change during recent years. In the era of rugged individualism and "bull of the woods" direction of largely uneducated groups, leadership consisted of physical strength and a show of force. Today factors such as broader education, labor unions, government regulations, improved standards of living, and the concept of individual dignity demand new ideas and patterns.

Today's effective leader must live by today's rules; the old ways not only are ineffective but often result in negative reactions. The modern leader must operate from a solid foundation of knowledge, usually based on formal education and company-initiated programs, and the practice of techniques founded on successful experience. He must lead through persuasion, through example, and through services rendered.

Great leaders come in assorted sizes and shapes. Some exert leadership through political position, some through mental brilliance, some through creativity, and still others through effective organization. Yet there are common denominators which can be identified and used as the foundation for developing effective leadership in business and industry.

During World War II, when our nation was confronted with the need for thousands of leaders in both industry and the armed services, it was discovered that no one really knew what leadership was or understood how to identify potential leaders. Since no criteria had been established, it was impossible to select potential leaders or to develop a training program for them with any degree of success.

Experiments have revealed that leaders emerge when there are problems to be solved. In the absence of problems, people remain an undirected mass; but when difficulties do arise, those who find it to their benefit to have them solved accept the leadership of the person who can point the way to acceptable solutions.

The common mental picture of leadership is that of a spellbinder before a crowd or of a corporation president at the head of the conference table. However, the supervisor who talks over the roar of a machine as he explains a change of production schedule is no less a leader. Regardless of reason or place, leadership denotes dynamic action, movement, activity, organization, purpose, goals, and human resourcefulness. Leadership functions best when it is up and going—when it is maintaining order and direction.

THE PRIMARY FUNCTIONS OF LEADERSHIP

The need for and the characteristics of leadership can best be understood by looking at its functions and what it seeks to accomplish.

Leadership renders a service. This is the most significant single statement that can be made about leadership. No leadership is exercised when employees are serving supervisors; it begins to function when the supervisor begins to serve the employees. He serves them by helping them solve their problems, using his superior knowledge of how to do the job in accordance with guides to improved work methods, increased motivation, and favorable attitudes toward the job. The quantity and quality of results should increase as a direct consequence of this service. The supervisor moves individuals toward fulfillment of their maximum potential, thus increasing their value to themselves and to the enterprise. Leadership thus multiplies the contribution of every individual who is its beneficiary.

Leadership serves the interests of the total activity as well as those of the individual. It is the men who accept and practice the philosophy of service through their knowledge and their ability to lead who become outstanding leaders. People are willing to follow a leader who helps them achieve mutually beneficial goals.

Leadership makes decisions. Movement and progress are initiated and continued through a series of decisions; indecisiveness results in no movement—only in waiting for someone who is both capable of making the right decisions and willing to do so.

The sales promotion department of a large company was beset by constant employee turnover and internal dissatisfaction. During an exit interview with one employee, it was revealed that the principal source of dissatisfaction was the fact that the department head was not a successful decision-maker. Because he delayed making most decisions until the last possible moment, he put everyone in the department under strain and made it almost impossible for the group to produce satisfactory work.

An important function of everyone who supervises is the process of decision making to meet both individual and project needs. This is not a reckless shooting from the hip but a calculated searching for and weighing of facts. The leader practices what he knows to be the successful techniques of decision making in order to keep resources oriented in the right direction, to keep them from becoming sidetracked, and to maintain satisfactory progress.

Leadership elicits response. The very nature of modern leadership requires persuasion. The environment in which leadership operates, even in the company framework, depends on people who are capable of persuading rather than issuing edicts or threats for results.

Sufficient human energy will be applied to a task only by those who respond willingly, and this will happen only after a supervisor has been able to convince them of the advantages of their response. An important function of leadership, then, is to communicate to others sufficient understanding to elicit this response.

The industrial supervisor who seeks to promote safety must be prepared with facts, figures, reasons, and a conviction that safety is essential before satisfactory results will be achieved. Then he must get others to see the importance of safety procedures and equipment in order to gain their willing participation. Leadership functions only as it leads others to sufficient understanding to motivate the response necessary to accomplish the task at hand.

Leadership achieves results. The moment of truth in leadership is the achievement of the result. For all practical purposes, leadership is guiding human energy in a definite direction for a specific purpose. Leadership which dies on the vine or falls by the wayside is like a ship which does not deliver its passengers and cargo safely into port —it has rendered a disservice because it has consumed resources without subsequent benefit.

Great movements in history—and successful companies—have aimed their arrows at great targets. But it was not the aiming or shooting of the arrow that left the mark; rather, it was the hitting of the target. Today's supervisor, too, leaves his mark by hitting his target with results. Excuses may be tabulated by the hundreds, delays may seem justified, but the only significant criterion is what has been achieved.

Leadership is a willingness to be different. Leaders are ordinary human beings who become stars in the game through a willingness to practice harder and longer, master their skills more thoroughly, and engage in those activities which promote growth. This often involves a different discipline and standard of performance from that followed by the nonleader.

PROFILE OF THE EFFECTIVE LEADER

The following list of activities is not a stereotype or a rigid mold into which effective leaders must fit. It is instead a set of guidelines for those who seek to enlarge the scope of their own service and influence.

Leaders maintain respect. It has been asked many times and debated at many levels: What should the relationship be between the supervisor and the supervised? Extremes of overfamiliarity or detachment can be detrimental to the group's mutual aims. The appropriate relationship can be summarized in one word: respect. The leader must respect the individuality, the dignity, and the needs of everyone in the group. He must, through example, integrity, empathy, and overall ability, deserve and receive the respect of others because of what he is and does. Unless he has the respect of others, they will disregard his attempts to lead them. The instinct, the impulse to turn toward another person for direction begins with confidence, builds on respect, and eventually becomes a willingness to follow. The supervisor who expects to lead must create the proper relationships with his people and retain their respect in order to merit their willingness to accept his leadership.

Leaders work effectively with people. The handling of people is leadership in action. Human resources are the principal asset of the leader, and it must therefore follow that his own contribution to the group effort will be dependent on his success in utilizing those resources.

Effective leadership must be based on an identification and skillful implementation of all the established principles of good human relationships, beginning with a knowledge of the fundamentals of psychology and moving progressively to a blueprint for effective team utilization. It is a recognition that everyone is an individual and must be dealt with as an individual. It is an identification of the response or job performance required for results and a willingness to exert the appropriate influence in order to bring about this type of job behavior.

Effective relationships with others involve the use of facts and a rational approach. But they must also go the extra mile—which is often the most decisive one—and make maximum use of emotional appeal. Emotional appeal involves an understanding of ourselves in order to elicit the desired reactions in others. Too often we think of it as being restricted to politics or moonlit nights. However, it is generally recognized that response to a sales appeal is based more on a subconscious emotional reaction than on a conscious rational process. It follows that most successful leaders have learned to practice the art of emotional appeal. Just as the advertiser knows the appeal of status, acceptance, and belonging, so must the production or office supervisor learn that emotional appeal can be used beneficially in human motivation.

Leaders are responsive to the needs and desires of others. Leaders must be sufficiently responsive to both the immediate and the long-range needs and desires of their followers if they expect to continue to lead. They cannot be all things to all people, but neither can they lead in a free society without being sensitive to the desires of those who are expected to follow.

Leaders are knowledgeable. Leadership hinges on knowing more about a subject and being able to supply more of the answers than one's followers. Willingness to follow depends on this ability to supply answers—and answers will be forthcoming only if the leader functions from a base of superior knowledge. The leader must understand the total situation: its past, present, and future, how it affects others, and how it is affected by other influences. He must have broad general information, the details of systems and procedures, and an understanding of the techniques involved in the business enterprise.

Leaders possess superior motivation. From the standpoint of achievement, knowledge is of no value until it is set in motion by motivation. A leader should have an intense desire to get things done and to involve others in this activity. He must recognize that he cannot motivate others until he is personally convinced and is stimulated into action. Motivation not only sets energy into motion but is responsible for keeping it moving, and it should be of such quantity and quality that it brings everyone else to the same point of energetic action.

The leader knows how to motivate others on the basis of their self-interest. Likewise, he can increase his own motivation by identifying and enlarging on those things which are to his own self-interest. If properly utilized, these in turn generate an insatiable need to move forward to greater goal achievement. The leader who is not highly motivated is not likely to motivate others. Since self-motivation is indispensable to his success, the leader who wishes to accomplish results through other people must recognize that their will to contribute is directly related to their conception of how this contribution will benefit *them*.

Leaders are inspired and enthusiastic. These qualities are closely identified with the mainstream of on-going leadership. There are unusual characteristics of enthusiasm that may be compared to those of a communicable disease. Enthusiasm is contagious; it spreads to all those within its sphere of influence. However, it cannot be spread unless it is first possessed by the leader.

Many managers who seem to be following all the rules of effective leadership come up short in their efforts to reach maximum potential for themselves and their groups because they do not possess—or have failed to transfer—the qualities of enthusiasm and enterprise. It is these qualities which cause other people to work with more dedication, hold on a little longer, and have more respect for the one who leads them, and it is these factors which mean the difference between success and failure.

Leaders tap and utilize every resource. The automobile which does not use the energy potential of every ounce of fuel and every cylinder has wasted power, reduced efficiency, increased operating costs, and slowed forward progress. Just so, the leader who accomplishes most and moves fastest is the one who recognizes and utilizes every resource available. And one who fails to utilize every resource not only impedes progress but wastes potential—people, machines, money, goodwill, organization, public relations. The superior leader recognizes the contribution each resource can make and then skillfully meshes them all into a smoothly functioning pattern which moves toward goal achievement.

Leaders capitalize on the organizational environment and the leadership of others. Part of the potential available to the individual leader is that of the organizational environment in which he works and the leadership of others who can contribute to his own accomplishment. He determines exactly where his duties and responsibilities fit into the organizational structure of the company—the people who supervise him, those on his own level, and those he supervises. A clear understanding of this function reveals what his responsibilities are as well as what they are not and gives him an opportunity to make every effort to improve his working relationships with these three groups.

The effective leader utilizes the leadership potential of other leaders. He learns from them, profits by their mistakes, enlarges on their successes, in order to move forward in his own area of interest. This he does by working within the acceptable framework of company organization and proper human relationships.

Leadership, then, is many attributes and qualifications. In addition to those already listed, others which contribute to greater effectiveness include reliability, ambition, judgment, moral courage, competitive spirit, the will to win, poise, and a willingness to work longer and harder than the followers.

GUIDES TO THE PRACTICE OF LEADERSHIP

The practice of leadership involves certain steps which can be identified and which, if practiced with skill, will result in both maximum leadership influence and goal achievement. If these guides are disregarded, the results will not be of the desired quality and quantity. The late Chester I. Barnard, known not only as president of the New Jersey Bell Telephone Company but as an outstanding thinker on management, has suggested the following four factors in leadership behavior:

1. The determination of objectives.
2. The manipulation of means.
3. The instrumentality of action.
4. The stimulation of coordinated action.

The ten-step guide for leadership achievement which follows embodies these factors, but the breakdown is different. This ten-step

KEYS TO IMPROVED LEADERSHIP

An essential characteristic of leadership is a striving for constant improvement. It follows that the leader himself must seek constantly to increase his own contribution. This does not come about by accident but must be the result of a deliberate and carefully planned approach. Experience has shown that when the leader improves his knowledge and skills by following the rules, he will increase his total contribution potential.

Be willing to accept additional leadership and responsibility. A department head in a large general office was asked to assume responsibility for an additional segment of the work. His reaction was that he didn't want it. He already had too much to look after, he felt—he couldn't take on additional work because he didn't have enough people or equipment to do it. He failed to recognize that if he agreed to do more work, the company naturally would provide the necessary people and equipment. Yet this same man was dissatisfied with his progress and salary.

Leaders who rise rapidly to high positions of responsibility have one trait in common—a willingness to accept additional responsibility. Too many people make excuses for themselves by saying that they have too much to do already, that it will be too much trouble, or that it is someone else's job. The successful leader recognizes that the only way to make a greater contribution is to be willing to accept greater leadership and work responsibility; and, of course, he must be capable of discharging that responsibility with efficiency.

Surround yourself with capable people. Every successful man has realized somewhere along the way that he could not handle all the details of his work himself. Unfortunately, many never move beyond this point. The wise ones choose capable people to help get the job done. The abilities of these people do not detract from the leader's role; they contribute to it. And as their contributions increase, the leader reaches higher levels of accomplishment.

Be dissatisfied. The fatal blow to progress is self-satisfaction. When we become smug about what has been accomplished, it is almost certain that no further progress will be made. Most executives look for subordinates who are dissatisfied in their present positions, in the hope that this dissatisfaction will bring about continuing improvement and growth.

After discussion it was decided not to promote a line executive to the position of branch manager because he was too satisfied to bring sufficient drive to the job. The man was a college graduate, had a brilliant mind, possessed excellent ability, and was capable of accomplishing almost any goal. He was in his early 40's, his children had finished college, his wife had an excellent job. He was able to meet his financial responsibilities with his present salary and to cope with the demands of his job with a minimum of exertion. He missed the promotion because he lacked sufficient ambition to be entrusted with more important responsibility. Had he been dissatisfied with his present salary, with the results in his department, and with his present responsibility level, he would have been a more aggressive leader and a prime candidate for promotion.

Put first things first. A dedicated leader often has to have a sense of values which is different from the employee's. He must be able to put things of first value first and not become blinded by details which will prevent the achievement of the really important goals.

Most men find the time and the resources for the things which they consider most important—whether these be fishing and golf or professional improvements on the job. It does not necessarily follow that a man has to exclude the one or the other, but in most cases he must ask himself bluntly what will give him the greatest reward. He should recognize that his accomplishments can be almost limitless if he is willing to pay the price by setting up a system of priorities in his personal and professional life.

Develop people. It is a basic human desire to want to improve, to make more money, to become more professional in every activity. Some people have a capacity for self-motivation and can move forward to some degree under their own steam. However, leaders need to recognize that one of their responsibilities is to accelerate the development of other people through training, example, and all the other means of helping each individual to realize his maximum potential. The employee will be grateful for the assistance and will respond with respect and appreciation.

Design a blueprint for growth and stick to it. A contractor does not build a house without a blueprint. However, after the blueprint has been approved, he must follow it unless there is sufficient reason for change, in which case new plans must be drawn. Leadership is not a finished state which suddenly bursts forth with mature fruit. It grows step by step. The blueprint should provide for this orderly growth and for a steadily increasing contribution on the part of the leader.

LEADERSHIP AND EXECUTIVE GROWTH

John A. Patton said it: "Ninety-nine percent of the people in this world want to be told what to do. Be in the other 1 percent." For those who have what it takes to be in the 1 percent group, the rewards are great in human satisfaction and material compensation. But this exclusive club is composed only of the ambitious, the dedicated, those who are willing to follow the roadmap which leads to effective human leadership.

The opportunity to lead, to shape the lives of others, to provide an authentic service to people and enterprises can be an experience equal in excitement and satisfaction to that offered by any profession or game. Take a new look at your leadership opportunity, plot a fresh and creative approach to it, elicit the mental and physical resources of your people, and your future can be unlimited. Your success as a leader now will determine your future.

The job of getting work done through others has its own peculiar tools and skills which must be understood and mastered if the job is to be done effectively.

3. Mastering the Skills of Managing People

FAILURES IN HUMAN MANAGEMENT stem principally from the failure to recognize and to master the essential human-influence tools and to use them conscientiously. It is in this area that the woods are full of "born experts" who find it easy to lead others. These pseudo-experts don't worry about tools or fancy guides. They close their eyes, blast away, and expect the results to be harmonious and successful.

The beginning of wisdom for the sincere supervisor comes with an awareness that he cannot practice his trade without being an expert in the use of its tools. Once he realizes this, he seeks to identify the essential tools and then exerts his full effort to master them. He is never satisfied but constantly strives for greater adeptness.

A professional basketball player was asked why he continued to practice so long and diligently, since he was already considered the best in the game. He replied, "I practice because if I don't, sooner or later I'll run up against someone who does, and then he'll beat me."

A CRAFTSMAN NEEDS TOOLS

A carpenter cannot build a house without the use of certain tools. He needs a hammer, a level, a saw, a wood plane, and a variety of other implements. But the mere possession of a complete set of tools does not make the man a skilled carpenter. He must understand the

The supervisor, like the craftsman, must possess certain tools for dealing with people.

exact purpose and use of each, and he must practice using them until he can handle them with a finesse and a skill that qualify him as a craftsman. He learns to work with wood and other materials. He comes to realize that not all woods can be sawed and nailed in the same manner. He learns that each kind of material is best suited for a particular purpose. He learns when to nail and when to glue, when to brace, and how much stress a piece of lumber will take. Then he fits each piece together in the right sequence and erects a structure that is proof of his understanding of the materials and the tools of his trade.

The supervisor is also a craftsman who must possess certain tools for dealing with people, and he must develop a real proficiency in the use of these tools. He cannot hope to mesh people into a team without specific knowledge of the necessary skills and a special effort to master them.

KEY HUMAN FACTORS IN SUPERVISION

The carpenter recognizes that certain factors must be dealt with during the construction process. Problems that require alteration, adjustment, and reinforcement must be faced and overcome. The supervisor, too, must be aware of the peculiarities of the problems he will be facing. The following list constitutes some of these potential problem areas.

Individual and group differences. As the carpenter learns to work with each material according to its peculiar characteristic, so the supervisor learns to recognize and work with variations in human nature that affect training, work assignments, adjustments to a given situation, and the appropriate type of supervision. There are some variations in the way a younger or older person should be supervised, some differences in the handling of men and women, special considerations for unique problems.

The supervisor should recognize the differences inherent in different individuals and groups and adjust accordingly. He should remember that he can operate within a certain human relations framework, but that he must develop the tools to deal with known variations and still fit the total into a smoothly functioning team.

Emotional behavior. This is probably the most difficult human problem with which the supervisor has to deal. Fortunately, it does not occur overtly too often; but when it does, it presents a real challenge. Emotional behavior is often unpredictable; it has little or no logical basis, and it may be unrelated to on-the-job factors. It may stem from family-related conflicts, economic problems, or poor physical or mental health. It often builds up like a head of steam pumped into a container until it explodes. When the explosion or crisis is over, the individual often regrets what has happened—but by this time he may have "told off" the supervisor and resigned.

Employee attitudes. Some people are a joy to work with; others try the souls of supervisors. The difference can usually be traced to attitudes. Some people cooperate willingly; others almost dare the supervisor to win their cooperation. Attitudes affect morale, training, group harmony, the number of supervisory problems to be solved, and certainly the work result. The supervisor faces his severest test as he attempts to cope with attitudes and tries to mold them in the direction of willing cooperation.

Background—heredity and environment. Philosophers and psychologists have argued since the time of Plato whether heredity or environment has a greater effect on personality, ability, and behavior. No attempt is made here to answer this eternal question; our premise is that people are what they are as a result of both heredity and acquired experience. This means that certain things can seldom be altered and that it is often a waste of effort to try. It also means that each man's knowledge, built-in reactions, and capacity for productive work or negative influence stem from his own experience. Since experience is composed of many environmental factors, their influence must be recognized. The supervisor logically seeks to understand those with whom he must deal. He recognizes each individual for what he is and concentrates on influencing the areas which can be changed.

Personality influence. Personality must be defined not in isolation but rather as it influences others. It is generally understood to be the impression one person makes on others, including appearance, speech, attitudes, and total manner. The employee's personality has a significant effect on his job adjustments and on whether he will fit harmoniously into the group. It is especially important when the job brings him in contact with the public and when he is being considered for supervisory responsibility. Personality is difficult to change, though certain external factors can be altered. Certainly the supervisor can gradually influence personality over a long period, but there is seldom a dramatic change.

Failure and frustration. When an individual is confronted with situations to which he cannot find solutions, the result is often frustration and internal conflict. Most people keep coming up for another try; but for some, prolonged frustration often results in conflict with others. Although conflicts cannot always be resolved to the satisfaction of the employee, considerable success can be achieved in preventing and eliminating frustrations which interfere with job performance.

Fairness. The problem of fairness with employees can be one of the most bothersome faced by the supervisor. Simply being fair in dealing with people is not enough. The supervisor must lean over backward to demonstrate to everyone that he is impartial.

In the bookkeeping department of a bank, three new girls reported for work the same morning. Two of them caught on quickly and required only minor assistance from the supervisor. However, the third girl was not as familiar with the procedures and required considerable attention from the supervisor during the first few days. Because this need was not made clear to the rest of the group, it was not too surprising that one of the older employees in the department was heard to say on the second day, "Well, it looks like the boss has a new girl friend, but I don't understand what he sees in her."

The desire to contribute. It is generally agreed that in most instances desire has a greater influence on job results than does ability. Although this is an intangible factor, it is the responsibility of the supervisor not only to provide the work that is to be done but also to influence the employee to *want* to do it. The supervisor can supply certain guides and incentives, but the crucial factor is individual response.

Supervisor-subordinate relationship. What should be the personal relationship of supervisor and supervised, not only on but off the job? This problem has been the undoing of many supervisors. Some have leaned too far toward being "one of the boys," while others have erred in the opposite direction of aloofness and have lost rapport with the group.

Employees have been heard to say, "I don't want to be a supervisor and have everyone hate me." Supervisors confess, "I simply can't get them to do what I ask. I guess it's my own fault, because we've been so close." Or they try to stage a popularity contest to get employees to like them.

The supervisor should do nothing which would obligate him to an employee, nor should he permit the employee to become obligated to him. Favors on or off the job which are clearly beyond the boundaries of this relationship may make it difficult for the supervisor to maintain the respect of the employee. The lending or borrowing of money may result in a strained relationship, especially if the money is not repaid as agreed. If the supervisor spends too much time with one of his employees on or off the job, he is subject to criticism. If he overcompensates in order to avoid showing favoritism, he may be unfair to this friend; if he doesn't, he may be accused of showing partiality.

This is a tightrope to walk, but it must be mastered by every supervisor. Obviously the size of the group, its make-up (does it include both sexes?), and other environmental factors affect the handling of this problem area.

Problems of human efficiency. How efficient are you? How efficient are other people? "Efficiency" is the term applied to the relationship of input to output. It is not possible to measure human efficiency by the same precise standards as machines; but, at the same time, the supervisor is faced with the responsibility of using available human energy in the most efficient manner.

How fast can an individual be expected to work? It is recognized that only a reasonable amount of pressure can be put on the employee to speed up the work process, but efficiency can be influenced substantially by the methods and organization of the work. Some employees seem to be busy all the time but accomplish very little; others do not appear to give their jobs undivided attention, yet they have far more to show for their time and efforts.

TOOLS AND TECHNIQUES FOR HANDLING HUMAN PROBLEMS

Many of the human factors which have been given special consideration in the previous section as potential human relations problems can also be approached as potential opportunity tools. Whether they remain problems or become effective tools depends largely on the decisive ingredient of appropriate leadership.

When a carpenter comes face to face with problems in his work, he tries to understand the structure he is building, examines the materials with which he has to work, analyzes the problems on this basis, and then decides what tools and techniques he can utilize most effectively. The supervisor goes through essentially the same process. He identifies the end results desired; evaluates the available resources of people, machines, and materials; anticipates the problems he will be facing; and then seeks to use the tools and techniques which offer the best potential for achieving the desired results.

It needs to be repeated that when the term "human resources" is used, the individual is not viewed as a working machine who is in turn working other machines. Rather, the basic concept is always one of an individual with psychological needs to be met and a value equal to that of any other person in the company. But the company's human resources are the corporate assets which most concern the supervisor.

An employee's time is purchased at great price by the company. It is a precious commodity and needs to be used profitably if the individual, the supervisor, and the company are to be rewarded fairly for their time and energy. And the individual deserves both the environment and the leadership that will enable him to make the best possible use of his time and talent.

The following is a list of some of the tools and techniques which the supervisor will need to utilize in discharging his responsibility to both the individual and the company.

The human equation. Just as the carpenter remains constantly aware of the properties of the materials with which he must work, so the supervisor must remain constantly aware of the special characteristics of his people. These give him certain fundamental guides and a predictable framework in which to maneuver.

Increasing knowledge. Training by formal program or personal example enables the supervisor to increase the quantity and quality of his department's output. It is this tool which can minimize the waste of time, energy, and materials. It is the technique with which the supervisor moves the total enterprise forward to improved results.

Motivation. If there is a secret weapon in the supervisor's arsenal, it is that of motivation. All his training programs, elaborate plans, sophisticated organization, and good intentions go for naught unless he can use this tool effectively. It determines how much is accomplished and how good the results are.

Emotional appeal. Again, it is often this tool which sets all else into motion. Facts and reason can be presented, but the stimulus of feeling becomes the spark that says, "Let's get going!" It turns from satisfying the employee's economic needs to satisfying his psychological, self-realization, and ego needs. It is this extra ingredient which accounts for total job-related satisfaction.

Force versus persuasion. The supervisor must be a salesman—he must sell his people on the idea that they should do certain things. One of his primary functions is that of getting people to see and understand what needs to be done and how it should be done. The salesman sells a product or service by getting the customer to understand its advantages; the supervisor sells a job-related course of action, recognizing that only if the employee applies himself willingly can the desired results be achieved.

Cause and effect. Many things do not occur on the job which should. Certain things do occur which should not. In each instance, certain causes or influences precede the subsequent action. Control of the causative factor can make something happen or keep it from happening. By manipulating this control factor, the supervisor can bring about that action which has the greatest contributory effect on job-related goals.

Appraisal of contribution. Every activity can be improved, but the only way to determine what needs to be changed is to appraise what is being done. The supervisor does this, not to find fault or criticize, but to discover areas which can be improved—everything related to the job process and the contribution of the employee.

Correction of failures. The supervisor's greatest service to other people is in increasing their job security and showing them ways to enhance their value to themselves and to the company. In any case, the correction of failures involves job performance, not the individual. This responsibility is often approached with fear and trembling by the supervisor; but, if skillfully handled, it can give him one of his greatest job satisfactions.

Work-related attitudes. Much of what a man does or doesn't do, how well he gets along with others, and, to a considerable extent, his value to the company and his job-related satisfaction depend on his attitudes. The attitude of the employee is a responsibility of the supervisor. He can mold it, but he must do so as part of the process of overall training on the job. It can be one of his most decisive tools.

Work methods. The carpenter must organize his work and know the appropriate sequence of steps to take. He cannot put on a roof until he has erected a frame that will support it. The supervisor, too, must organize his tools and his methods of getting the work done. Some may be efficient, but others may need to be changed.

Results through communication. Most job-related problems can be solved through adequate understanding. This understanding is based on two-way communication where both the supervisor and those supervised are kept informed of one another's problems and what is expected of each. The use of this tool must be initiated by the supervisor, and he is accountable for its continued functioning. But he must have the cooperation of the employees, who must supply the other half of the information needed.

Counseling. Employees often need someone they can turn to for understanding, and the logical person is the supervisor. Counseling is a tool that is often underrated, but one that offers a special opportunity for the supervisor to be of service to his people. The extent to which employees turn to their supervisor for personal assistance is the surest test of the relationship between them. Counseling is a highly specialized tool and requires both a delicate touch and self-discipline on the part of the supervisor if it is to serve the best interests of the employee and not interfere with job requirements.

Organizational framework. Every job-related human activity takes place within a human and company framework. This framework is normally structured to afford the greatest opportunity to each employee to make a job contribution and assure specific results. It should be used to move toward a more streamlined and refined organization in order to improve group harmony and efficiency.

Day-to-day conversations. The frequent conversations which the supervisor has with each employee provide the bridge for the application of the many techniques available to him. These talks are used to inquire, to inform, to instruct, to guide, to correct, and to persuade. The other management tools lose much of their potential effectiveness in the absence of skillful on-the-job conversation.

Creativity. Man's growth, his culture, his technology, his standard of living are the result of his continuing creativity. The supervisor who is himself creative and can encourage others to be creative can often develop new work methods, new processes, and new products.

Work standards and goals. Almost every activity has stated or implied standards of quality and quantity. Since these standards comprise the criteria for judging progress and results, they should be fair and they must be thoroughly understood if they are to lead to job improvement.

THE LEADER AND HIS TOOLS

It is inconceivable that a supervisor could achieve appropriate goals without using the tools of leadership. Without these tools he would have almost no effective contact with people and certainly no means of influencing them. Just as the carpenter cannot practice his trade without tools, neither can the supervisor. It is possession of tools and skill in their use that give man potential mastery over his environment—in this instance his work environment.

The supervisor must recognize from the start that the process of directing people successfully is a highly specialized art. The right turns in the road must be taken and the best mode of transportation used.

If you were to hand a set of carpentry tools to a man on the street and ask him to build a house, the results would probably be disastrous even if he knew what the tools were and what they should be used for. Just so, familiarity with the tools and techniques of handling people does not of itself guarantee that an effective, productive team will be built. The tools and techniques of leadership are certainly necessary, but equally important is skill in their use. The following list provides some of the steppingstones to the more effective use of leadership tools.

Self-motivation. The athlete becomes great only in proportion to his willingness to practice and to exert extra effort. He cannot be forced to excel; he must want to excel to such a degree that he will develop exceptional skill and performance.

It is possible to force the manual worker to engage in a certain amount and type of muscular motion. But leadership involves mental processes, rational application, and deliberate effort. The leader cannot be forced or threatened into skillful use of the tools of leadership. Just as the baseball pitcher must want to pitch a winning game, so must the leader want to lead successfully. The skills of supervision do not improve by accident. They change for the better only as the supervisor is motivated to apply his knowledge and refine his skills.

Thoroughness. This is probably the one most important skill that identifies the exceptional executive. Lack of thoroughness leaves a supervisor out on a limb, causes most of his errors, results in his most serious embarrassment, and leads to most of the mishandling of his human relations responsibilities.

Like the artist and the scientist, the executive must be concerned with every small detail. An important part of many middle management development programs, for instance, is to have every participant undertake a research project. This is done to dramatize the process top management must go through in making decisions, including the gathering and evaluating of every essential detail.

The higher a man rises in management, the less margin he has for error because the consequences of error are more expensive and affect more people. He learns that the best way to prevent error is to be sure that nothing is left to chance, that nothing significant is left out of consideration, and that careful planning serves as the framework for all action. When a top executive conducts a meeting, he should seldom be surprised by any action taken. If he has sampled opinion beforehand, he can gauge what motions are going to be made and what action the group will take. When he plans a program, he wants it timed and outlined to the last detail; he wants everyone informed about what he is expected to do and what is to be accomplished. Only then does he consider the success of the meeting assured.

Most of us have worked with the young executive who comes running into our offices about once each day with a proposal for a new project. In most instances, a few questions reveal that the man has not thought his idea through and analyzed the consequences of the proposed action. The truly outstanding executive is the one who is the most thorough. He not only determines whether the swimming pool is full of water before he jumps, but he finds out the depth and temperature of the water and all the other details necessary to insure that he will enjoy the swim and come out safely.

The neophyte supervisor grows in proportion to his ability and willingness to be thorough. His thoroughness prevents errors which would cause others to lost respect for him and would interfere in his relationship with his people. The manager who fails to use this tool consistently and skillfully may be likened to the carpenter who neglects to use a level in the construction of a house: The floor will not be level, the studs will not be perpendicular, the ends of the lumber will not fit, and the result will be grotesque. The supervisor builds the same type of human relations structure when he neglects the habitual and skillful use of the tool of thoroughness.

Before taking action, the supervisor or top executive should ask himself the following questions:

- Have I considered every significant detail?
- Have I talked with all the people involved or affected?
- Has anything been left to chance?
- Am I positive that my information is completely correct?
- Am I so familiar with the facts, the people, the consequences of contemplated action that I can predict the outcome?

Thoroughness ought to become as automatic as stopping and looking both ways before stepping out into a street. The supervisor should develop some system of daily reminder that the absence of thoroughness can lead to disaster, whereas its skillful use can become a key to leadership success.

Emotional control. Before it is possible to control others effectively and consistently, we must master our own emotions. There are, of course, strong leaders who have been emotionally unstable, but they are rare exceptions; in most instances, such leadership has eventually been disastrous.

One bright young man with two years of college education worked in the stockroom of a large Eastern manufacturer. About every three months this young man asked the personnel director when he could expect to be promoted or given more responsibility. The young man had every qualification for leadership except emotional control. About as often as he inquired about his future, he engaged in a violent argument; and many of these disagreements would have reached the fighting stage if someone else had not stepped in. Would it have been reasonable to recommend this man for supervisory responsibility? Could he have earned and retained the respect of others? What would have happened the first time an employee crossed him in some way? The obvious answers to these questions explain why this man never became a part of management. He eventually resigned, and the company was not unhappy when he did.

It is a sobering fact that a man can spend a working lifetime building a respected reputation for stability; then, with one irresponsible outburst, he can destroy it in seconds and have to start up the long hill all over again. Kipling stated it well: "If you can keep your head when all about you are losing theirs. . . ." This is a picture of a business leader—the man who becomes the stabilizer, the man who calms others, the man whose example of emotional control leads others into an unemotional pursuit of the task to be done.

Emotional control does not mean curbing or eliminating strong feelings and convictions. A man must be willing to take a stand, have convictions and deep feelings, and be dedicated to what he believes to be right and what he wants to accomplish. It does mean, however, that judgment, facts, and logic should guide his thinking. He cannot let his emotions lead him into dealing in personalities and making decisions on the basis of his personal likes and dislikes. He must be willing to take and give criticism unemotionally. He must accept the fact that some criticism of him may be unfair and some of it may be tactless. But regardless of circumstances, he must have the poise to deal graciously and objectively with other people in light of the merits of the situation.

The skill with which the manager uses the tools of supervision is affected substantially by his objectivity. The energy generated by strong feelings should be directed into constructive rather than destructive channels. It is characteristic of outstanding leaders to have strong feelings, but their success comes only when they have learned to master and guide this energy in the right direction.

Supervisors should recognize that emotional control is important to their success as leaders of other people and that setting the right example for others is half the battle in leading others. Just remember that the manager who merits respect today is not one who uses a show of force, aggression, or emotional assault; he is a calm, persuasive, logical person who can lead others by making skillful use of the tools of leadership.

Tactful relations. Tact can become the supervisor's secret weapon for success—or the lack of it can become his instrument for professional suicide. To the casual observer, successful leaders seem to possess a sixth sense for saying and doing the right thing at the right time. They know how, by words and action, to make others feel important, to give them a sense of belonging on the team, and to calm troubled waters before a storm gets out of control.

The supervisor who feels it is unnecessary to be tactful usually finds himself in trouble because he can no longer influence other people. Tact is the lubricant that keeps the machinery of human relationships functioning smoothly. It is the lifeline that leads away from strained feelings and negative impulses.

Observing effective executives in action becomes an object lesson in tact. They use the right words instinctively, sense what needs to be said in any situation, and keep their human relations insurance paid up each day with tact. They have a radar sensitivity to the feelings and reactions of others, and they guard against saying anything that would upset or offend.

Initiative. What contribution does a carpenter's level make if it is never taken out of the tool chest? Many potentially useful supervisory tools gather dust because the supervisor hasn't the initiative to get acquainted with them. Remember that whatever value the tools of human relations have, they can make no contribution until they are put to use.

The supervisor must have the courage to get the ball rolling. He must recognize the problem, decide what needs to be done, and then set about getting it done. Lack of decisiveness or the courage to translate decisions into action can be the supervisor's undoing. If the tools he is now using are not accomplishing the desired results, he should have the courage to try new or different ones.

The comfortable thing about an employee's job is that he has someone telling him what to do: His need for initiative is limited, and he does not have to engage in the mental gymnastics of decision making. However, the supervisor's success is dependent on his initiative, and the higher he goes in management, the more this becomes true.

Mature judgment. Along with the initiative to use the tools of his trade, the supervisor must have the judgment to decide which tools will be most effective and to what extent they should be used. An incorrect tool can be more harmful than no tool at all; also, the overuse of certain ones can be damaging.

The supervisor needs to exercise mature judgment in the use of his tools and understand their exact function. He should be aware of what each can be expected to do and what it cannot be expected to do. No one tool supplies the productive effort needed to get the job done; no one tool compensates for the improper use of others. Effective supervision is dependent on the exercise of judgment to use the tools needed at a particular time, with a particular person, to get a specific job done.

Attempting to understand man can be the most frustrating and, at the same time, the most satisfying human experience. It becomes more satisfying than frustrating in proportion to man's intelligent and systematic approach to solving the human riddle.

4. Understanding Human Behavior

KIENZLE AND DARE state in *Climbing the Executive Ladder* that "few things will pay you bigger dividends than the time and trouble you take to understand people. Almost nothing will add more to your stature as an executive and a man. Nothing will give you greater satisfaction or bring you more happiness."

"Not one person in 10,000 ever really tries to understand people," says psychologist Donald Laird. It is for this reason that anyone who does understand people has an almost limitless potential for success. For the past 50 years, top responsibility and top pay have gone to the men who have known how to mold individuals into strong productive teams that have moved companies to success. Management has recognized that no matter how many technicians and specialists it employs, the talent of greatest value is the leadership that makes everyone else productive and profitable.

It is conceivable that during the next 50 years more progress will be made in the field of human understanding than in any other. This statement becomes more reasonable when we remember that very little progress has been made to date in utilizing man's potential. It has been estimated that man functions mentally at considerably below 40 percent of his potential. If this were stepped up by just 10 percent, the possibilities would be fantastic. And this is precisely the opportunity facing the executive who unravels the mystery of the human will to produce.

Top producers and top salesmen are not necessarily promoted to

The best study of man is man himself.

supervisory responsibility. Rather, demonstrated ability to get along with people, to understand them, and, more importantly, to accomplish results through them are of decisive importance.

Clarence Darrow, one of the most famous and successful trial lawyers of this century, insisted that even where laws are concerned, "the most important thing is to make the judge want to decide things your way, then give him a point of law that will give him a reason for doing what you have made him want to do."

MAN'S BEHAVIOR CAN BE UNDERSTOOD

The best study of man is man himself. History, literature, psychology, government, industry—everything that has influenced man reveals his nature and behavior pattern. The first step in understanding man is to remember that he is human. This is obvious, but it needs to be said. As part of management, we sometimes forget that the worker thinks, has emotions and desires, is changeable, and must endure disappointments. He is concerned with the status of his job, whether he is making any progress, and what his wife and his neighbors think about the place where he works.

He is closely linked to his job—often more so than the supervisor because he may have fewer outside interests. His job gives him a sense of importance, and through it he hopes to discharge his family and community responsibilities. His feelings and attitudes toward his job are not always expressed verbally; in fact, he often does not recognize them. Yet the job must offer him many things.

How difficult is it to understand man and his behavior? Not too difficult. The entire history of mankind is the story of what he wants and doesn't want, of what causes favorable and unfavorable reactions, of what elicits his will to produce and what does not; and all these things have been recorded in the books and in the experiences that others are willing to share with us. Our sole responsibility is to be wise enough to look, to listen, to learn, and to respond.

Find out what a man wants; supply it, and he will respond to your wishes. Find out what things are important to him on the job; supply them, and you have a good worker. The key is for the supervisor and the employee to agree that the same things are important. The following table, developed by the authors of *Improving Individual Pro-*

ductivity (American Management Association), shows how foremen and workers rated the important aspects of job satisfaction. Note the diversity of opinion in these ratings.

Job Conditions	*Worker Rating*	*Supervisor Rating*
Appreciation for good work	1st	8th
Feeling "in" on things	2nd	10th
Help with personal problems	3rd	9th
Job security	4th	2nd
Good wages	5th	1st
Work that keeps you interested	6th	5th
Possibilities for promotion	7th	3rd
Personal loyalty to workers	8th	6th
Good working conditions	9th	4th
Tactful discipline	10th	7th

The most significant fact about this table is that workers and supervisors rated the first three factors at opposite ends of the scale. This makes for some obvious misunderstandings. When the employee does not get the type of supervision he wants, he is dissatisfied with his job; when the supervisor does not get the results he wants from the employee, he is disappointed with his own accomplishment and with the reaction of the employee.

Experience has indicated that employees generally seek the following tangible and intangible compensations from their jobs.

Recognition for good work. There is nothing so discouraging as not being appreciated. In the employees' eyes the supervisor always spots the mistakes but seldom sees the things that are done well.

Recently a management expert was asked to study morale and working conditions in a plant producing garden tools. As one shift was changing, he asked a workman how he was getting along. The reply was unenthusiastic. Upon further inquiry, the man revealed his gripes in these words: "You know, I produced 179 hoes today. Two of them were rejected and had to have further work before they would pass inspection. Well, you know what? All I heard from the supervisor was about those measly two bad hoes. Not once did he even hint that I had had a pretty good day and made 177 perfect hoes."

According to one television commercial, man never outgrows his need for milk. The supervisor should recognize that neither does man outgrow his need for recognition. Recognition should be specific— for a particularly good piece of work, for a large sale, for better-than-average results. Don't be afraid to be generous with recognition, but be honest and sincere and give it fairly to all who merit it. Appropriately used, it results in greater production and better morale.

An interesting job. Have you ever heard an employee say that he wanted a dull, uninteresting job? We spend a large portion of our waking time at work, and we want it to be interesting and satisfying. Many people change jobs just to get away from work that is dull and unchallenging.

Every employee needs to have the interesting aspects of his job pointed out. Therefore, not only should the supervisor know more about the job and its relationship to other processes, but he should make sure the worker is aware of the significance of what he does. This develops a pride in the work and increases both quality and quantity of results.

Early in World War II, a number of bombers performed below standard because they were not put together properly. Someone conceived the idea that there needed to be a closer link between the aircraft plant worker and the plane crew. In order to accomplish this, a movie was made. It began by showing pilots boarding a plane and taking off for the combat zone. Then scenes were filmed of planes in battle, of planes disabled and landing back at their base badly damaged. When this movie was introduced into aircraft factories, the message was obvious—every screw, every rivet, every foot of wire, every minute detail was important to insure the safety of the crew and the success of the mission. The improvement in both quality and quantity of work was immediate and substantial.

Proper pay. What is proper pay? The answer is probably different in the opinion of the union leader, the company president, and the employee. Many old-line managers believe that pay can solve all the problems associated with production. They say, "Put it in their envelope and forget all this fancy stuff about employee benefits and bowling teams." But would this procedure be successful? Have the highest-paying companies eliminated their employee turnover, guaranteed their production schedules, erased their need for real management leadership, and made obsolete the need for understanding people? The answer is an emphatic *no!*

What, then, is the role of money in relationship to employee job satisfaction? One manager put it this way: "Never pay people in money alone." The amount of pay as well as the basis for it should be fair as measured against three standards: (1) pay in proportion to the contribution value of the job performance; (2) pay at a rate which has a realistic relationship to other jobs in the company that have comparable duties and responsibilities; and (3) pay at a rate comparable to that being paid elsewhere in the locality for the same type of work.

The employee needs to understand the basis of his pay, and he needs the assurance that increases are based on merit and not solely on the personal opinion or whims of the supervisor.

Proper pay represents far more than money; it is an indication of what the company thinks of a man, the value it places on his service. One man who was being considered for a key executive job said, "When I know what the company intends to pay for the position, I will know what it thinks of the job—whether it is an important job or not."

The employee wants and is entitled to proper pay. But the successful supervisor pays the employee additional intangible wages, including recognition, praise, proper training, understanding, and respectful leadership.

An environment of understanding. Every human being wants to be understood. The employee's need to be understood is related to his sense of security—his feeling that the supervisor will at least try to understand his problems on and off the job. So there must be no psychological barriers between the supervisor and employee; instead, there should be an environment of free and easy communication. The supervisor must be an interested listener, because understanding involves more listening than acting.

Opportunity for growth and promotion. The employee wants to feel that he has the opportunity to make more money and to be promoted to a better job. Company practice with regard to promotions from within, merit increases, and programs of employee development demonstrates growth and promotional opportunity.

The supervisor has a responsibility to bring to the attention of the employee those things which have a direct effect on his growth prospects. Since opportunities for pay increases and promotions are related to the financial health and growth of the company as a whole, the employee should be aware that he enhances his own opportunity by making a greater contribution to the company, thus enabling it to grow.

Job security. Security has been an oft-debated subject in recent years. The accusation has been made that employees are more concerned with the security of the status quo than with the challenge and opportunity of growth. It is contended that modern man has sold his birthright for government regulations, union contracts, and company policies that assure his sense of security and his job.

The employee wants and needs emancipation from fear, from capricious or irrational decisions, and from unjustified action. He wants the comfortable feeling that satisfactory work will assure him his job and the means to provide the necessities of life for his family.

It is the company's responsibility to provide maximum job security, consistent with its ability to provide continuing jobs and with the merits of the individual's performance. But company managers resent any attempt by individuals or organizations to use security as a barrier behind which to hide laziness or lack of responsibility. They believe that security should have a direct relation to the employee's value on the job—that the best employee ought to have the greatest security and the least satisfactory employee deserves the least job security. The employee should recognize that what he can expect from a particular job is related to his contribution on the job.

The need to render a service. Many decisions to accept or reject jobs and to stay or leave are contingent on the amount of service these jobs render to other people. Although motivation stems largely from concern for self, there is also a tremendous satisfaction connected with service to others. Other things being equal, the job which affords more opportunity to serve others has more appeal and offers more compensation to the employee. Teaching, social work, the ministry, and many other fields offer opportunities for service to others. But the satisfactions that go with providing such service need not be limited to a few professions. The production worker who assembles refrigerators is contributing to the general health of many families; the textile worker provides warmth and comfort to many; the bank employee is important to our economic safety and security; the insurance salesman affords us a measure of peace of mind. It's up to the supervisor and the company to help each employee see how his work benefits others.

A favorable work environment. In what type of environment would you rather spend eight hours of every working day—one that is bright and cheerful or one that is drab and filled with tension? The employee, too, wants working conditions that make him look forward to his job.

The company has the principal responsibility for creating and maintaining favorable working conditions—pleasant associates, safe machines, clean restrooms, comfortable temperatures, appropriate equipment, reasonable hours, and a host of others. And it must insure that each employee works within an efficient organizational framework which lets him know his job and does not frustrate him with too many bosses. The working environment is a composite of many things, most of which the company controls. This requires management's attention to human relations within the employee group and especially to the qualifications and leadership skills of the supervisor.

It is significant that the most important influence on the working environment is not the physical setting or equipment; rather, it is the type of supervision the employee receives. Surveys have shown that one of the principal reasons people give for resigning from their jobs is dissatisfaction with supervision. It is the supervisor who assigns work, indicates how it is to be done, and reviews what has been done. It is the supervisor who makes the employee feel favorable or resentful toward his job and the company.

Respect for and confidence in the organization. What type of people do you like to associate with—those in whom you have confidence or those in whom you have no confidence? What type of company do you prefer to work for—one whose future, whose policies, and whose management you have doubts about and are suspicious of most of the time or one that commands your respect? The answers to these questions are obvious, and it is for these same reasons that an employee wants to be able to respect and have confidence in the company where he works.

Desire to belong. Man is social by nature; he needs acceptance; he wants to belong to the club, to the church, to the employee group. When he's left out, he's lonely and unhappy. He looks to his job for the opportunity to be a part of something important. He wants to take pride in his job, his associates, his supervisor, and his company. It is a wise supervisor who welcomes the new employee, gives him the feeling of belonging and being accepted, and then insures that on-the-job conditions give him the same feeling.

When company executives are asked what they have done within the past six months to keep the top half of their employees from becoming dissatisfied and leaving, the usual answer is that raises have been given. But the answer should also be more personal. Has the supervisor spoken to the employee as an important fellow human being—inquired sincerely about his family, communicated that the company is pleased to count him part of the organization and is proud of him? The man who is thus recognized is less likely to slacken his efforts or to seek more favorable conditions elsewhere.

A proper understanding of the preceding job-related factors must take into consideration that they vary greatly with individuals and are not presented in any order of importance. The young person may be more interested in opportunity; the older person, in security; the head of a large family, in money; and the working wife, in the opportunity for self-expression. The particular interest may also vary with economic conditions. During depression times, job security may be most important; when jobs are plentiful, other factors are of more interest.

It is the supervisor's responsibility to know what each employee expects from the job. Then, through his leadership and his interpretation of the job to each individual, the supervisor attempts to see that the expectations are realized.

SOURCES OF JOB-RELATED SATISFACTION

This is a free country; man is not obliged to work for a particular supervisor or company. In essence, he sells eight hours of his day to a company and expects certain things in return. Since he would probably get about the same pay from several companies, why does he work for one in particular? The answer is that the one company provides him with *more* of the things he wants in connection with the job.

It follows that the company which can provide the employee with the greatest number of the things he wants, and to the greatest degree, will merit his will to contribute. How are these things provided? Top management controls some, but the majority come from the immediate supervisor. It is the supervisor who recognizes good work, gives understanding, influences security, recommends pay increases, provides the chief element of the working environment, and in general acts as the link between the employee and the company. The supervisor is also the employee's principal source of information about what the company thinks of him as an employee and what it thinks of his work.

The supervisor's primary function is to direct human energy toward achieving a specific type of job performance. This he can do only when he has a thorough understanding of people, their motives and reactions to their job environment; so he must be accurately informed regarding the total situation and especially the factors which influence human contribution.

Understanding is recognizing that reactions are influenced by facts and reasons. But subconscious factors based on feeling and emotions also must be recognized and controlled. Although the salesman sells with facts, the clincher is often the emotional appeal. It is essential that supervisors realize that the feelings and emotional reactions of employees are a vital influence on job performance.

LAWS OF HUMAN ASSOCIATION

We are all more alike than different. We have individual characteristics and degrees of needs, but in the final analysis we are similar. It is significant that there is a common psychological base governing our culture and our sense of values. This varies with different societies and at different times according to the mores of a particular group. However, the decisive influence of Biblical teachings on Western civilization's value structure and behavior patterns has accounted for an unusually consistent pattern of thought, stable criteria for right and wrong, and a solid base on which to build our human relations laws.

We make calculated predictions concerning our physical and mathematical environment on the basis of existing norms. An accurate sampling of human reaction reveals predictable patterns which, when charted, invariably form a bell-shaped curve. This means that behavior patterns can be anticipated if we know the laws and the predicted reactions. The following examples of psychological laws of human contact illustrate the accuracy and importance of predictability.

Anxiety of the initial contact. In our first contact with a new idea, new product, new situation, or new person we are inclined toward caution and anxiety. When a new employee reports for work, he regards the company, the supervisor, and the job with a considerable amount of apprehension. The supervisor can eliminate this uncertainty by making the person feel welcome and a part of the group. William Allen White is credited with saying, "A stranger is a friend I have yet to meet."

When the supervisor suggests a new machine or new procedure and the employee is reluctant to accept it, this does not mean that he is stubborn and uncooperative; he is simply exhibiting normal anxiety. It becomes the supervisor's responsibility to eliminate this feeling by carefully explaining the change.

Strong social need and reaction. Most of us want to be with other people, and we want to belong to groups. When a sailor who had been adrift on a life raft for 38 days was finally rescued, he said that what he had missed most was human companionship and that sheer loneliness had almost killed him.

On one particular job the secretary seldom stayed longer than six months before resigning. Finally it was observed that the location of her desk so isolated her that she did not have any opportunity to talk with the other people in the office. When the desk was moved to bring her in close contact with others, the problem was solved.

Thus social need can be an important factor in the productivity of the employee, since job performance may be the measure of acceptance by the work group.

The need for approval. The need for approval can often be more important than material goals. The strongest incentives often involve honor, prestige, titles, and other forms of approval. People may accept and remain in lower-paying jobs than their talent could command because family and friends express greater approval. For example, a bank clerk's position often carries more prestige and status than that of a service station manager but not always more salary. The prudent supervisor recognizes this strong desire for approval and permits the employee to obtain it through top job performance.

The will to win. Some societies are almost completely devoid of competition, and their members placidly accept certain roles in life. Not so the American. He must be up and doing and winning. He wants to win at golf, at cards, on the job. This response to competition may stem from the caveman's search for food in competition with other cavemen. Theirs was a time of the survival of the fittest or strongest. Although modern law restricts man's competitive instinct, it is still very much in evidence in almost every phase of his personal and business life. The merchant engages constantly in the game of letting the customer win. Getting a bargain or a marked-down item implies to the customer that he has gotten more than he has paid for.

The company can capitalize on this human quality through the use of incentives, contests, prizes, and activities which permit winning. And the supervisor must recognize and use this competitiveness to stimulate interest and production. A word of caution is in order, though: Excessive competition can be harmful. When one person interferes with the rights of others, then it has gone too far.

Satisfaction of physical needs. Much human energy is exerted in satisfying physical needs for food, clothing, shelter, and self-preservation. When men earned very little, they had little time or energy left for anything else except meeting their physical needs. Now, as the result of improved machines, refined techniques, and shorter working hours, other factors are becoming more important.

Resistance to change. We are creatures of habit. We like to go to work at the same time every day, eat lunch at the same time, perform our jobs in the same way, and we resist efforts to make us change. Since this reaction is predictable, the supervisor who wants to transfer an employee or change his working conditions must be prepared to overcome resistance.

Response to subconscious forces. Icebergs are seven-eighths submerged, and the same thing frequently seems true of the reasons for human behavior. It is important to recognize that people seldom know why they react in a particular way. The supervisor needs to be aware that behavior is not always logically explainable. This knowledge should make him less frustrated as he deals with people.

*   *   *

No supervisor can be completely effective unless he recognizes and responds to the basic laws controlling human response. To ignore or go contrary to these laws can be disastrous; to understand and conscientiously observe them can lead to more effective leadership. Those in leadership positions have the opportunity to use effectively both the time and the energy of their employees. Failure to do so results in waste. The more thoroughly the supervisor understands people, the better his chance of meeting the challenges of leadership.

Who ever said that leading or supervising people is easy? The fact is that a man is given a position of leadership because someone has faith in his ability to rise to the challenge, deal with difficult problems, and find the right answer most of the time. The exciting game of leadership reserves its greatest compensations for those who face these challenges boldly and emerge winners.

Beginning with the first work experience, attitudes begin to form regarding the work, the supervisors, and the company.

Beginning with the first work experience, attitudes form regarding the work, the supervisors, and the company. Some are carried along to new jobs and gradually intensify. The lazier a person is mentally, the less logical his thinking is, the more easily he is influenced by others, and the more willing he is to assume their views.

Individual attitudes are greatly influenced by prevailing opinions. Local customs exert a predictable influence, and tribal attitudes become part of the religion or law of the group. Almost the same type of situation can develop in a company.

Ready-made attitudes are often adopted from others. It is surprising how willingly people accept ready-made attitudes, make them their own, react accordingly, and suffer the consequences without examining them critically to determine whether they are justified. We are cautious about contamination in the food we eat. Yet we open the doors of our minds and fail to guard against contamination from many opinions that come our way.

We dislike hand-me-down clothing, but we are willing to wear worn-out attitudes. When employees accept ready-made opinions without analyzing them and then base decisions and reactions on them, they may be jeopardizing their future by ignoring their capacity for independent judgment. The danger is that one strong-willed person in an employee group can transfer his negative attitude to the entire group.

Attitudes may be based solely on one dramatic experience. The employee who is humiliated in front of others may assume that all supervisors are unfair. One mouthful of distasteful food doesn't make us swear off eating for the rest of our lives, but one dramatic or emotional experience can establish fixed reaction patterns in the unthinking person.

Over a period of time a hierarchy of attitudes develops within a company. These influence the ease with which new policies can be established and reveal the actual relationship between manager and employee. Attitudes vary from department to department and from area to area of the company.

Attitudes prevail toward races and national groups, the opposite sex, other employees, and new people; toward company policy and benefits; toward the supervisor. These determine whether management's action is interpreted with understanding and cooperation or with suspicion and resistance; therefore, they have a substantial effect on its success.

The significant influence of attitudes on what can be accomplished offers convincing evidence that attitude development and maintenance is too important a responsibility to be ignored or left to chance. However, attitudes can be influenced and controlled, and the manner in which this is handled constitutes the very foundation on which most other management skills are built.

SIGNIFICANT FACTS CONCERNING ATTITUDES

Some things that are known about attitudes can be of real value in understanding and influencing them. It is possible, on the basis of this information, to predict the potential development of certain attitudes and therefore to alter conditions so that those attitudes which are detrimental will not develop.

Attitudes develop quickly. It has been said that for the new employee the first minute on the job is the most important minute and that the first day is the most important day. The new employee is usually uncertain and impressionable. If he is ignored or left to the chance influence of an employee who has an ax to grind, it is probable that a negative attitude will develop. It is because of the importance of first impressions that every possible step should be taken to insure that the new employee feels welcome, wanted, and convinced that the company is a good place to work. The supervisor who is warm and friendly and who demonstrates his helpfulness and availability has a favorable influence on the attitudes of the newcomer.

Attitudes are long-lasting. Attitudes develop quickly and, once developed, have a permanent effect on patterns of behavior. Attitudes are rigid. Once they have firmed up about the supervisor, the work, or the company, it becomes a real challenge to alter them.

Attitudes are interrelated. If an employee has a very strong attitude toward one phase of his job, it probably influences and determines his reaction to other phases. If he considers the supervisor to be unfair, he is likely to think the same way about policies, pay, working conditions, benefits, and the company as a whole. If the supervisor refuses to change a man's vacation schedule, for example, the reaction may be that "he picks on me every opportunity he gets."

This is why it is important that the supervisor explain very carefully the reason for his decisions and actions—he cannot afford to let pockets of discontent develop which might spread like a cancer.

Behavior stems from attitudes. Strong feelings are often associated with attitudes. A prejudice is one type of attitude, more often associated with race, religion, or groups of people than with individuals apart from the group. Moods often cause temporary reactions which are based more on momentary emotions than on logical thinking. Although attitudes are consistent and predictable, moods may cause temporary variations in behavior and attitudes.

Individual attitudes differ. Although group attitudes are important factors in the work environment, those of the individual are the primary concern of the supervisor. People bring with them the prejudices and opinions which were developed in an earlier environment or on previous jobs. It is necessary for the supervisor to learn these attitudes in order to work more effectively with his group and its members. Because people differ, and their ideas differ too, the supervisor has to seek to promote the best possible group attitude while at the same time making allowances for individual differences.

RESPONSIBILITY FOR ATTITUDE DEVELOPMENT

The supervisor is in the best position to influence each employee's adjustment to the job and, in particular, his attitude formation. This is a responsibility which he cannot avoid or delegate. Moreover, he should remember that it can't be handled successfully once a year but requires constant attention. Once the supervisor recognizes his responsibility for the creation and maintenance of attitudes, he must then develop effective practices for dealing with them.

Recognizing attitudes. How do you recognize an attitude when you see one? If we agree that attitudes have a significant effect on work, we must acknowledge the need to identify them in their early stages and initiate immediate corrective action where necessary.

When an individual holds a strong opinion, consistently reacts in the same manner, and refuses to change when the facts, situation, and other influences change, he is displaying a form of intellectual dishonesty—a refusal or unwillingness to recognize that the situation can change and that a single event should not form the foundation for future conclusions. This is evidence that an attitude problem exists.

Many people make no serious attempt to keep their attitudes from showing. They quite willingly admit: "I don't like the boss and I don't care who knows it." "You can't blame me for being stubborn. I get it honestly from my dad—and he was certainly a fine man." "It's too late in life for me to change my thinking now." "I'm no eager beaver, but I once tried cooperating with the boss and it didn't get me a thing. Never again!" All a supervisor has to do to spot potential attitude problems is merely to listen.

Predicting attitudes. Basic to the success of every supervisor is the ability to anticipate employee reaction and job behavior. The same holds true about attitudes. Though there are significant exceptions, as a general rule an employee's reactions to certain aspects of the job carry over to other areas. This principle is often applied in making decisions regarding work and benefit changes. Leadership for change is usually channeled through those who are known to be strongly cooperative, because they are likely to come through with favorable reaction to the proposed change. By the same logic, those who are not particularly cooperative will probably react negatively to the proposal and should not be used to initiate it.

Measuring attitudes. The politician needs to know not only which way people think on an issue but also how strongly they feel; both affect the way they vote. Accordingly, the supervisor must be concerned with those attitudes which affect the work and morale of the group because they, in turn, affect the quantity and quality of job results. He needs to know, in short, not only the existence of attitudes but also their strength.

Opinion and morale surveys attempt to discover the existence and strength of attitudes in the employee group. These surveys may be undertaken by company personnel but are usually conducted by an outside firm. Attitude-rating scales can also be used. These often ask the employee to consider a given issue and, on a scale ranging from mild to strong, indicate the point which represents his feelings.

The alert supervisor can learn the strength of employee attitudes in yet another way—through casual conversation and interviews. And the use of a properly instituted and supervised suggestion system also gradually reveals a profile of employee attitudes and depth of feeling, since suggestions may be symptoms of attitudes.

GUIDES FOR CHANGING ATTITUDES

First, we should remember that attitudes are established patterns of thinking and behavior in which the individual feels comfortable and secure. So he is not likely to change until he recognizes that his needs can be satisfied in a better way.

Regardless of the supervisor's elaborate care with new people and his attention to his present people, unfavorable attitudes often appear on the job. It then becomes desirable for the supervisor to change them by channeling employee thinking and reaction in a more favorable direction.

Substitute a desirable attitude for an undesirable one. The small child holds tightly to a sharp instrument until a more desirable toy is offered as a substitute. Similarly, the supervisor has little success in asking an employee to give up an idea unless another is offered to take its place—one that better serves the needs of the employee.

Interview and motivate. The process of substituting the more desirable attitude is usually handled through interviewing and motivating, by showing the advantage of the new one to the extent that the employee voluntarily relinquishes the old. For example, if an employee objects to having women working in the department, it's up to the supervisor to convince him that this attitude could jeopardize his chances for promotion. The employee can be told that the women's presence may represent a real opportunity for him, as an experienced employee, to assist with their training and that, by proving that he is capable of dealing effectively with all types of people, he increases his value to the company.

Seek only a small or gradual change at first. A major change in attitude is more than the employee may be willing to make and more than the supervisor should request. Instead of asking a man who objects to working with women to devise and carry forward an elaborate training program for all the women in his department, he should be asked to help the one woman who works next to him on the grounds that he has proved that he is an excellent worker and knows the job thoroughly. It should be pointed out that this will increase his standing in the eyes of his associates. Once he finds out that she isn't so bad, he may be willing to render the same assistance to others.

Ask for change on a trial basis. It is understandable that people may be reluctant to make permanent changes, but they may appear unreasonable if they refuse even to try something. Once they try a new idea or work method and it doesn't prove "fatal," they often find they really like the change. Though they seldom admit it immediately, their willingness to try the same thing another time indicates their acceptance.

Show the big picture. Try to understand the situation from the employee's point of view. Often he has not had the opportunity to see and understand the overall picture and cannot know how a change will affect his job. The supervisor should explain the change and show how it fits into the total picture.

Affect a permanent substitution of the desirable attitude. The purpose of attitude change is to replace an undesirable opinion with one that is favorable. When such a change has been accomplished, it should not be neglected but should be nurtured and maintained. Too many supervisors make the mistake of changing an attitude and then forgetting it; then they're surprised later when they discover that the attitude has reverted to its original state.

THE SUPERVISOR'S OWN ATTITUDE DEVELOPMENT

The attitude of the supervisor exerts a significant influence on that of the employee. Whether or not an opinion is expressed orally, it is communicated by everything the supervisor does. To build positive attitudes he must have positive attitudes himself. The employee's opinion of the company, his confidence in it, his understanding of its policies, and his predisposition to act in a particular manner are influenced more by the supervisor than by any other single factor.

The supervisor develops his own attitudes by recognizing what they are and then engaging in the effort necessary to make them what they should be. If his attitude is negative or weak in a particular area, he should ask himself why, then take steps to change it. He certainly can't afford to jeopardize his future with faulty attitudes which affect his own job performance as well as that of everyone he supervises.

A supervisor who understands and controls the factors of causation is also able to control what the employee does on the job.

6. The Key to Controlling and Changing Behavior

MANY SUPERVISORS who try to understand the reasons for certain job reactions reach a state of frustration and give up, convinced that there is neither rhyme nor reason to the riddle of human behavior. Yet before they throw in the towel they ought to recognize that they must understand and control human behavior on the job if they are to meet job responsibilities. The supervisor will have minimum success in changing job behavior unless he discovers its causes; he will have even less success if he attacks the end product of the activity rather than the contributing causes.

WHY PEOPLE BEHAVE THE WAY THEY DO

It has been stated that whatever a man does, he does it for a good and sufficient reason. For every action or reaction there is a cause. The ability to accept and be appropriately guided by this principle can be an important key to success in working effectively through other people.

Consider the case of Harry Baker, bank cashier. The supervisor began to realize that Harry was falling down on the job. He mentioned the situation casually, but no improvement resulted. Harry continued to come in late about twice a week; he was out a couple of days without satisfactory explanation; he was falling behind in his work, and he was irritable with customers.

Before the supervisor called Harry into the office, he decided to investigate further. He learned that Harry had been with the company for seven years. During this time his interest had been high, his volume of work had been consistently near the top in the department, he had been punctual and dependable, and he had worked harmoniously with other employees and customers. Additional checking revealed that it was just within the previous five weeks that Harry had fallen down on the job. He had been absent and late more during these five weeks than during the rest of the seven years. This sudden change was a tip-off that something was seriously wrong.

The supervisor called Harry into the office and asked how he liked the job and whether anything about it was unsatisfactory. Harry was pleasant but insisted that there was nothing wrong.

During the conversation, however, he revealed that his wife had been ill for several weeks and had not been able to get out of bed. He had had to look after her and assist the children with their studies at night. Then, in the mornings, he'd have to prepare breakfast, get the children off to school, and try to whip things into shape so that he could leave his wife for the day.

Consider what this man's reaction might have been had he been bawled out without a chance to tell his side of the story. He might have said, "You work seven years with a good record, and then something happens that you can't help and—pow! They jump on you with both feet. Maybe this isn't such a good place to work after all." This incident demonstrates that supervisors who attack the *result* without analyzing the *cause* commit serious errors of judgment and often aggravate the situation rather than correct it.

A basic principle of causation is that behavior doesn't just happen; it is caused. When we begin looking for the causes of behavior, we are headed toward a better understanding of why people act as they do.

It is easy to see the cause-and-effect relationship in the physical world. The laws of physics state that a body at rest tends to remain at rest, that if pressure is applied to an object it will move in the opposite direction, and that when in each instance we know the cause —the force acting on the object—we can predict the effect or result.

If we stick someone with a pin, we can anticipate the effect. Words —"Stop!" "Run!"—can stimulate a physical response. Movies move us to tears or laughter. Doctors make use of chemicals and hormones to cause a desired effect in the body. All this is based on the fundamental principle that behavior (reaction effect) is equal to the organism (human being) plus the stimulus (cause). This means that only two factors account for behavior—the individual and the environmental influences. A change in either changes the result.

The supervisor who wishes to change the job behavior of the employee, then, needs to change either the individual or the influences that act on him.

ENVIRONMENTAL AND CULTURAL INFLUENCES

The factors that influence behavior stem from two principal sources: adjustments to the physical and human environment and adjustments to a contemporary culture. The culture in turn is the techniques, activities, and symbols making up the individual's adaptation to his environment.

Much of man's reaction is conditioned by repetition which develops habit patterns. A woman and a young child coming suddenly upon a snake are likely to react differently. The woman will probably have a violent conditioned reaction; the child may show no fear—may even try to pick up the snake and play with it. The fear and the violent reaction of the woman are gradually transferred to the child as a result of exposure. In the same manner, the reactions of employees are conditioned over an extended period of time until eventually they become fixed and automatic.

We generally judge others by our own standards. This may not be sound because we frequently do not know why we do things. Also, we tend to forget that the other fellow is in a different situation, comes from a different background, and has had different conditioning. It is especially difficult to discover the real causes for behavior when they are submerged below the conscious level and when the individuals themselves are not aware of why they react as they do.

Since such a strong case can be made for causation, we may tend to believe that mankind is a rudderless boat that is moved by the winds of influence. There is no denying the substantial relationship between cause and effect, but one additional element must be taken into consideration: man's willpower. Man can, if he wishes, override causes and make decisions according to his own rational conclusions.

People behave the way they do because of the sum total of heredity, acquired experience, and the forces acting on them.

In deciding whether to cooperate with or oppose a change of company policy, the employee may not be exercising willpower so much as weighing the relative merits of the possible courses of action. Which pathway corresponds to his own best interest? What factors cause him to lean in the direction of cooperation? What factors cause him to oppose the new policy? It is doubtful that his final decision will represent a deliberate weighing of these factors so much as a response to their relative pressures and the personal advantages involved. Modern psychologists doubt the strength of willpower. They think that whether the employee acts wisely or unwisely depends not so much on the force of will as on which causation factors are strongest.

People behave the way they do because of the sum total of heredity, acquired experience, and the current forces acting upon them. It is obvious that physical needs influence behavior and responses. But the need for recognition and the satisfying of other nonphysical drives can also be identified as influencing behavior.

Among the factors influencing a man's reactions are age, length of time on the job, health, family, temperament, education, personality, loyalty, and training. These may change with time and with the changing moods of the individual. If the supervisor is to discover and influence employee behavior, he must know his employees as individuals. The better he knows them, the better he is able to understand the influences which cause them to act as they do.

The employee is an organism constantly adjusting and reacting to his total environment. Lighting, noise, monotony, other people, leadership, and the efficiency of the machinery all are elements of causation. But, in addition, factors outside the plant must be taken into consideration. If a man is under emotional stress at home, it may show up in his work. Such influences are not constant but fluid; they operate with varying degrees of force on different days.

CHANGING BEHAVIOR BY CHANGING CAUSES

A well-known headache remedy advertises, "For frequent or recurring headaches, consult your physician." This is a recognition that aspirin can cure the symptom (headache) without affecting the cause (illness). The supervisor who wants to change job performance or reactions is wise to concentrate on the cause. He must ask *What?* and *Why?* He needs to analyze both performance and job adjustment to determine where a change is needed and then bring an appropriate influence to bear on the cause in order to affect the result.

Exploring causation presents the supervisor with one of his most serious challenges. He is engaged in basically the same type of pursuit as that of the psychiatrist. Of course, the supervisor is seldom dealing with a disturbed personality, but he has to observe, question, and analyze in order to discover the true situation. Part of the difficulty in making such an analysis lies in the fact that the individual is constantly influenced by many competing stimuli, and the supervisor needs to know which stimulus is at work at the moment. It is worthwhile noting that many habits and patterned reactions go all the way back to childhood; the current effect is but a reflection of the causation factor.

One young office worker was on the verge of being discharged because of excessive errors in her work. It was her responsibility to keep accurate records of all items sold, their size, price, and color, and the names of manufacturers. Not only did she make far too many errors, but she was so late in completing the records that the primary need for them had passed before they were available.

When the employee was called to the office, she could not explain why she made so many errors or why it took her so long to complete the work. The condition of the machines was reviewed, and she was asked whether she received the correct information on time and whether she was experiencing difficulty with anyone on the job. She was happily married, she said, and the situation away from the job presented no problems. Finally, as a shot in the dark, the girl was asked if she had ever worn glasses. She replied that she had—beginning with the third grade—but that she had not worn them for about five years. She had made an appointment to have her eyes checked about three months before but had not kept the appointment. It was agreed that she could remain on the job only on condition that she determine immediately whether she needed glasses. She did; and with them her work so improved that she became an outstanding employee.

Many of the human problems facing the supervisor stem from causes rooted deep within the personality of the individual. The employee who forever complains is exhibiting a symptom of hidden problems. Making constant excuses for failure and exhibiting apparently groundless antagonisms are other outward manifestations of inner conflict. It is the supervisor's responsibility to view these complaints, maladjustments, and conflicts; ferret out their causes; and take whatever steps are necessary to eliminate the unsatisfactory behavior which may, in fact, be the result of poor supervision.

For example, a new employee in the shipping department was seen loafing frequently during his probationary period. He completed all his assigned jobs on time, and the results were satisfactory. But the supervisor decided not to keep him as there was no place in the department for loafers. When the employee was confronted with the reason for his discharge, he was amazed. He stated that he had completed every assignment to the best of his ability. During his first day on the job, one of the older employees had told him that when he got through with each shipment, he was to return to the loading platform and wait there until he received another assignment. He had been doing this because he understood it to be the correct procedure.

The man was not discharged but asked to remain on the job. The true situation was pointed out to the supervisor; the man was given proper instructions; and he proved to be a good employee. Had the job been explained properly in the beginning and had there been proper supervision and adequate communication between supervisor and employee, such a misunderstanding need never have developed.

It is difficult to change an individual's behavior. Each man tends to have fixed attitudes, to be confident of his acquired experience, and to react in a way that has proved satisfactory in the past. He has a natural tendency to resist change and probably will not recognize that any fault or failure rests with him.

The need for change confronts the supervisor with the task of interviewing the employee, getting him to see the cause-and-effect relationship, and convincing him that the only way to correct the situation is to correct the cause. The self-interest of the employee should be used in this connection as explained in Chapter 8 on motivation. The supervisor must approach the problem knowing that the employee is likely to resist the change and that he may fail to recognize that the cause lies within himself. This requires great patience, thorough planning, and careful follow-up. One attempt seldom produces a cure.

In many cases, it is easier to change the environment than the individual. But this can usually be accomplished only within limits. It may not be feasible to transfer the man to another department or even to another machine, and it is doubtful whether the workplace can be completely rearranged. However, it *is* possible to check the condition of the machine, the condition of the raw material, and the workload.

If the work environment seems to be causing trouble, ask the employee for suggestions. He may admit that there is nothing really wrong with the machine but that he resents being given the most difficult assignments. This could be corrected by reminding him that he is assigned the more complicated work because of his superior skill and that he is being paid a higher rate than the men doing less difficult work.

The important principle to keep in mind is that the environment is a causation factor. If it is not possible to change the physical situation, the supervisor may be able to accomplish the same result by talking with the employee and getting him to recognize *why* it cannot be changed, to understand that a proper adjustment has to be made to conditions as they exist.

CAUSATION AND ITS EFFECT ON SUPERVISION

If supervisors are to make an accurate and objective appraisal of job behavior, they must recognize the cause-and-effect relationship. If they expect to change response or behavior as they affect job performance, they will have to discover and change the cause. The following guides should be helpful:

- Develop the habit of assuming that there is a cause or a combination of causes which brings about the conduct of the individual on the job.
- Follow this up by conducting an open-minded search for the cause—whether on or off the job.
- Remove or alter the cause so as to bring about a more desirable result.
- Use the cause-effect principle to enhance productive behavior as well as divert wasteful activities to useful achievement.
- Recognize that in some instances, even after the cause has been discovered, no constructive action can be taken.

- Avoid blaming the individual or pouncing on the wrong thing in an attempt to bring about change. This will prove frustrating to the supervisor and upsetting to the employee. Threats may occasionally force the employee to make certain changes, but the old groove will soon be found unless permanent changes are made through the alteration of causes.
- Examine closely the expected results in the light of what is necessary to bring them about.
- Be especially alert to changes in job performance or behavior. When the employee has a record of loyalty and satisfactory job results, look for an explanation if these should suddenly change.
- Provided the cause can be discovered and changed, then the chances are that the job performance will return to normal.

Causes of trouble which merit the attention of the supervisor might come to his attention in the following ways:

- Personal observation.
- Production and attendance records.
- Complaints from the employee.
- Complaints from other people.
- Morale surveys revealing problems which bother employees and which may be interfering with their job performance.
- Exit interviews.

Although exit interviews come too late for the individuals involved, they can reveal certain changes which need to be made. When employees resign, in most instances the reasons they give the immediate supervisor are not the real ones. They may have resigned because the workload is unequal, or because others won't do their share of the work and they can't meet production quotas, or because the supervisor shows favoritism, or one employee runs the department and tells the supervisor what to do, or because someone is stealing in the department and "I don't want to get involved," or simply because "my supervisor and I just don't seem to hit it off."

The wise supervisor must take an objective look at the employee's performance as well as his behavior. If he expects to change results, he must discover and change the causes. If he approaches this responsibility with an open mind, he serves the best interests of the employee, the company, and himself.

All possible roadblocks should be eliminated and the way smoothed to facilitate and speed progress toward goal achievement.

7. Minimizing Frustration for Improved Results

Pathways to goals are not straight, uneventful roads which are traversed with ease and surety. Rather, the journey is often thwarted, delayed, detoured, or stopped completely. When this happens, the goals established for the enterprise will not be met, individuals will be disappointed, and a tag of failure will be hung on the activity.

Frustration can be described as the failure to attain a desired goal, resulting in abnormal behavior. The individual proceeds without complications until barriers are confronted over which he is unable to move. The first or even the first several confrontations with insurmountable barriers may do no harm; but when the individual begins to feel that the barrier will never be overcome, then negative problems often result, minimizing the job contribution, creating additional supervisory problems, and posing a serious threat to the job security of the individual and the goals of the department.

Controlled laboratory experiments in animal psychology have proved to be most revealing as guides to human behavior. One such experiment is to induce frustration in a normal, healthy, growing white rat. Through a careful control of food, the rat is induced to solve maze problems in order to satisfy his hunger. The decisions necessary to obtain food are quickly learned. When the maze is changed, the rat soon learns to solve the new problem. Finally the maze is altered in such a way that no predictable pattern of action leads to the food. After a short period during which the rat tries to find some solution, there is a dramatic change in its behavior. The rat now trembles, turns in circles, loses all desire for food, bites indiscriminately at everything close by, no longer makes any effort to solve the problem, and is apparently willing to give up and die.

Human behavior can change almost as drastically. The individual starts out with the confidence that he can lick the world, get the job done, win a promotion, earn an increase in pay, and experience bushels of satisfaction from the terrific results he will achieve. Along the way, his timetable is often thrown off schedule—he doesn't get the raise or the promotion he expects, and this causes him severe disappointment. In most cases the employee's reaction is philosophical; he vows to work harder and be more deserving at the time of his next performance review. His energy continues to be oriented toward the job and its purpose.

The real problems enter the picture when disappointment becomes so severe and sustained that the man engages in abnormal problem solving and activity which is not related to goal achievement. The supervisor must now be concerned with the potential loss of production and a deliberate interference with the contributions of others which could drastically curtail the success of the department. This situation requires quick and careful attention.

SOURCES OF FRUSTRATION

Frustration can result any time a person expects to satisfy a desire but fails to do so. The more a man is led to expect from the job, the greater his frustration if these expectations are not fulfilled. The individual often does expect too much from a job. He may have ambitions and aspirations beyond his ability. He may fail to recognize that to receive a promotion, increased compensation, prestige, self-satisfaction, and all the other things he wants, he must be willing to pay the price in hard work and the type of contribution which merits these things. Too often he blames others for his failure to get what he expects.

If the supervisor has oversold an employee on the possibilities of the job, he is asking for future trouble. It is the supervisor who interprets and explains the company's decisions and actions. He can do much to remove the sting of disappointment by learning to anticipate and forestall it.

There are many situations over which the company and those in it

The journey toward goal achievement is often thwarted, delayed, detoured, or stopped completely.

have little or no control, but which often affect the job-related satisfaction of the employee. Economic conditions change; the need for
a particular product diminishes; old, worn-out machinery is replaced
with a new type; or the company is not growing enough to make
promotions available as fast as desired. All these mean possible disappointment for the employee.

The company may fail, for example, to establish an expected new
supervisor's job, so that one less promotion is available. It may lose
an order for its product which would have enabled it to expand. It
may fail to keep the promises it made at the time of hiring the individual. It may deal too much in personalities; favorites may receive
undue consideration. Pay increases and promotions may not be
handled properly.

Frustration, like any other behavior pattern, is caused—it doesn't
just happen by accident. The supervisor's awareness of possible
causes helps him determine whether frustration is likely to result
when certain combinations of circumstances and individuals are
mixed together. The following will offer some guides.

Level of tolerance. Some people are very exacting—they are said to
have a place for everything and to want everything to be in its place.
Such a person is likely to have definite expectations about his job,
and the slightest deviation causes him severe disappointment. On the
other hand, some people have a broader tolerance range. Their picture of what they can expect from the job is not as precise, and it
takes rather severe jolts to disappoint them. Because these wide differences in reaction can be expected, it is essential for the supervisor
to know his people extremely well as individuals.

History of frustration. The supervisor can anticipate that certain
employees will be disappointed at the slightest setback if they have
often exhibited frustration in the past. Established behavior patterns
are a tip-off to what can be expected in a given situation.

Pressures and needs of the moment. If a man has promised to buy
his wife new furniture because he expects a salary increase or promotion next week, he is going to experience great disappointment if
neither is received. When a father needs extra money to keep his son
in college, failure to get a raise may cause frustration. And the man
who has been bragging to everyone that he is going to get a promotion often blames the supervisor or the company if it doesn't come
through.

Interpretation of the situation. A man's attitude toward the supervisor and the company may well determine how he interprets events which affect him on the job. He may see only the most painful and disappointing aspect of every event. Some people assume that each situation is considered on its merits; others consider any unfavorable decision as proof that the supervisor is picking on them and will never let them get ahead. The amount of frustration which results from any given situation is substantially influenced by the individual's interpretation.

Seriousness of the incident and time span involved. Most people can shake off minor disappointments and can endure stress for a reasonable period of time. But serious disappointment or prolonged stress requires the supervisor's special attention lest it affect job performance.

SYMPTOMS OF FRUSTRATION

Just as certain cloud formations indicate the probability of rain, so do certain behavior patterns indicate potential frustration. When the supervisor recognizes the true nature and causes of these patterns, he can often find solutions to the problems by rechanneling employee activities into productive job performance. The following three patterns are tip-offs that something may be wrong.

1. *Change in job performance.* When a man has been on the job for several years and has a good overall record, something, as we have seen, must be afoot if this changes suddenly or even gradually. He has demonstrated through the years that he knows how the job should be done. Change is an indication that his attitude, his feeling, or perhaps his overall interest has altered. Productive activity could now become meaningless or even destructive in nature.

2. *Increase in emotional behavior.* Reactions which have been rational and unemotional may suddenly become emotional and irrational. Not only does the supervisor have difficulty explaining why the employee does certain things, but the man himself often seems confused as to why he feels or acts the way he does. This emotional reaction could show up in relationships with other people or in job performance.

3. *Increase in non-goal-directed activity.* If a man has a clear understanding of the job to be done and the type of activity neces-

sary to get it done, few problems result so long as he directs his efforts to meet this goal. However, when much of his activity becomes pointless, when he moves in circles or hints about getting even with someone, or even when he simply fails to accomplish anything constructive, then frustration is a possible cause.

FOUR PATTERNS OF FRUSTRATED BEHAVIOR

The supervisor has justifiable concern when any of the four behavior patterns that follow appear on the job, since they tend to replace useful productive activity with almost senseless confusion.

1. *Excessive aggression.* An overly aggressive person may attack—physically or in some other way—the object of his displeasure. Modern law and custom deter most forms of physical attack; thus the attack may be made verbally or through negative attitudes. Often considerable damage can be done by attacking the character, the reputation, and the job being done by the person who is the object of displeasure, especially if this is the supervisor.

The aggressive person has a chip on his shoulder; he throws his weight around because he has been frustrated. He exhibits such symptoms of aggression as excessive criticism, constant grievances, damaging or careless use of equipment, failure to get along with other people, and a certain belligerence in all contacts.

It is not the intention of this discussion to imply that all forms of aggression are harmful or undesirable. A hustling salesman, a conscientious supervisor, and a top worker are often fairly aggressive. This sort of aggressiveness should be encouraged so long as it is directed toward goal achievement and does not interfere with the rights of others.

2. *Regressive tendency.* When we regress we go backward, and when the adult goes back, he goes back to childhood. Take a look at these immature behavior patterns: name-calling, violent arguments, loss of emotional control, pouting, crying, blind following of a leader, refusal to accept responsibility, belief in rumors, inability to think logically and objectively. Although these are characteristic of children, they are all too often found in adults on the job. This type of job performance is harmful rather than helpful to the supervisor's effort to build a productive team.

3. *Abnormal fixation.* Extreme stress can cause compulsive behav-

ior which continues even though it accomplishes nothing and has no value. It may go hand in hand with the employee's refusal to accept change. Frustration seems to freeze the old patterns and prevent the acceptance of new ones—often in those who have lost self-confidence.

4. *Resignation.* This negative form of behavior is most frustrating to the supervisor. It is not resigning from the job—rather, it is a state of giving up. Frustration which results in resignation causes loss of production in the individual and has a demoralizing effect on the group as a whole. The individual may avoid serious trouble and escape discharge, but he is seldom good enough to deserve more money. He is the type of person who has been on the payroll for many years on the same job, often with very little change in salary or responsibility.

A man who had been employed for many years in a major department store was quick to tell new employees that they would never get ahead with the company because the company would not promote him. However, he failed to state two important facts—first, that he had been head of the department for five years and had lost money each year; and second, during his years with the company dozens of others had passed him on their way up the executive ladder. Here was a man who exhibited all the symptoms of resignation to his unhappy state of affairs and blamed it all on the company. His one aim in life seemed to be that of instilling in others the same unproductive resignation.

PREVENTING AND REMEDYING FRUSTRATION

Although frustration can be one of the supervisor's most difficult problems and one that can drain away tremendous productive potential, it should be encouraging to know that most frustration can be prevented to begin with or eliminated if it exists. It is in this area that the supervisor must know his people thoroughly and be willing to take the time to do the things which need to be done.

In his attempt to minimize potential causes of frustration, the prudent supervisor recognizes at all times that a major reason for frustration is the failure to achieve an expected goal. He should be constantly alert to circumstances in the department as well as to the aspirations, long- and short-range, of the people who are his responsibility. If he is, he will be aware that a promotion which makes one person happy will disappoint several others who had hoped to get the same promotion. Also, changes in work schedules, machines, and systems can result in anxiety and confusion. These situations challenge the supervisor to take the necessary steps to prevent frustration before it occurs.

A knowledge of the employee and the pressures he is operating under at the moment supplies the supervisor with valuable information. Though frustration may affect a whole group, in most cases it is an individual's reaction to an event that touches on his own personal expectation.

An ear to the ground can detect problems in their early stages before they become serious and while they are still comparatively easy to handle. The battle is half-won if frustration can be detected early, so that the supervisor can counsel with the individual and alter those circumstances which can be changed.

There are many approaches the supervisor can use to minimize frustration in the work environment. Among the most sensible preventive measures which can be taken are the following.

Avoid impractical promises. Do not encourage the employee to anticipate results beyond what he can reasonably expect to achieve. Serious mistakes are made in setting unrealistic goals when employing people. However, a mistake is also made if no reasonable goals are set.

Goals should not be so small and meaningless that they offer no challenge; rather, the approach should be one of caution lest the job be oversold or the mark set so high that the employee cannot reasonably expect to reach it. If either is done, disappointment and potential frustration are inadvertently built into the situation.

Set recognizable intermediate goals. A child does not attend school for 12 years without receiving some indications of progress. Tests, grades, report cards, and promotions mark the steps along the way. In the same way, the supervisor and the company should provide signs of progress—pay increases, added responsibility, opportunity to learn some new phase of the job, or other indicators that the company is aware of the employee's presence, wants him to grow, and believes in him.

Offer encouragement and reassurances. The individual who remains on the same job and at the same pay rate for an extended period may feel that he is making no progress—a sure source of disappointment and frustration. The supervisor can do much to prevent these reactions by helping the man understand what progress he is making while still on the same job—he learns every day, does his job better, merits more confidence, is closer to the next step up.

Clarify the employee's responsibility for his own goal achievement. Make certain that the man has a realistic understanding of what he must contribute to the job in order to reach his goals. The company cannot assume total responsibility for seeing that he reaches certain levels of pay and status; it provides the opportunity, but he must contribute the work, the extra study, the response to job requirements if he expects to attain his goals.

Face up to realities when necessary. Although the supervisor wants to keep his best foot forward and put the best possible construction on all difficulties, occasionally there are situations which he should not try to ignore or hide. If he is weak, he may attempt to sweep them under the rug, pass the buck, or shift the responsibility to someone else. However, this only causes delays and permits the problems to become more serious.

Employees do not always get everything they expect from the job. Not everyone can be given a promotion, and few people get as much money as they think they are worth. The supervisor's severest challenge in preventing frustration is in being honest with people when the reasons for their failure must be faced. He is not going to work miracles and make all his employees happy every time, but he should explain his actions and make every reasonable effort to keep his employees informed.

WHEN THE EMPLOYEE REACHES HIS CEILING, THEN WHAT?

An oft-debated question is whether to tell an employee when, in the company's judgment, he can't go much further. Every company needs qualified people who will stay in their present jobs and continue to get the work done year after year—including those who are not ambitious and anxious to move up the ladder as well as those who have limitations for additional growth. However, certain individuals are not going to be satisfied with limited progress, whatever the company's judgment and their own limited contributions. They will continue to push and become more dissatisfied with each passing month. It seems only fair to them, as well as a protection to the company, that they be informed of this judgment. Then, with all the facts in their possession, they can decide for themselves whether to remain with the company.

The desire to contribute and the application of effort are the two greatest determinants of on-the-job results.

8. Motivation for Maximum Job Contribution

THE SUPERVISOR who effectively coordinates the various influences leading to proper employee motivation can direct a beautiful symphony of production music. If he is not skilled in the use of motivation, he is in for a frustrating and disappointing career of trying to accomplish results through other people.

Motivation involves the human will to work, to contribute, and to cooperate. Motivating is causing activity to occur which leads to desirable results. As one psychologist has said, "The application of psychology consists chiefly of the manipulation of stimuli so that they will set off the desired habit patterns." This states the supervisor's responsibility for managing the employee and his work environment in order to effect those job performance patterns that will produce the required results.

In those areas of religious and civic activities where volunteers are a major source of manpower, leaders must rely exclusively on motivation to get the job done. Since no salaries are involved, the volunteers cannot be forced to participate. The total success of this type of activity is dependent on effective motivation. In a sense, many industrial situations fall into a similar category. It is accepted that a company pays a salary and that this can be stopped. But the difference between what mere presence on the job can achieve and what the conscientious desire to make a contribution can achieve is the difference between success and failure. Therefore, no business can be satisfied with only the voluntary effort of the employee; each must be motivated and stimulated to greater effort.

THE FINE ART OF MOTIVATION

The stairway to effective motivation includes discovering each individual's needs and desires; identifying how these needs can be satisfied; communicating to the employee that his desires can be achieved by following the recommended procedure; enhancing the desirability of the needs in order to make them more attractive; convincing the employee that his goals are worth the effort required to attain them; providing the technique whereby the employee can attain these goals by following the advocated course; and initiating and maintaining employee activity which will insure the accomplishment of these goals.

These steps provide a real challenge to the supervisor. They may seem deceptively simple, but they involve most areas of leadership. The supervisor must know his people and their individual needs. He must know how these needs can be realized through the work environment. He must be able to convince the employee of the desirability of good work and full effort. He must instill better work habits by providing training, effective leadership, and other factors which will pave the way to increased motivation and productivity.

It is difficult to recover tomorrow the production lost today or to sell enough next month to compensate for this month's failures to sell. To keep both production and sales high, motivation must be kept high. And just as the salesman must be motivated to sell, so must the customer be motivated to buy. It isn't enough for the salesman to say he wants to meet his quota for the day or to win a selling contest—these are of interest to the salesman but not to the potential purchaser. If a customer is to be stimulated to buy he must be given the answer to the question, "What's in it for me?"

To motivate employees to accomplish maximum results, the supervisor must appeal to them in a way that elicits a positive response. Such an appeal should take into account the following:

1. The goal and activity must be of interest to the employee.
2. Appropriate information must be presented.
3. The presentation must be convincing.
4. The process must be provocative.

Few people are endowed with enough self-motivation to guarantee that they will give every task their full attention and effort. It isn't that they are habitually unwilling to respond, but if employees were

Motivating is causing activity to occur which leads to desirable results.

completely self-motivated and were performing each task to the best of their ability, there would be far less need for supervision.

Company standards are set to utilize the full potential of the employee, and the supervisor's function is to see that the standards are met. If the employee does not apply himself to the job, the goals will not be met. So, in reality, we are concerned not so much with motivation itself as with the ultimate fulfillment of the goals.

HOW PEOPLE CAN BE MOTIVATED

The foundation on which motivation can be built is not a lot of pretty-sounding platitudes or social activities. Before the supervisor can initiate activity, institute change, or elicit extra effort on the part of the employee, a few simple questions must be answered: "How do I benefit? What do I get out of it?" Let's face facts—neither the production employee nor anyone else will vary the way he performs his duties until he is shown that there is a better way and that it is to his benefit to follow the better way.

Several factors influence human action and reaction. People respond to the need for food, shelter, air, self-preservation, avoidance of pain, and bodily comfort; to love, parental instincts, social drives; to a desire for security, beauty, happiness. Most of these have to do with physical comfort or satisfaction. They also respond to other drives and needs, including the opportunity for self-development and for promotion, financial compensation, desirable work in a pleasant environment, the opportunity to render a service, respect from others, social status, fair and helpful leadership, and an opportunity to influence their own future. These form the nucleus of job-related desires and become the doorways through which the supervisor can channel his motivation efforts.

FACTORS WHICH DETERMINE RESPONSE TO MOTIVATION

The laboratory experiments used in motivating rats to find their way through mazes demonstrate clearly the principles of motivation. Among the factors that determine response, let us discuss four.

1. *Strength or intensity of the drive.* The degree of hunger determines whether the laboratory rat moves from the starting position,

GUIDES FOR EFFECTIVE USE OF MOTIVATION

The supervisor must keep in mind that employee motivation is not effected by an isolated incident. It is developed by the total atmosphere of the department, the confidence the employee has in the supervisor, and the way the tools of supervision are used. The following specific areas should be considered in seeking an improvement in motivational effectiveness.

Make appeals specific. High-sounding platitudes seldom change mediocre performance into total effort. Instead, the supervisor has to get down to brass tacks. "The more specific the stimulus, the more immediate will be the response," according to one psychologist.

It is not enough to say "Work harder, produce more, and you'll get ahead around here." The job applicant wants to know what the training program contains, how long it will last, what salary will be paid, and what can be expected when the training is completed. The employee is more likely to respond if the supervisor says, "Joe, I know how you can earn 25 cents more per hour."

Emphasize the positive. People have to believe in themselves to accomplish extraordinary feats. The supervisor can apply this principle by expressing his confidence in the employee, calling attention to his assets, reminding him of his successes, and then conveying the message that the goal that has been set is designed especially for someone with his qualifications.

Make use of symbolic appeals. The salesman cannot prove to the customer that a $6,000 automobile will provide faster transportation than one costing half as much. Therefore, if he expects to make the sale, he must use secondary stimulators and other symbols to create desire—comfort, luxury, prestige, pride, and a dozen other factors which have little to do with transportation. Similarly, the supervisor must appeal to the employee's pride, to his wish to be well regarded by his associates, to his yearning for the extra security and prestige that additional money can afford him, and to his desire for the satisfaction a promotion will bring him.

Make effective use of words. Joseph Conrad stated, "Give me the right word and the right accent, and I will move the world." Words can make tears flow; they can incite mobs to action; they can lift men to lofty endeavors; they can soothe injury; they can cause mayhem. Words form the foundation for one man's influence over others. The supervisor who expects to influence employees is dependent on the skillful use of words.

Combine motives skillfully. A single motive, if strong enough, can provoke action; a combination of motives elicits greater response. The supervisor needs to discover the interests of the employee and to gauge the strength of those interests in order to so use them that each complements and strengthens the others. The impact of a combination of motives may be compared to the impact of a coordinated team of football players; together they are far more effective than even the superstars can be alone.

Develop a sense of responsibility in the employee. The amount which a given department can accomplish is limited if every employee must be prodded continually. Instead, the supervisor should help each worker in his department to develop a sense of responsibility, because the productive employee is the one who is well informed about production goals and company objectives, who understands that good performance is in his own self-interest, and who recognizes that his own effort affects the survival of the enterprise that provides him with his livelihood.

Early in his career C. H. Greenewalt, chairman of E. I. du Pont de Nemours & Co., Inc., used to report to work an hour early each morning and stay an hour longer than the rest of the employees in his department. When told that Du Pont did not require such long hours of work he replied, "I'm working for Du Pont from 8:30 to 5:30; the rest of the time I'm working for myself. I want my work done better than that required to just get by. I want to know that it is as perfect as I can make it." This willingness to sacrifice immediate pleasures for long-range rewards is an example of the self-motivation and sense of responsibility that can help a man along the road to the leadership of one of America's largest corporations.

PUTTING MOTIVATION INTO PRACTICE

Theories do not produce results until they are effectively translated into action. Thus the principles of motivation must be put into practice by the supervisor before improvement will result. The suggestions that follow can facilitate the theory-to-practice transition.

Make maximum use of the most effective tools. The mechanic has a special tool for each task and completes the job successfully by selecting the correct tool and using it skillfully to perform its unique role. In selecting the most appropriate tool for motivating employees, the supervisor must give consideration to the personality of the individual, the goal to be reached, the timing, and the long-range aims of both the individual and the company.

Resolve conflicting motives. Little can be accomplished so long as motives are in direct conflict with one another; one set of motives must dominate before action results. Most of the decisions which employees are forced to make are not between good and bad but between alternatives with only shades of difference. When conflicts arise in deciding between courses of action, the temptation is to select the one which leads to immediate results even though the greater future gain has to be sacrificed. Impulsive decisions are usually those offering immediate satisfaction. The supervisor's responsibility is to assist the employee with an honest evaluation of both sides of the decision scale. If he can inspire and motivate the employee to plan and work for the long-range goal through an appropriate selection of conflicting motives, he will have rendered a real service to the individual and to the department.

Use competition to motivate. Most people like to compete and have a strong desire to win. Winning gives them a sense of satisfaction and boosts their ego. Often the best way to stimulate one department to greater production is to show what another department is doing. Competition adds interest and zest to the job, gives the employees something to talk about and something to take pride in, and serves as a production stimulator.

The employee's response depends on how effectively the supervisor explains the situation and on the desirability of the reward. Competition can vary from elaborate companywide contests to one man's effort to better his own record. If some phases of the job are not appealing or exciting, competition may be the best way to stimulate interest. Job-related housekeeping, for example, is uninteresting but necessary; a clean-up campaign with prizes offered for the best department is often the most effective way to achieve results.

Use incentives to motivate. Incentive can take a variety of forms, but if structured properly and explained to employees, it can become one of the supervisor's most important motivating tools. Money is the best all-round stimulator, but intangible incentives also produce dividends of extra effort. The most commonly used incentives are piece-rate pay scales and commissions on sales. In each case, the employee is paid in proportion to his contribution—a form of incentive that is direct and easy to understand. However, in many areas it is difficult to pay on the basis of production. When this is the case, department incentives or some type of profit-sharing plan can be used.

One large national company employed 1,200 people in a storage and shipping warehouse where there was no reasonable way to establish incentives for individual employees. The company called in a management consultant who studied the situation, established a standard operating cost for the warehouse, and initiated a program whereby a fixed percentage of any improvement in this cost figure would be shared with employees, payable monthly and prorated according to salary. The employees were told that this was not a scheme to get them to produce more, but simply a way for them to earn more money. Then they were shown how they could cut down on the use of supplies, avoid waste, streamline work procedures, and get the job done quicker. By the end of the third month they were making an average of $28 extra per month. And because they were proud of their accomplishment, they continued to show steady improvement.

MOTIVATING EMPLOYEE COOPERATION

The supervisor has a clearer understanding of the importance of cooperation when he is aware of the difference between a cooperative and an uncooperative employee. Among the characteristics typical of the cooperative employee are these: He tends to cooperate fully at every opportunity; he trusts the supervisor's instructions and the company policy; and he has a favorable attitude, is well adjusted on the job, and generally goes along with what the supervisor and the company wish to accomplish.

The uncooperative employee, on the other hand, needs to be sold or almost forced to cooperate. He approaches most tasks negatively and discharges them grudgingly, and the quantity and quality of his results reflect this forced effort. He does only what he is required to do and seldom puts forth extra effort. He has a tendency to be suspicious of most instructions and work assignments. He complains and gripes about other people and about the company in general. He is afraid he will do more than his share of the work. And he consumes a disproportionate share of the supervisor's time and emotional energy. This opposite side of the cooperation coin indicates clearly that the leadership required to create and maintain a cooperative workforce is a vital part of every supervisor's job.

Cooperation requires knowledge, identification, and action on the part of the employee. He must know the goals, identify himself with them, and take action to make the goals a reality. The supervisor must not only be familiar with pertinent factors but must also make sure that his employees know them. Cooperation is a dynamic process, with both the supervisor and the supervised contributing their own ideas and methods to achieve an established goal. There are several techniques which the supervisor can use to promote and motivate cooperation.

Provide adequate training. People are more willing to do things which they do well and from which they derive a sense of accomplishment. If the employee understands how to do the job and is skillful in performing the required activities, he is inclined to work more cooperatively.

Keep employees informed. Employees are more inclined to go along if they know where they are going. It is much easier to be a cooperating member of the team if you understand the game and know which signals and plays will be used.

Provide dependable leadership. An employee's experience with the supervisor determines whether he is willing to depend on what the supervisor says. If he has confidence in the supervisor, he is motivated to cooperate rather than to question; he returns in kind the degree of cooperation he receives.

Build positive attitudes. Attitudes set the stage for cooperation or for lack of cooperation. If the employee has a positive, trusting attitude, cooperation is likely to be a companion trait.

Work for the interest of the employee. It is much easier to cooperate with someone who works for your interests and is willing to go to bat for you. Employees need someone to champion their cause. It is often difficult, despite the open-door policy stated in employee handbooks, for rank and file employees to make direct contact with top management. To the employee the supervisor is the vital link with management. The supervisor has an opportunity to win the cooperation of his people if he works consistently for their best interests.

Give instructions properly. Use the "let's do it" approach instead of giving orders. Make it easy for employees to cooperate by making certain that instructions are clear, brief, and easy to understand. When asking for cooperation, be willing to explain "why."

Provide safe and favorable working conditions. Avoid tensions in working conditions. The supervisor has the responsibility for insuring that machines and procedures provide maximum safety. He should also create a favorable environment in which to work.

Ask questions. Telling people may produce a defensive reaction, but asking their opinion motivates cooperation. An executive of a well-known company learned that the best way to sell was to ask enough questions to find out how the product could best be used by the customer. Customers complimented him on the way he sold—he didn't use high pressure and seemed to know just what they needed. Still other successful executives and supervisors have learned the secret of asking, "Would you mind?" and "What do you think?" That is, asking enough questions to make certain that all the information is presented. Getting across information through the proper questions is more effective than imparting the same information with an emphatic statement.

Be a leader—not a boss. The supervisor's example is a stronger influence than his words. Proper leadership makes it easy for employees to cooperate—they simply follow the example of the supervisor. Employees have to work *for* a boss but can work *with* a leader.

It is the supervisor's responsibility to create a cooperative work environment and provide the leadership which will encourage employee cooperation. He should approach this area of responsibility the same way a salesman approaches a customer—if the customer doesn't buy, the salesman hasn't sold. If the employee is uncooperative, the supervisor must recognize that he has failed in his efforts to develop a cooperative response.

JOB INTEREST AND MOTIVATION

The activities in which we excel are those which interest us. Those which do not interest us are performed with little enthusiasm, with no effort for improvement, and consequently with minimum success. Interest is the intangible nourishment which intensifies the desire to improve both performance and results.

Everyone wants an interesting job, but each individual has his own idea of what is interesting. To one person, an interesting job must present challenges to be met and problems to be solved. To others, a job is interesting if it is important but doesn't require much decision making. The real task of the supervisor is to identify the aspects that are of interest and communicate them to the employee. The degree of interest in the job, in the department, and in the total work environment has a direct bearing on employee turnover, grievances, and job results. Job interest does not appear on the balance sheet, but its effect is there just the same. When motivating employees to take more of an interest in their work, the supervisor should recognize that certain job-related factors influence the degree of interest an individual is likely to have in his job:

- Attitude toward the total work environment. If the employee believes in the company, the supervisor, and the importance of his job, the job becomes more interesting to him. His attitude is central to the formation of the other factors which determine job interest.

- Progress on the job. Most employees begin the job with interest, but this can wither away if insufficient progress is made. Progress can be recognized by salary increases, promotions, or other rewards. It is much easier for an employee to maintain interest if he feels that his day-to-day effort is leading him forward.

- Quality of supervision. Interest is influenced by the attitude of the supervisor. Imaginative leadership eliminates frustration and maintains harmony, assuring a more interesting job.

- Associations on the job. For many employees the associations developed on the job are the most important factor in promoting job interest. Strong social units are often developed, and the employee looks forward to being with the group. This association with the group can supply an important portion of the satisfaction and interest which the job offers the individual—especially in repetitive or routine work which affords the opportunity for conversation while the work is being done. For example, in some clerical, sales, and manual jobs, the proximity of the workers and the low noise level make social exchange practical during working hours.

- Challenge. For many employees challenge and interest are closely associated. College graduates make unsatisfactory taxi drivers—because the job is not challenging, they have too many accidents. When an employee finds no challenge in the job, it becomes boring and holds little interest for him.
- Satisfaction. Many employees enjoy working with people. This contact with others is the focus of interest and part of the intangible compensation the individual is seeking from the job environment.

There are many factors which tend to minimize or destroy the interest needed for maximum job performance. For example, when the supervisor fails to recognize good work or to show appreciation for superior effort, the employee quickly loses interest. Every opportunity should be taken to say to the employee, "You handled that well; that was good work; keep it up." Mediocre workers can often be stimulated to top production if appropriate appreciation is shown.

If the supervisor loses the respect of his employees, they will lose interest in the job. No one likes to work for a supervisor who lacks the necessary knowledge, does not give honest answers, plays favorites, mistreats employees in any way, fails to communicate necessary information, or is unable to organize the work and provide the necessary leadership.

Often the temporary employee—or the employee who plans to resign—has little interest in the job. Since a temporary job offers no prospect of security, increases in pay, or promotion, the employee has no motivation to try to make good.

Although poor health is a factor over which the supervisor has little control, it certainly influences job interest. If the employee's physical energy is being sapped by illness, pain, or emotional strain, he is unable to exhibit a vital and enthusiastic interest in his job. And home problems that worry the employee will almost certainly result in a lack of interest.

The "bad apple" is an enemy of on-the-job interest. Workers are more easily influenced by a disgruntled employee than by a productive and interested one. Casual disparaging remarks can be especially detrimental to the newer employee who is seeking answers and who is developing feelings about the job. If positive answers are not given by the supervisor, the employee often falls under the influence of a "bad apple."

However, every job can be interesting if it is important and if its relationship to other company activities is understood. Employees on identical jobs have varying degrees of interest in the work, since interest is influenced more by the individual's interpretation and emotional reaction than by what is actually involved in the job. The supervisor cannot depend on the job to generate its own interest; he must actively assist the employee by motivating him to develop a more dynamic interest in the job.

For example, the supervisor can emphasize the interesting aspects of a task. He knows more about the job than the employee; he should explain facets of the job that the employee might not otherwise notice. If a man can see his job from a new perspective, what now seems dull or routine may be seen as interesting and even exciting. Operating an elevator can be viewed as excessively dull—or as an opportunity to insert a pleasant note into the lives of many people every day.

The supervisor can also keep the employee aware of the importance of the job. To a business every job is important. If it were not, money would not be paid to have someone do the job. The employee needs to understand the importance of his particular job—the service he renders, the product he makes. We often treasure possessions not because of their material value but because of the value we assign to them. When the employee is doing work he considers important, he takes great interest in the job.

Employees need to have a clear picture of the goals they are expected to meet. The establishment of quotas or goals not only stimulates interest but also serves as one of the surest ways of increasing production. Whether it is a safety standard or a production goal, the employee should understand the mark he is attempting to hit. Goals should be high but not unrealistic; they should be explained clearly; the employee should be given every possible assistance in meeting them; and he should be kept informed of his progress toward those goals.

Job interest may be heightened by explaining the employee's relationship to other jobs. A job must be viewed in its relationship to other company activity in order to be interesting and meaningful—and productive. Whether his job is processing papers, producing bolts, or selling insurance, the employee must understand how his contribution relates to the success of the company.

Both the relationship of the supervisor to the individuals in the department and the relationships of employees with one another are crucial factors in determining job interest. This is often revealed when transfers and other changes are discussed with employees— resistance usually centers not around changes in the work but around changes in the work groups. An employee is often reluctant to leave the familiar social environment because he is uncertain about how he will fit in with the new group.

Finally, an employee is less likely to lose interest when the supervisor is concerned with and interested in his activities. To be engaged in an activity in which no one else is interested causes the individual's own interest to die.

MOTIVATION AND EFFICIENCY

Efficiency is a concern of every employee in every company. Efficiency does not mean an incessant struggle to produce more at the expense of one's health. Rather, it means the elimination of waste— wasted motion, wasted material, and wasted time.

The efficiency of an automobile is stated in miles per gallon. This efficiency is affected by the condition of the motor, the speed at which the car is driven, the terrain over which it moves, the skill of the driver, and other variables. It is more difficult to measure human efficiency. How do we know how much effort an individual is exerting? The amount produced is not a reliable criterion. Observation is not reliable; often the person who seems to be busiest has the least to show for his efforts at the end of the day. On the other hand, a man who seems to be wasting time may accomplish the greatest amount.

Efficiency is concerned with human input as it relates to the quality and quantity of results. The efficient person makes the best use of machines, raw materials, time, effort, and of the investments the company has made to create and continue his job. The employee may rate his efficiency in terms of the amount he earns or on the basis of units produced in a given time. The supervisor may judge efficiency by the relationship of departmental production to the number of employees. The company and the stockholders are likely to consider return on investment the most important criterion of efficiency.

During the past 50 years, psychologists, efficiency engineers, and managers from first-line supervisors to company presidents have given increasing attention to the efficiency of employees. Efforts have been concentrated on elimination of superfluous motion, more efficient arrangements of the work area, changes in the design and speed of machines, and more scientific placement of individuals on the job.

Frank and Lillian Gilbreth, pioneers in time and motion studies, once made a systematic study of bricklaying and found that by eliminating unnecessary motion the number of movements could be reduced from 18 to 4, with the result that each man's output was increased from 120 to 350 bricks per hour. A great deal of research has since been concentrated on increasing efficiency, and industrial engineering and "human engineering" are the subjects of many courses now included in company training programs and college curricula.

Certain identifiable factors are obstacles to efficiency—fatigue, noise, boredom, poor lighting, inefficient supervision, lack of sleep, worry, lack of interest, inadequate training, poor health, lack of energy, and a host of others. All these factors affect efficiency in varying degrees. Studies have been conducted to measure the effect of these obstacles, and serious attention has been given to physical design, planning, and administrative organization in order to provide employees with an efficient work environment. The following steps are helpful in motivating maximum day-to-day efficiency on the job.

Make certain that the work environment promotes efficiency. Are the machines still as efficient as they were or have they slowed down with age? What are the condition and quality of the raw material used? Are all the people in the organization making the appropriate contribution? If someone is letting down on the job, this may interfere with the work of others. Have the methods used in the department become obsolete? Can a more efficient method be substituted?

Many significant factors affecting quality, quantity, and efficiency of work are for all practical purposes beyond the control of the employee. The supervisor should identify the factors which he can influence directly and provide, within the limits of his authority, the most efficient work environment for the people in his department. He has the further responsibility of bringing other factors—those which interfere with employee efficiency—to the attention of management and of pressing for their correction. If the employee is to work efficiently, he must be provided with the most efficient machines, methods, materials, leadership, and surroundings possible.

Anticipate the employee's point of view. No matter what kind of environment the company provides, the employee will be no more efficient than he wants to be. Many employees are merely putting in time. They are not loafing; they work at a leisurely pace from the beginning to the end of the work period. Their purpose seems to be to consume time rather than to complete the task. This type of performance does not meet the company's goal or improve the individual's opportunity for more pay or promotion. The following illustration shows the thought processes an employee may go through in deciding whether to respond to motivation.

What's in it for me?	*What will it cost me?*
I'll make more money, since I'm on an incentive basis.	I'll have to put forth more effort.
The supervisor says it will make me more valuable to the company.	It means I'll have to get in on time, be on the job every day, and waste less time during the day.
I'll gain the approval and recognition of the supervisor.	I'll have to give up visiting with other people during the day.
My name will be posted as one of the top producers in the department.	Some of the other employees may think I'm an eager beaver trying to impress the boss.
The other employees will think well of me if I help win the company contest.	If I work harder and produce more during the contest, the boss will expect me to do the same all the time.
I suppose the better I work, the better my chance for promotion.	I'm not lazy, but I don't know whether I want to work that hard.
I believe I'll enjoy my work and get more satisfaction from the job if I know that I'm doing my best.	Will it be worth the price I'll have to pay?

And so it goes; the employee decides whether to put forth the extra effort necessary to work faster and produce more. But he doesn't go through this procedure all the time; he develops an attitude toward the supervisor and the job that determines his reaction to any attempt to encourage increased effort.

Communicate the benefits of efficiency to the employee. The results of efficient performance should result in benefits to the employee. Efficiency becomes desirable to the employee when it is linked to job security, more pay, promotion, profit sharing, job satisfaction, and overall value to the company.

Keep employees busy. Efficiency becomes a habit if a man works at a steady pace. It is when the employee stops and lets his mind wander that errors occur. The myth that employees who work more slowly are more accurate and more efficient is false; generally, the rapid worker is also the more efficient. The supervisor therefore needs to plan to keep the employees busy and working at a fast pace for top performance.

Continue training. A company continues to exist and grow only in proportion to its success in improving its operating efficiency. The only way this can be accomplished is through improvement in the mechanics of the operation and in the performance of the personnel. Both the supervisor and the company have a responsibility to continue training in order to achieve this improvement. Only in this way can obsolete methods of operation be replaced with more efficient procedures.

Promote understanding of efficiency standards. Most jobs have standards of efficiency. The production operation may allow no more than 5 percent rejects, the sales operation may be permitted no more than 10 percent in returns, the cost estimators may be limited to a 2 percent margin. Whatever the standards, employees must be familiarized with them. Standards of efficiency serve as guides as well as goals; they are meaningless unless the employee understands them and relates them to his own job.

Supervise closely at the beginning and end of the work period. Most errors are made and most inefficient work is performed at the beginning and end of the work period. Once the supervisor recognizes this, he should be able to compensate for this lack of efficiency by his presence and attention to the operation at these crucial times.

Take prompt action if work continues below standard. The supervisor must not ignore inefficient performance by assuming that it will automatically improve in time. He has a responsibility to exert every reasonable effort to bring each employee to an acceptable standard. If this is not reached within a reasonable time and maintained thereafter, certain definite steps should be taken. In some instances a transfer to a more appropriate job may be advisable; in other instances the company may not be able to justify retaining the employee in any capacity.

Encourage pride in workmanship. When an artist paints a picture, a cobbler makes a pair of shoes, or a carpenter builds a house, the finished product is a testimony of the craftsman's pride in his workmanship. The worker who completes an entire process and has a finished product to prove his skill usually takes pride in what he does. But the assembly-line worker or the bank clerk is involved with only a small phase of the overall operation. It is easy for him to lose this pride in workmanship. Since the employee's individual effort may be almost indiscernible, the importance of his contribution must be emphasized by the supervisor.

Expect the employee to work efficiently. Employees generally perform according to what is expected. If the supervisor shows that he expects efficiency, the employee is likely to exert the effort necessary to justify this confidence.

SELF-MOTIVATION

The mature employee should come to recognize that it is in his own self-interest to meet the goals set for his job. Though the supervisor may have had to point this out initially, the employee should supply his own motive force the second time around. Maturity of this kind is not a factor of age; it is instead an ability and a willingness to respond to the requirements of the job.

This self-motivated employee recognizes that job security is related to job performance. He recognizes that his compensation must be a realistic reflection of his own contribution. He accepts the fact that in order to derive satisfaction from the job—recognition, status, approval, and security—he must merit them. He is aware that his own dedication, initiative, compulsion to excel, and willingness to improve will determine his progress on the job. He accepts personal responsibility for his job performance and his future role with the company. He welcomes the assistance of the supervisor in clarifying and strengthening these things, but he is willing to work at them on his own initiative.

What has just been said about the employee applies with even greater validity in the case of the supervisor. If the employee is expected to supply a sizable portion of his own motivation, the supervisor should be expected to supply an even greater portion of the motivation necessary to discharge the duties and responsibilities of his job. As a means to self-motivation, the supervisor should identify the goals of his department; list his own personal goals; identify the ways in which his own goals can be attained through meeting the goals of the department; work out a specific program for realizing his goals; and recognize that he must supply his own initiative and motivation.

Writers and leaders throughout history have recognized the importance of self-motivation. The Roman poet Virgil put it this way: "They can because they think they can." So the supervisor must recognize that it is his choice; it is up to him. Eric Hoffer put it another way in *The Passionate State of Mind*: "We are told that talent creates its own opportunities. But it seems that intense desire creates not only its own opportunities but its own talents." And in the words of one of the nation's leading businessmen: "I believe we make our own ability, talents—even genius through hard work and self-discipline." And the president of a large insurance company once said: "Determine what you are living for, what you are working for, what you are trying to accomplish, and support that philosophy with faith and energy and courage. Know where you are going, and be on your way."

Appropriately handled employee correction can be the supervisor's greatest opportunity for contributing to the achievement of goals: the employee's, the company's, and his own.

9. Correction: The Unique Opportunity

THE FOOTBALL COACH improves his team's chances of winning by correcting the techniques of the players; the parent teaches his child by furnishing corrective guidance; and the supervisor corrects the performance of his workforce to improve results. Yet many supervisors play the role of ostrich by ignoring the need for correction. In so doing, they neglect a primary responsibility of their position and render a distinct disservice to all concerned.

The need for correction is present in every leadership position, and the skill with which it is handled can be a decisive factor in the success of the department and in the professional progress of the leader. Yet no other supervisory responsibility is so misunderstood. It is neglected and delayed because the supervisor does not have confidence in his skill in correction techniques and is afraid he may make someone unhappy. It is misunderstood because many supervisors fail to realize its purpose and the unique opportunity it presents.

We all know men like the mild supervisor who has been on the job for years. He's calm, works hard himself, and doesn't see too much of what goes on in the department. He ignores most minor incidents and laxity. But when a situation is brought to his attention by higher management or has become too critical to be ignored any longer, he pounces. Almost invariably, the employee is resentful and feels mistreated; the supervisor is upset; and the situation is not corrected.

The football coach improves his team's chances of winning by correcting the techniques of the players.

What could have been handed calmly, if dealt with skillfully before it became too serious, now assumes the proportions of a major incident. Such a supervisor commits many of the errors commonly made in connection with the correction procedure.

CORRECTION DEMANDS TOP SKILLS

The proper handling of correction demands mastery of the best leadership skills. There is no unique leadership involved in assigning work, prodding for more production, or discharging those who are unsatisfactory. When supervision is limited to these activities, the best interests of the employee, the company, and the department have not been met. The real test of leadership is rather in leading employees to improvement through correction and training.

Many leaders make the mistake of thinking they have to be one of the boys so that they will be popular and well liked. The fallacy in this belief is that no business enterprise is created for the purpose of staging a popularity contest, and the good guys are not always the most effective ones in getting the job done. The supervisor who is overly concerned about his popularity often lets mistakes go unnoticed, settles for unmet production standards and half-way loyalty —and the result can be a breakdown of productive activity in the department.

Still other supervisors err in the opposite direction. They think they have to be disciplinarians and let people know who is boss in order to get things done. They consider their main function to be that of enforcing a complete set of rules and punishing offenders. They are of the old school which believes that it takes toughness and a show of strength to get things done through other people.

The need for correction arises when a failure has occurred. Failures of omission and of commission can occur on the job. The employee fails to meet job standards when he neglects to do something which he should have done or when he does certain things which he should not have done. In either case, the supervisor has the responsibility of effecting a correction so that established standards will be met. The purpose of correction is to make the adjustments in job activity to meet these requirements. Every company sets certain policies and rules to protect the rights of all concerned and provide for orderly activity.

The need for correction may come to the attention of the supervisor in a variety of ways: He may observe an infraction of a department rule; an employee may make a complaint or request assistance; other employees may bring the need to his attention; a check of production records may reveal that standards are not being met; or a higher executive may indicate that work or policy standards must be improved. In any case, the urgency and the seriousness of the situation that needs correction determine the way it is handled.

Once the level of acceptable performance has been established for the department, the employee is considered satisfactory so long as he meets the standard. If, through negative attitudes or faulty habits, he deviates from the norm by engaging in job performance which is less than satisfactory, it is the supervisor's responsibility to help him return to acceptable standards. It should be noted that the supervisor's concern is with correcting the *performance*, not the individual. This overall view of correction should help the supervisor in keeping correction on an impersonal and objective basis.

THE UNIQUE SERVICE OF CORRECTION

Correction is a direct and deliberate effort to bring about a change in job performance or work-related behavior so that it will more nearly meet the standards established for the job. When this is accomplished, the benefits will be felt not only by the employee but by the supervisor and the company as well.

Service to the employee. Every person who wants to do a good job and increase his value should be receptive to constructive evaluation. If unsatisfactory work is ignored and permitted to continue, it will jeopardize his job security, reduce his job satisfaction, decrease his value, and certainly eliminate any reasonable possibility of promotion. Thus the individual who is permitted to continue without correction is being given unfair and inappropriate leadership. When the supervisor seeks to bring about the desired correction, the employee may not agree initially that he needs to make a change and may reject the criticism. However, it is the supervisor's responsibility to bring about an understanding of the need by relating it to the man's job security, his desire to increase his earnings, and his overall growth with the company.

Service to the supervisor. Certain standards of production are expected from each department; when these are not achieved, the supervisor is not meeting the requirements of his job. And he cannot meet these standards when his people fail to make the necessary contribution. He must therefore recognize that an inherent part of his job is to maintain appropriate work standards and behavior. Just as it is in the employee's self-interest to respond to correction, it is in the supervisor's self-interest to engage in the appropriate procedures to bring about the correction.

The supervisor's problems and his department's accomplishments are directly related to the number of failures which occur in this area of responsibility. The time lapse before they are corrected and restored to normal standards is an indication of his skill in handling people. The greater the time involved, and the greater the deviation from standard, the more negative reflection there is on the supervisor, his capacity to manage his people, and his departmental goal achievement.

Service to the company. The company is committed to pay the salaries of its employees at an agreed rate even if a specific employee's value falls below this level. Since the company's ability to grow, expand, and provide greater job opportunities is the direct result of employee productivity, the entire organization is harmed by employee failures and strengthened by top performance. And because supervisory leadership is the key to meeting standards, the supervisor who does not see to it that all employees receive the required training and correction is not meeting the standards of his job and does not personally deserve the recognition of increased pay or responsibility.

Admittedly, correction is not the most welcome of supervisory tasks. But the service it renders should be sufficient motivation for the supervisor to tackle it with sincerity and understanding. With this supervisory tool he can do more than just correct errors; he can increase production, restore employee self-respect and confidence, and build a loyal workforce. By discovering ways to help employees correct faults which minimize their value to the company, he can lead them from failure to success. And if he succeeds in this effort, he will have performed his finest act of supervisory leadership.

THE APPROPRIATE APPROACH TO CORRECTION

The most important aspect of correction is the supervisor's own attitude and understanding of its purpose—not to punish, browbeat, embarrass, belittle, or grind an employee into the ground; not to be unduly critical of the man personally or of what he does apart from the job, provided it does not adversely affect his work or the well-being of the company; but to make an objective analysis of job standards and job performance and then to seek correction where needed.

Before the supervisor proceeds with correction, he should recognize the following dangers.

Never correct in the presence of others. To do so causes embarrassment to the individual involved as well as to all bystanders.

A regional supervisor visited one of the company's branch units and called several things to the manager's attention which needed correcting. The manager immediately called two supervisors over and proceeded to remind them that they had been told about these things a dozen times and that there could be no excuse for failure to correct them. This was done in the presence of the regional manager, a group of employees, and several customers. As a result, the manager lost the respect not only of the regional manager but also of the employees and the customers, and he failed to correct the situation.

Never correct while angry or upset. When this is done, the correction becomes personal and cannot be kept objective. It will therefore fail to bring about the desired results and may so upset and infuriate the other person that his loyalty and job contribution will be lessened rather than improved.

Never correct in haste, before facts are completely checked. The wise supervisor learns quickly that things are often not what they seem. If his action is based on inadequate information, his handling of the situation will probably be wrong and unfair.

For example, a report was received late one evening that an employee had several items in a bag and planned to take them home at the end of the work period. The man was stopped as he was leaving the building, sent to the superintendent's office, and asked about the company property he was taking out. He explained that the items had been damaged and had been given to him by the supervisor as toys for his children. A quick check did indeed reveal that this information was correct. An apology was made to the employee for the embarrassment and delay. As a result of this incident the supervisor was reminded that a record should be made of discarded items and the employee removing them should be given a copy as his authority to take them from the building. It is hasty action of this type which can cause the supervisor his most embarrassing moments.

Recognize the purpose of the correction. The goal is not to bawl out a man but to correct a job situation. It is to restore right habits, confidence, and maximum contribution. Hasty and improper handling often causes just the opposite: more errors, less production, resentment, and hurt feelings.

Beware of hearsay. Every supervisor is at times bombarded with hints, gossip, and innuendoes that certain things are going on which he should know about and which should receive appropriate action. These things should not be ignored, but they should certainly be kept in perspective, viewed objectively, and not be allowed to build up like a head of steam. Corrective action should be based on facts which he has personally verified, not on allegations or hearsay.

Consider the case of two women who worked side by side in the personnel department. Both had been with the firm for a number of years. One, Margaret, was friendly, talkative, and generally well liked. The other, Judith, was efficient, hard-working, aloof, and a bit brusque in her manner. Outwardly, the two women were cordial. But, in fact, Margaret often complained to the supervisor that Judith antagonized people by snapping at them and ruffling their feathers. The effect of these complaints, extending as they did over a long period of time, was comparable to that of drops of water wearing away stone; the impact on the supervisor was so great that he reprimanded Judith for her way of handling people, and she resigned.

Only after she had left and others had to be trained to do her work did the supervisor realize his mistake. Because he had listened to the hints and innuendoes of a tale-bearer, he had lost a capable and efficient employee. Had he instead investigated, determined Judith's need for counseling to help her learn to deal with people more tactfully, and offered a less receptive ear for Margaret's efforts to downgrade another employee in order to improve her own status in the department, the interests of the company as well as of the supervisor would have been served better.

Do not delay correction unduly when it is clearly needed. The old adage about an ounce of prevention is good advice when it is applied to correction of faulty habits, work, and attitudes. The longer correction is delayed, the more entrenched a habit becomes and the more difficult it is to dislodge.

The personnel director of a large warehouse operation talked with one of the supervisors concerning the excessive amount of time involved in filling orders in his area. The supervisor indicated that some of the employees were not getting in on time and others didn't seem to have enough interest in what they were doing. He cited the case of one man who had developed a habit of coming in 15 to 20 minutes late every morning. When asked what he had done about the situation, the supervisor replied that he hesitated to try to correct such a good worker for fear that he would quit. Further investigation revealed that the man had been coming in late for so long he now considered lateness to be his privilege. Efforts were made to correct the situation, but it had been permitted to continue for too long; the employee thought he was being picked on and eventually resigned. It is significant that this "indispensable" employee was replaced by another man who worked faster and more efficiently.

THE CORRECTION PROCEDURE

The correction procedure should follow a definite pattern if maximum results are to be obtained, though there will be considerable variation in its use to fit the situation. To begin with, the supervisor has to take some preliminary steps before he talks to the employee. First, he should try to eliminate any personal bias he may have concerning the situation and the man so that he can be as objective as possible. Second, he should look at the incident from every angle— how it affects other employees as well as the company and himself, what type of employee he is dealing with, and so on. Third, he should investigate the entire situation—get all the information; be thorough in considering all the facts; check all the conditions leading to and surrounding the incident; and consider the seriousness of the infraction. When necessary, he should consult with others, particularly his own supervisor. His next step is to consider the validity of all information and check whether it is based on facts or just hearsay. Finally, he should review to make certain that he has not overlooked any pertinent information.

In making his analysis of the problem, the supervisor must consider many points and seek answers to many questions, since the cause of the incident often influences the way it should be handled as well as the consequences to the employee. What were the apparent motives of the person involved? Was the incident brought about because of lack of training or information, misunderstanding of instructions, development of poor habits, or deliberate rebellion against the stated policies of the company? Is there evidence of poor supervision, improperly planned work procedures, or off-the-job problems? Is the employee interested in the job, or is it one he feels he shouldn't be doing? Is the job too easy or too difficult? Would a transfer to a more (or less) difficult job solve the problem?

If it is found that correction or penalties are in order, the various types need to be considered. The most common is the oral reprimand, which involves a complete discussion of the event and the admonition to see that it doesn't happen again. In an increasing number of cases a written warning is given and a copy of the information put in the man's record. This becomes especially important if recurrences might force the discharge of the man. Also, it has some effect on the man's eligibility to draw unemployment compensation.

A severe form of discipline is a suspension, involving loss of both money and respect. This is seldom used because the company loses the services of the employee, and the additional workload, in a sense, punishes other employees who were not involved.

The ultimate punishment is discharge. If the employee has a good record before the incident, this is seldom necessary; but if he has had previous warnings and his attitude remains negative, the best course of action may be an outright discharge.

In correcting and disciplining an employee, the supervisor is in essence disciplining every employee in the company. When one man fails to meet the standards of the job, the action taken represents the policy of the company as far as other employees are concerned. It is considered to be an indication of—

- What constitutes a failure or breach of policy.
- Whether the policy means what it says.
- The company's attitude and policy toward violators.
- The supervisor's ability to handle the problems associated with correction and policy enforcement.
- What will happen to other employees if they violate the same policies.

Correction, like every other activity, can be handled more effectively if done at the right time, in the right place, and with the right approach. It is generally agreed that correction should preferably take place near the beginning of the day, certainly before the end of the work period. This gives the employee and the supervisor time to talk again during the day if either so desires. It also gives the employee time to cool off or work off any resentment before he goes home.

The location of the correction interview must provide privacy. The purpose of the correction interview—to restore job performance to acceptable standards—isn't likely to be accomplished if a man is criticized in front of other people. Only if the employee is acting in a dangerous manner which could cause injury to others or damage to the company's property should the supervisor step in and take the action necessary to avert disaster. And even in this type of situation the follow-up correction should be handled in private. Few emergencies are acute enough to justify public embarrassment.

As a general rule, be as easy as possible but as firm as necessary in order to insure appropriate corrective action. Beware of any form of automatic approach. Companies may suggest penalties for infractions, but most of these are intended as guides and not as absolute rules.

CONDUCTING THE CORRECTION INTERVIEW

After preparation and analysis of the situation, the supervisor should be ready to handle the problem and make the correction through an interview with the employee. It is recommended that the interview be conducted as follows.

Arrange for the interview. Select a private place and make time available during which neither party will be interrupted. A correction interview which is broken off in the middle or conducted piecemeal is seldom effective for the employee or easy to handle for the supervisor. Take the man away from his place of work when he can best be spared and when his absence will be least conspicuous.

Plan your approach. If necessary, write down the pertinent facts surrounding the situation. Don't plow into the interview without a clear concept of what you believe to be the problem and alternate ways in which it might be handled. If you have notes and a carefully planned step-by-step approach, you are less likely to become emotional and lose control of the interview.

Always begin with a question. This lets the employee know you are willing to listen—it gets him in the act. Never launch into a long and emotional tirade the moment he enters the room. Instead, proceed cautiously; there is no hurry, and it is not necessary to strike the first blow.

Listen to learn. Listening isn't just refraining from talking. It is also demonstrating that you are willing to consider what the man has to say. Get his side of the situation—his reasons or justification for his action. What he reveals often helps you get to the bottom of the problem. Perhaps his justification for disregarding the rules is that he has so much work to do that he can get it done on time only by ignoring the rules.

Obtain agreement on the facts. After the employee has told his story, restate it and make certain he agrees with your interpretation. Only when there is agreement can you know that you are both talking about the same set of facts and that the correction will deal with these facts.

Retain control of the interview. Although the employee should be encouraged to tell his side of the story, the supervisor should not lose control of the conversation or permit the interview to be diverted from the problem at hand. He should remain calm even though the employee reacts with an emotional outburst. Recognize that it is only normal for him to try to justify his course of action. But remember that it takes two to argue and that he will not remain at a high emotional pitch if the response is calm and unemotional. The important thing is to maintain an open-minded judicial attitude with a minimum of self-assertion. Get the employee to see that it is a business problem, not a personal affair, and that it must be handled because it affects his work.

Weigh all evidence carefully. This includes the new evidence that the employee may reveal. If his reasons are not justified, tell him why. However, if he has a reasonable explanation for his action, perhaps changing the work procedure, giving the man some extra help, or bringing the rules to his attention will be all the correction required.

Seek advice when needed. If the employee offers additional information, the supervisor is often well advised to delay his decision until he has had a chance to evaluate the new evidence. He should seek as much help and advice as seems necessary. Consulting with his own boss is not admitting that the supervisor is unable to handle the situation; rather, it indicates his sincerity and thoroughness. His supervisor will appreciate being consulted; after all, what eventually happens could affect him, too.

Keep in mind the objective to be achieved. The purpose of correction is not to punish or embarrass but to avoid repetition of the incident and to insure that the rules will be followed in the future. This should obviously influence the supervisor's attitude and the techniques he uses in the interview.

Consider company policy and practices. How is this type of incident generally handled? Does the company have a prescribed procedure? Is there a broad framework within which the supervisor is expected to operate? His handling of this matter should not be too far out of line with what is being done in other areas of the company. If his decision sets a precedent, it could affect many other employees.

Fit the correction to the individual. The fair approach is not to use the same type of correction for every individual but to tailor the action to each person and to each situation. Consider such factors as length of service, past history of offenses, seriousness of the incident, the employee's attitude, his willingness to make the correction, what he has said to others about the incident, and the reasons he gives for it. He may not agree with the ultimate decision, but he is likely to understand and accept it as being fair if it takes into consideration all these factors.

Fit the correction to the incident. The driver who overparks at a parking meter does not expect the same sentence as the drunken driver whose speeding and reckless driving result in the death of a pedestrian. By the same token, the employee does not expect severe or harsh punishment for minor infractions of the rules.

The most significant service which the supervisor can render during the whole correction procedure is to provide a specific plan of action which will lead the employee back to acceptable performance. The cardinal rule is, don't just criticize; be constructive.

Make certain the employee understands. During the correction interview, make certain the employee understands your decision and the course of action he is expected to follow. If necessary, write it down and give him a copy.

Close the interview pleasantly and restore self-confidence. The purpose of the interview is not accomplished if the employee leaves like a whipped dog. The interview should be closed pleasantly but firmly. Don't neglect to remind the employee that his dependability and loyalty are highly regarded and that you have confidence in him and his ability to do the job correctly. Encourage him to ask questions if there is anything he does not understand. Invite him to talk with you in the future if he is confronted with unusual problems. When he leaves, he should feel more secure in his job and have greater confidence that the supervisor is interested in him and is there to help him.

Conduct a follow-up interview. The employee deserves a follow-up interview even though it may be short. If he is now doing a good job, the supervisor should recognize the improved performance and compliment the man on his response to the earlier interview. This lets him know that he has not been forgotten and that his good work has been recognized and appreciated. If, on the other hand, it is discovered that he has not made the correction, then a much firmer approach is in order.

After every football game the coach views films of the game in order to learn what the players did well and where they must improve their techniques. Immediately following the handling of a correction situation, the supervisor should also review his techniques to determine what went well and what needs to be improved in order to do a better job next time. Among the areas he should review are whether all pertinent information had been gathered and properly evaluated; whether his understanding of the incident was altogether correct; whether the employee had confidence in the supervisor, an adequate understanding of the rules and policies, and a fair opportunity to express his point of view; what the supervisor or the employee might have done to prevent the need for correction; and what guides the supervisor can use for the better handling of similar situations in the future.

When an employee was called on the carpet by the plant manager for violating the no-smoking rule in a storage area, he said he fully understood this rule and admitted that he had violated it. The plant manager explained the need for the ban on smoking as a fire prevention measure and emphasized that if the employee smoked in the area again he would be discharged. The employee indicated that he understood. Two weeks later, when he was again caught smoking in the area, he was discharged. Failure to be firm when the situation requires firmness can weaken the whole structure of company policy and cause a general breakdown in adherence to these policies.

GUIDES IN THE EFFECTIVE USE OF CORRECTION

The supervisor should keep the following points in mind when attempting to correct the performance of an employee. First, do not correct too frequently. If used too often, correction is annoying and ineffective. It is generally better to handle most minor incidents as part of the continuing on-the-job training. Only the more serious incidents should be taken up in correction interviews.

Second, relate the correction to self-interest and job security. The employee who is expected to make a change must understand how it will affect him. The clearest way to do this is by talking in terms of his own good.

Third, motivate the employee to make the correction. Help him work out a definite program as to time and method for making the correction. Remember that the man is more likely to make the correction if he has good reasons for doing so—reasons which are meaningful to him.

Finally, be firm. Employees respect firmness if it is fair. There is no area in which firmness is more important than in the correction of faulty habits or work performance.

TIPS ON MAINTAINING GOOD DISCIPLINE
AND A PRODUCTIVE ENVIRONMENT

The best way to handle correction is to prevent incidents which require it, just as the best method for handling an accident is to avoid it. The company and the supervisor can eliminate much of the need for correction by eliminating the causes for breaches of company rules and unsatisfactory work. The time and effort spent in prevention will pay rich and lasting dividends to all concerned. These guidelines will prove useful:

1. Make certain that you, as the supervisor, know and understand all policies, prescribed work methods, safety rules, and customer relations guides.

2. Make certain that your employees understand the rules, the reasons for them, and why it is in their best interest to follow them. Training, communication, and personal example are excellent guides for this purpose.

3. Instruct your people carefully in the proper work methods. Most incorrect work is the result of not knowing how or of developing incorrect habits.

4. Make certain instructions are clear and the employee understands fully what is expected of him. The results will be no better than the instruction or the understanding the employee has of what he is expected to do.

5. Take the steps necessary to prevent errors—but don't pounce on the employee. He will not appreciate it, and such action will certainly not merit much respect for the supervisor or make the correction easier.

6. Ask yourself, "How could it have been prevented?" This question should be asked after every accident and after every job failure; when the cause has been determined, appropriate action should be taken to insure that it will not happen again.

THE SUPERVISOR'S OWN ATTITUDE AND CORRECTION

This chapter would not be complete without recognizing that the supervisor has a stake in his own correction. He should recognize that he, too, may fail to carry out his own duties and responsibilities perfectly. The degree to which he can discipline and manage himself determines how much supervision he requires.

The supervisor should constantly have before him the production goals of the department, the company's policies, the standards of the department, and the duties and responsibilities of his job. He should be prudent enough to compare his own job performance with these standards and correct unsatisfactory results. He may be resentful of any criticism about the way he is doing his job. But he had better be smart enough to recognize that his handling of such criticism—the way he accepts it, the way he acts on it—is an important factor in his future, whether he likes to admit it or not. To discharge his duties and responsibilities in the most efficient manner, he must not only seek guidance so as to avoid mistakes but also develop an attitude of accepting all correction gracefully.

The supervisor faces a severe challenge in resolving grievances and in installing change. The failure to neutralize an employee's grievance or overcome his resistance to change can result in the breakdown of effective job performance.

10. Guides for Handling Complaints and Changes

F ROM THE INDUSTRIAL STANDPOINT a grievance is anything in the work situation which the employee considers wrong, unjust, or unfair. He does not have to present objective grounds for his grievance; what is important is that he reacts according to his feeling. Although some grievances are based on factual situations that can be determined accurately, others stem from intangible feelings and are very difficult to understand or explain.

TWO TYPES OF EMPLOYEE COMPLAINTS

A *correction interview* is usually initiated by the manager when he has some criticism about the employee's performance or conduct on the job. On the other hand, a complaint arises when the employee feels that he has a grievance against the company or the work environment. Complaints, whether real or imagined, create a gulf between employee and supervisor, and so long as they remain unsettled they affect job performance.

There are two basic types of complaints: first, those the employee comes right out in the open and talks about; second, those he says nothing about. When his grievances are unexpressed, the symptoms show up in his work and his attitude. The out-in-the-open type is much easier to handle because the supervisor can talk it over with the employee, get his reasons for his dissatisfaction, and attempt to resolve the problem. The unexplained complaint presents the more critical challenge because it is difficult to pin down, identify, and root out. Whatever their form, grievances are usually reflected by indifference, absenteeism, irritability, reduced production, and failure to get along with other people.

POSSIBLE APPROACHES TO HANDLING GRIEVANCES

The best way to handle complaints is to prevent them from arising in the first place, just as preventive maintenance is the best way to avert machine breakdown. Two prevention steps are suggested:

- Maintain an atmosphere promoting the highest morale. Watch for symptoms and danger signals, and handle complaints before they become too serious.
- Maintain open lines of communication. This allows complaints to be brought to the supervisor's attention before they become critical. If the supervisor keeps himself accessible and is alert to employee feeling and thinking, situations can be handled on a preventive basis.

In handling real or imaginary grievances, the supervisor should follow certain patterns of approach.

Learn the basic cause. What really caused the complaint—not just the superficial reason but the real causative factor?

Try to understand all the factors involved. You may think that the employee's complaint is silly and completely off base, but remember that if it weren't bothering him, he wouldn't come to you with it in the first place. He deserves your sympathetic understanding—even though your approach may have to be firm.

Assist the employee in facing the realities of the situation. The employee may be using imagined complaints or company errors simply to cover his own inadequacies. If this is the case, try to make him see the situation in its true light.

Attempt an explanation or settlement as soon as practical. The sooner a grievance is resolved, the easier it usually is to handle. Also, since it probably interferes with the employee's work, it should be resolved at the earliest reasonable moment for his benefit. This is not to suggest that a decision should be made before the matter has been

When an employee has a grievance, the supervisor probably won't have to start the conversation.

thoroughly investigated and all the facts determined. But delay may cause the complaint to become more serious.

Consider the advisability of additional training. Bringing the employee to a satisfactory level of production may eliminate the basis of the complaint, since failure to meet the standards may cause the employee to look for excuses.

Use a firm approach or direct orders when needed. Recognize that objective firmness could be the most appropriate solution.

Find a replacement if necessary. If all reasonable effort has been made to help the employee adjust to the situation but without success, attempts may be made to transfer the man. However, discharge may be the logical solution. Remember that no man should be permitted to infect other employees with disloyalty or the habit of constant complaining.

A FOUR-STEP GUIDE TO HANDLING GRIEVANCES

The words "grievance" and "complaint" are used interchangeably here, although they do not mean the same to everyone. It should be noted, however, that some of what follows may not apply in instances where a grievance procedure is spelled out in a union contract. Where a contract exists, it should be studied carefully so that the supervisor's handling of grievances will conform to the contractual agreement.

Settling a grievance is not the most pleasant task a supervisor is called upon to perform, but if it is handled correctly it affords a real opportunity to be of service to both the employee and the company. The following four-step method is recommended.

1. *Receive the grievance properly.* The way a grievance is received is important because the way a man is treated when he makes the complaint may have a significant influence on the ease of handling as well as on the outcome. Regardless of how angry, upset, or loud the man may be, invite him in calmly and courteously. In all probability, you won't have to start the conversation. Ask him to tell you about his problem if he doesn't volunteer the information. No matter what he says, let him have the opportunity to say it. He deserves a hearing. Give him your entire attention and hide any irritation or impatience you may feel.

While he's talking, take a few notes. This impresses him with the importance you attach to his story. After he has gone completely through the story and has stopped talking, ask him to repeat it. It's surprising how much calmer and less explosive the situation appears during the second telling. Then, after hearing his story for the second time, repeat the essential parts in your own words. It is important that you get across to the man that you understand his complaint; so ask him if your interpretation is correct.

The difficulty may be one that you can resolve during the conversation; if so, handle it accordingly. If what he has brought to your attention requires further investigation and study, tell him why. Be sure to thank him for bringing the matter to your attention and to tell him when he can expect a decision.

2. *Get all the information you need to make a decision.* It is important that you give the matter your prompt attention. Make the investigation as complete as is necessary; check every angle and talk with all the people who may be able to shed light on the situation. Make appropriate notes of your findings—this prevents forgetting or misquoting at a later time.

Check whether company policy or the union contract clearly spells out what action is to be taken. Find out if other supervisors have set a precedent in similar situations. Consult with your own supervisor; perhaps he has some definite ideas about what should be done. Such checking of company policy, contract clauses, precedents, and upper management opinion insures that your decision will not be reversed at a later time.

Examine the employee's record. Is he a habitual complainer? How often has he been absent? What is his record of production and cooperation? What does his job performance rating show? The answers to these questions help you interpret the complaint in the context of the man's overall record.

3. *Take appropriate action.* If you have completed Steps 1 and 2 adequately, you should now be in a position to act. If the company is in the wrong, make the correction. If the complaint centers around something which cannot be changed, tell the employee why it can't be changed. If the employee is in the wrong, then stick to your guns. Should you touch a sensitive nerve when you give him a decision that does not agree with his view of the complaint, your best position is calmness, firmness, and a shield of facts.

Above all, don't let yourself be bulldozed into a compromising position. If you have done a thorough job before making your decision, and no new information has been inserted which would justify changing that decision, then stick to it. It may not be to the employee's liking, but once you bring him to a point of agreement on the facts which entered into your decision his honesty will compel him to respect it.

4. *Engage in follow-up action.* The initial decision is only the first step in taking action on the complaint; follow-through is necessary until the problem has been completely eliminated.

In most instances a complaint is indicative of the company's failure to make a change or of the employee's failure to understand company procedures. The causes for most complaints can be eliminated if the atmosphere in the department is conducive to high morale and if lines of communication are kept open. Handling of complaints provides the supervisor with an opportunity to assist the employee with his job adjustment and provides the company with identification of needed changes.

SKILLFUL HANDLING OF CHANGE

We live in a world of change. Never before in human history have so many changes taken place within so short a time. Almost one-fifth of American families move each year. Communications, transportation, new products, and new ideas are altering our total environment. Most of us take pride in our up-to-date thinking and habits. But many of us still tend to resist change in our interpersonal and job relations because in the orderly and familiar ways lies security.

If a company is to survive in today's dynamic environment, it not only must be able to react to changing conditions quickly but also should anticipate them far enough in advance that its policies, organization, personnel, and products can be adapted in sufficient time to maintain a sound competitive position. The ability to introduce change with a minimum of resistance is one of the key skills of progressive management.

A new machine, a new technique, a new product, or a new system can make all the old ones obsolete. The growing companies, those that are offering better jobs to employees and larger returns to stockholders, are the ones which have a pattern of continuing adjustments. Their products are constantly improved through research; new uses are found for old products, and new products come from their laboratories every year. Not only have they changed their products, but they have altered their organizational structure and have been able to persuade their people to accept this without detrimental opposition. Management foresight and adequate planning are the tools that have overcome resistance and have assured the flexibility which was clearly in the best interests of the companies.

TYPES OF JOB-RELATED CHANGES

Change can take many forms, but we shall deal here with the ones that affect the employee and his job environment.

Changes in tools, machines, and equipment. Almost every organization has experienced difficulty with employees who resist new tools, machines, and equipment as possible threats to security or status. Several years ago, for example, cash registers were to be installed in a sales department. The department head was completely opposed, and no amount of reasoning about the advantages seemed to have much effect. Finally, a register was installed for a three-month trial, and the supervisor was told that if at the end of that time she still wanted it removed, consideration would be given to her request. By the time the trial period was over, however, she was so pleased with the speed, convenience, and accuracy of the cash register that its removal would have caused as much trouble as its installation had caused originally.

Changes in methods and procedures. Method and procedure changes imply that the company has learned a better, more efficient way than the old system offered. Certain employees will react almost automatically in a negative way when confronted with a new method. But the road to bankruptcy is paved with "We've always done it this way."

Changes in personnel. People are more willing to accept environmental changes than human changes. To the individual, personnel adjustments—new employees, a new supervisor, a decrease in staff—signal changes which could work to his disadvantage. People have a way of adjusting to each other, establishing rapport, and forming socially knit groups; personnel changes tend to threaten this balance.

Changes in the organizational structure. If two departments are merged into one, or a supervisor is assigned to manage an additional department, or the department is split or is shifted to a different division in the organizational structure, the employee's reaction may be one of uncertainty about his own future. And his response may be the same if he is himself transferred to a different department or plant or is assigned new responsibility.

REASONS FOR RESISTANCE TO CHANGE

In an earlier chapter it was pointed out that one of the basic human characteristics is resistance to change. When confronted with change, the individual is faced with a choice—to accept it as having a potential for benefit or to resist it because of the possible disadvantages. The question is whether to disturb the comfort and security of the status quo for the uncertain possibility of greater benefit.

It should be pointed out that not all employees resist change, but management would be wise to recognize that there is a very real tendency on the part of most people to do so. Consequently, the actual installation of change should be preceded by adequate planning and communication in order to minimize resistance. Just because management can see an advantage in making a change and can even prove this to the employee, there is no automatic guarantee that the employee will leap on the bandwagon. The following are some of the more common reasons for resistance to change.

Economic considerations. Will automation replace the individual? Will new standards be set that he may not be able to meet? Will the economic value of his skills be reduced? The employee's real concern is for the future of his job and income. If he has heard rumors of automation replacing hundreds of employees, he is unlikely to be enthusiastic about a machine that can perform his job faster and at one-tenth the cost. Since economic considerations are perhaps the primary reason for resistance to change, this uncertainty must be met and resolved before the employee will accept the change willingly.

Possible inconvenience. We all tend to cling to the old ways lest we make life more difficult. We develop a vested interest in our habits and patterns of behavior. Learning new ways requires the expenditure of both mental and physical energy as well as time. So we often reject anything which upsets our routine and causes inconvenience.

Uncertainty about the unknown. The new way is always strange, threatening, laden with uncertainties—even when it is an improvement. Many employees have turned down promotions and opportunities for more pay because they feared the change and lacked confidence in their ability to do the work.

Threat to social relationships. The social group is an important factor in the employee's job satisfaction. The work group becomes almost a second family. If this group affords the employee identification and acceptance, change often represents a threat because it may jeopardize the relationship.

Resistance to changes affecting status symbols. Location of desks and offices, titles, company privileges, and a host of other symbols come to be attached to particular jobs. Employees are inclined to resist anything which affects these status symbols. Though a change may in fact be trifling, it looms large if it seems to touch on status; if it removes any one of the outward evidences of status, however small, it may—to the employee—signal the undermining of his job security.

GUIDES FOR REDUCING RESISTANCE TO CHANGE

The following suggestions are those which have proved most successful in minimizing employee resistance to change.

Insure adequate understanding through effective communication. People fear the unknown; they trust and accept the things they understand. The real job of communication is to bring the employee to the point of understanding by eliminating the uncertainties, the hidden threats to job and security. The goal is to make the unknown known and thus acceptable. Research, planning, and the most effective techniques of communication should be a part of the process of providing employees with all the facts. Management and supervisors should not succumb to the temptation to color information concerning change to the point of misleading their employees.

Consider economic incentives. Money is still highly effective in gaining the attention, interest, and response of an employee. Since change may represent an economic threat to him, the surest way to overcome the resistance this creates is through economic incentives. Whenever possible, therefore, the employee should be assured that he will continue to make at least as much money as he has been making in the past. And if the possibility of greater earnings can be offered, it will be an added inducement to accept the change without further resistance.

Promote acceptance through group decision making. It is easier for employees to accept a decision that they have had a share in making. Not all changes can hinge on employee preference or democratic vote, but practical ways can be found to involve the work group in the final decision making. For example, the whole matter could be brought to their attention at a group meeting or in personal letters sent to their homes, or it could be handled on a departmental level by each supervisor. This in itself becomes an effective means of communicating the necessity for the change as well as its nature.

Maintain an environment of continuing improvement. The supervisor is the key to making a smooth change. If he has a close relationship with the members of the work group, they will tend to accept his word. And if, over a period of time, he has instituted small changes from which the employees have benefited, he will have created an environment in which change is accepted as a natural part of the work situation.

Make changes tentative. It is not always possible to make changes on a tentative basis, but the advantage is obvious where this technique is practical. If a new product or the installation of expensive machinery is involved, permanent changes must be made. But in instances involving the transfer of an employee or a minor change in procedure, it may be possible to permit the employee to try it out on a temporary basis. He is usually much more willing to accept a change if he has the feeling that he can return to the old and familiar way if the new one doesn't work out.

Interview and motivate. There is no substitute for the old-fashioned technique of sitting down and reasoning together. The success of this device rests squarely on the degree of skill the supervisor is able to bring to bear on the situation. He must be fortified with facts so that he can show the employee the necessity for the change and remind him of past changes which have worked out to his advantage. This method gives the supervisor the opportunity to discover the reasons for any resistance and to supply the best answers available.

Even if the answers do not entirely satisfy the employee, he will at least have had an opportunity to talk about the situation and learn the truth, which is in itself reassuring.

Follow up. It has been said that change is the only law of survival and the only constant. This is perhaps another way of saying that the company, the supervisor, and the employee should be conditioned to continuing change. The best way to accomplish change and minimize employee resistance in the future is to handle today's change effectively.

To insure a smooth transition and continued acceptance by the employee, small adjustments should be made as needed. Bring to the employee's attention the benefits the change has brought to him. Remind him that change is a way of life in a modern progressive company that expects to grow and offer even better jobs to its employees in the future. Gradually, the employee will be conditioned to trust the supervisor and the company to make changes which will be in his best interest. But it should be remembered that resistance to change is a normal employee reaction and overcoming it requires the skillful use of human leadership tools.

Learning draws back the curtain on a wonderful new world of knowledge and progress. The retention of learning for future use may well be the key to success for both the employee and the supervisor.

11. Techniques of Learning

How IMPORTANT are learning and retention to the supervisor? Should they be left to educators or training directors? If the supervisor ever expects to train new employees adequately or if he expects to improve the quantity and quality of work now being done, he must make efficient use of learning processes.

The whole on-going process of growth is dependent on the individual's ability to learn and to translate what is learned into favorable change. Unless the company and the individual are satisfied to stand still, learning must take place. The efficient application of learning techniques is the responsibility of the supervisor; his skill in teaching should enable the employee to meet profitable production standards with minimum expenditures of time, energy, and money.

Learning has been described as a modification of behavior. This may be subject to debate; perhaps learning could occur without any apparent change in behavior. But supervisors have to be practical people. For all practical purposes, training time and effort have been wasted until a change has been effected. From the standpoint of both supervisor and company, learning is useful or purposeful only when it results in increased production, in less time required for the job, or in increased overall efficiency.

The on-going process of growth is dependent on the individual's ability to learn and to translate what is learned into favorable change.

THE LEARNING MACHINERY

Many of our reactions are not the direct result of learning but are instinctive and automatic. We don't have to learn to react to bodily discomforts, for instance. The supervisor's concern is not with the behavior patterns and reactions that are beyond his influence. Instead, his attention is centered on those actions and reactions that respond to learning.

Single-cell animals, such as the amoeba, react to various stimuli in the environment. The amoeba possesses sensitivity, mobility, and conductivity despite its lack of nervous tissue. However, because it lacks a nervous system it cannot store up the effects of its experiences, as can higher forms of animal life, and therefore is unable to profit from learning.

Humans possess a very complicated communication system comparable to the wires of a highly complex computer. This tissue of the nervous system is both modifiable and retentive. The regions of possible change are called synapses (junction points across which nerve impulses pass); numbering in the billions, they furnish the neurological basis for intelligence and learning. As these synapses are used, changes occur; experience is retained; and repetition of the same or similar actions is made easier. In this manner, learning occurs—at least according to one theory. The nervous system's modifiability, sensitivity, and capacity to conduct impulses determine an individual's learning capacity. Although this feature is influenced by heredity, it is developed largely through use and acquired experience.

BASIC LAWS OF LEARNING

As a man goes through life, his everyday experiences are constantly creating new tendencies. A tendency to act in a certain way because of having acted that way before is referred to as "learned behavior." This law of learning, which can also be called the *law of retention*, is applicable to the teaching of new patterns as well as to the correction of undesirable learning.

Laboratory experiments, controlled psychological tests, and experience have revealed that certain basic laws govern the manner in which learning takes place, the most efficient methods of learning, the amount that will be learned, and the time required for learning. This set of laws can serve as a practical guide for the supervisor as he seeks to promote learning in the employee group.

The law of frequency. Each time an activity is repeated, impulses are communicated through the nervous system, modifications are made, and the resulting changes make it easier for the same impulses to go through the system on subsequent occasions. Advertisers apply this law when they use oft-repeated slogans; teachers apply it when they call for repeated drills, whether verbal or physical. Similarly, the supervisor who wants to implant a new skill asks the employee to repeat a job operation many times; the more frequently the activity is performed correctly, the more likely it is to be learned and remembered.

As an activity is repeated, it moves from the conscious to the subconscious level—from the awareness that to achieve a desired result certain prescribed steps must be followed to the habit of acting automatically without thought or analysis. A baby has to learn to lift a spoon to his mouth; as an adult, he will go through the process without thinking. It has been estimated that more than 60 percent of our activities require no conscious thought but occur as the result of learning which has developed into fixed patterns of behavior.

The supervisor can make good use of this law of frequency by recognizing that performing a job correctly one time does not guarantee that it has been learned. An employee may have to perform the job correctly many times in order to guarantee learning. Repetition of the work cycle should therefore continue to the point where correct performance becomes a habit.

The law of intensity. We experience many things which make little or no impression on us; an influence may be so insignificant that no learning takes place and forgetting is almost instantaneous. Other influences are so strong and other experiences are so intense that they make lasting impressions and will be remembered for years. Because of this the supervisor should attempt to make the learning experience dramatic and intense. The use of visual aids, demonstrations, and other learning gimmicks will help to make a deep impression and thus increase the probability of learning.

The law of recency. What has been learned most recently is most likely to be remembered; but if learning is not applied quickly, much of it will be lost. Advertisers know this. They urge us to "go to the corner drug store right now" because the longer we put it off, the greater the chance we will forget; there is a predictable falling-off of response with delay. Since the supervisor can anticipate that an activity performed only recently will be easy for the employee to repeat, but that one not repeated for many months is likely to be forgotten, he should arrange for the repetition of newly learned actions to insure that they are retained.

Carrier-based pilots know the importance of this law of learning. So exacting is the technique of landing a plane on the deck of an aircraft carrier that training takes months of intensive work. Yet if a pilot makes no carrier landings for an interval of 30 days he is required to practice the entire procedure before he is allowed to make actual landings again.

The law of duration. A short, concentrated training program usually does not result in as much permanent learning as one which can be extended over a longer time span. People reach a saturation point; they have limits on what they can absorb in a given time. Usually, more learning takes place if the same training—the same actions, the same amount of information—can be distributed over a longer period. From a practical standpoint, the supervisor needs to take this into consideration in planning training. He may do better, for instance, to separate a complex operation into various parts, teach one part at a time, and allow for enough practice so that it is completely learned before going on to the next part.

The law of effect. The effect that learning has on the individual will influence the amount that he learns. Experiments have demonstrated that when learning has a pleasant effect, it produces the best results. The supervisor can speed up the learning process by recognizing and praising evidences of learning and by emphasizing the pleasant effect —increased job security, more money, a better chance for promotion— and by making sure the employee has a sense of personal accomplishment.

The law of association. It is almost impossible for a man who has just emerged from a jungle culture to learn the hundreds of things necessary to meet the requirements of a job on a production line. He has very little with which to compare or associate the new information. Since learning is largely a matter of associating the unknown with the known, he is at an almost total loss. The person who knows most about a subject finds it easiest to learn and assimilate additional information. The student who has mastered two languages finds it easier to learn a third and easier still to master a fourth.

The supervisor needs to recognize that the current knowledge of the employee will determine the starting point for his job training and will influence the speed with which he can learn related information. Every effort should therefore be made to associate new information with what the employee already knows and understands. One teacher put it this way: "In teaching literature, you have to start at the present understanding level of the student. If this happens to be the comic-book stage, then that is where you have to begin. If you start too high, you pass over the head of the student and he will never catch up. Start with what he knows, and then you can bring him along to the higher ground." This applies with equal validity to the supervisor who must be concerned with training.

METHODS OF LEARNING

It is significant that people learn principally by three basic methods. Not all of them produce the same results. Some are more costly than others. A careful analysis by the supervisor will determine which he should use to promote maximum learning in his people. Each of the following methods has a special function; if the wrong one is used, the results will be costly and disappointing.

The trial-and-error method. If a chicken is placed on one side of a wire fence and food is placed on the other side, the chicken will have difficulty getting to the food. Even if the fence is short and open at both ends, the chicken will stick its head through the fence, try to crawl through it, try to fly over it. It will do these things again and again, never stopping to figure out the solution to the problem. After much trial and error, the chicken may, by accident, wander around one end of the fence. A little learning has taken place; the next time, the chicken is likely to get to one end of the fence a bit sooner. The trial-and-error method of learning has its value; sometimes it's the only way to find the answers.

Consider, however, the tremendous cost, the waste of time and materials, and the number of unhappy customers there would be if all new employees had to learn their jobs through trial and error. Yet this is precisely what has to happen if the supervisor does not take the time to train new people. Too often, through neglect or lack of interest, the new employee is left to his own improvisations to learn his job. This obviously is too expensive to the company and too detrimental to the development of the employee. Neither can afford this type of learning, and it therefore is the responsibility of the supervisor to guarantee that employees are not left to sink or swim.

The imitation method. A dog's intelligence level is higher than that of a chicken, and it would probably solve the food-and-fence problem differently. If the dog saw people going around the end of the fence, it would be able to deduce that it could follow suit. The dog would thus have learned to solve the problem by the imitation method, and the next time it would quickly go to the end of the fence to reach its goal.

Imitation has a place in learning and is used successfully in apprentice programs; it is often the best method to learn manual skills. Demonstrations which can be imitated promote learning. This is the reason a new employee is often placed alongside an experienced man and asked to imitate his work procedures.

Imitating correct procedures and techniques has a tremendous advantage over the trial and error method, yet it is not the most efficient way to learn because it takes excessive time and does not lend itself to all types of information.

Logical analysis, or the reasoning method. If a man were on one side of a strip of fence and a desirable object were on the other, he would simply look the situation over, recognize that he was not fenced in, and figure out the best way to get to the other side before committing himself to a course of action. He would thus save a tremendous amount of time over the trial-and-error method; he would not have to be taught by the imitation method. Man applies information that is stored in his brain and deduces solutions by logical analysis. This is the most efficient learning method; it is the most direct, the least time consuming, and the most economical. To be used appropriately, this method requires preparation and the development of a definite program which will promote maximum learning.

The supervisor needs to make a careful analysis of the methods used in his department both for training new people and for teaching new techniques and improvements to the more experienced employee. No supervisor can afford to permit the use of inefficient teaching and learning methods any more than he can justify the use of inefficient machinery.

DETERMINANTS OF LEARNING

A certain amount of learning will result from coincidental exposure or casual association, but the amount is limited and haphazard. To promote maximum learning in minimum time demands a more deliberate approach. Limited learning does occur despite indifference or resistance; however, greater learning results when the subject receives undivided attention and is approached with a deliberate intent to train. The supervisor therefore needs to devise methods which hold the learner's attention and maximum interest.

METHODS OF GAINING ATTENTION

Public speakers, sales managers, and advertisers use many methods to get the initial attention of people. The variety of gimmicks used is almost unlimited, and they all serve a useful purpose if they gain the attention of the person to whom communication is directed. The *objective* determinants of attention include *change*, such as motion or relocation; *uniqueness or novelty; size;* and *color.* These are overt techniques to gain attention. The circus barker shows just enough of his unusual collection of oddities to arouse interest. Store windows feature moving displays to draw the eyes of passers-by. These techniques are valuable to the supervisor too. To gain and hold the attention of those he must train, he has at his disposal many visual aids that attract attention initially and retain it throughout the learning process.

Gaining attention through *subjective* channels, on the other hand, involves sitting down with the employee and reasoning together. It is an appeal to the individual to meet his own needs through additional learning. For example, a man must learn the job initially and must later learn to do more difficult work in order to support his family and meet his financial obligations. Learning is a means to this goal. Beyond that, every person has special interests which can be satisfied only through additional learning. A man may in fact spend more time learning about his hobby than he does learning to do his job better. When these special interests relate to a man's work and when that relationship is emphasized during on-the-job training, he will learn more and learn it faster.

A man equips his car with safety belts because he is concerned about the safety of his family. He buys insurance to help meet their need for security. And he should learn to perform his job in the best manner to meet his own need for security and for growth.

STEPS IN THE LEARNING PROCESS

The individual goes through certain steps in learning and retaining what he learns. The supervisor needs to make a close study of these steps and to make use of them in order to understand and promote learning in his people. The first step is *set*, or *adjustment*. This refers to the degree to which the individual wants to learn; his attitude must be receptive in order to have fertile soil in which to plant the seed. The second step is *selection of contributing factors*, such as motions or procedures essential to adequate performance. A clear understanding of what is to be learned enables the learner to select and include those factors which contribute to the final goal. These are then made a part of his knowledge and skills.

The third step is the *discarding of noncontributing factors*, such as wasteful procedures. Certain factors are negative and actually interfere with the learning process. These need to be identified and discarded. To improve requires a gradual focusing on correct techniques and a complete elimination of those which make no contribution or actually interfere with learning. The *fixation of learning* is the final step in the learning process. Learning has not become permanent until it can be repeated and becomes fixed in the response pattern. And even at this point, attention must continue in order to insure that negative habits do not develop inadvertently.

It is within the framework of these four steps that the supervisor must plan and execute training so that he can bring the learner to the point of satisfactory retention of the knowledge and skills required by the job.

INFLUENCES ON LEARNING ACHIEVEMENT

How much learning will the employee achieve? The answer is significant to his success as well as to the achievement of the department as a whole. The following factors should be considered in order to understand the learning process and to promote maximum learning.

The influence of motivation. The amount of learning a person achieves is determined by ability plus motivation. Motivation, then, is one of the two necessary ingredients. If the desire to achieve a goal is increased, the determination to learn becomes greater and learning is increased.

A bright and capable young man was coasting along, making no effort to expand his knowledge because he considered that he was doing his job successfully and there was no point in exerting himself. The supervisor pointed out that some changes were contemplated, additional supervisors would be needed, and these positions would be filled by promoting from within. This was motivation enough; the young man asked the supervisor's advice about what training would best prepare him, took company-sponsored courses, and was ready when there was a new opening for a supervisory job.

The effect of age. "You can't teach an old dog new tricks" is an oft-repeated cliché that has caused both supervisors and employees to miss tremendous potential improvements. Facts simply do not support the theory that older adults cannot learn. An objective evaluation shows that the ability to learn increases through the early 20's, levels off through the early 50's, and has an almost insignificant decline thereafter unless senility sets in. Our ability to develop new physical skills that require strength, quick reaction, and muscular coordination does decrease as we grow older; the best years for the athlete are his 20's and 30's. But the ability to acquire knowledge does not decline as rapidly as is popularly believed.

Often what seems to be a limited ability to learn may instead be a lower energy supply and lessened motivation. Typically, the older person clings to the status quo and resists learning new techniques if he begins to feel less secure and less confident in his ability to cope with new experiences. This seeming lowered ability to learn is a defense mechanism which may stem from a fear of failure; since age alone makes it more difficult to get a new job, there is motivation to hang on to the security of existing knowledge, status, and skills.

When the supervisor who works with older people understands that much of their resistance stems from insecurity and that they are able to learn, though they may be reluctant to do so, he will encourage them and instill the self-confidence that will promote learning.

And where admissible, he should modify training procedures to suit an individual's pace.

The impact of education. The more education a person has, the more he can acquire. This is based on two facts: Educational achievement is in itself an indication of learning ability, and acquired knowledge is a foundation for additional knowledge. Since learning is largely a process of associating the unknown with the known, not only innate intelligence but also acquired knowledge and vocabulary are significant factors in learning. For instance, a 14-year-old child may be handicapped when competing with adults by the very fact that his vocabulary and understanding of word symbols are limited.

Often an employee already knows a considerable portion of what he needs to know to do a new job. If he is new to the company, he must learn new procedures and perhaps also learn to operate a machine that varies somewhat from the one he ran on his last job. If he is transferred within the company, he must learn the routines of the new department and perhaps also the operation of a new machine. But in neither case does he have to learn everything about the job from scratch; in each case he brings to the job what he already knows, and he adapts this knowledge to the needs of the new situation. The same is true when a football player takes up baseball—the speed, coordination, timing, and other factors he used in one sport are equally useful in the other.

The influence of conditioning. Learning can be stimulated by subconscious association. Ivan Pavlov's experiments on conditioned reflexes are a case in point. Pavlov, a Russian physiologist, knew that when food was presented to a dog, its saliva would flow. To test his theory that reflexes could be conditioned, he presented dogs with two stimulators at the same time—food and the sound of a bell. Eventually, as a result of conditioning, the reaction was transferred to the bell, and the dogs' saliva flowed when the bell was sounded even though no food was offered at the time.

The supervisor can make use of the principle of conditioning by presenting more than one phase of a job at the same time. If, for example, the more unpleasant aspects of a job are presented with the pleasant, the employee may be conditioned to cope with the unpleasant factors and to consider them unobjectionable. Thus the presentation of related aspects of the job in conjunction with each other may speed the learning of both.

The pace of presentation. It is generally agreed that people learn at different rates, depending on both ability and experience. If the supervisor attempts to present too much new information to the learner at one time or to present it too fast, considerable waste or spillover will result. The situation may be compared to the attempt to pour liquid into the mouth of a jug too quickly; only so much can pass through the neck at once, and the excess is spilled or wasted. So the supervisor's training methods should be adapted to the employee's learning pace in order to minimize wasted effort.

CHANGING INCORRECT LEARNING

The supervisor is often faced with the need to change the incorrect habits an employee brings to the job or has acquired on the job. This can often be more difficult than teaching him something from the beginning; the elimination of old patterns delays acceptance of the new, because each time the individual follows a new technique he has to overcome the old habit. The best course for the supervisor is to substitute a stronger and more desirable learning pattern. Once the new pattern has been acquired, it should be used frequently.

An efficient method of study is of utmost importance to the supervisor and the company, as is the learning environment. The amount of time the individual devotes to learning is one of the least significant factors affecting the amount he learns. Of greater importance are motivation, interest in learning, and the efficiency of study techniques. The more systematically a learner tests or reviews new information, the faster will learning be achieved. Of course, if an employee has only half a day to learn to operate a machine, the process must be speeded up to meet the demands of the situation. Generally, the less time available, the more testing and repetition are required for satisfactory learning.

The supervisor should recognize that saturating the employee with too much information in too short a time results in the employee's learning less than would otherwise be the case. There seems to be a correlation between the period of time over which the activity is experienced and the actual retention of knowledge; the longer the period, the more is learned.

When information must be memorized, experimental data show

that, instead of focusing on small units, the information should be read through from start to finish and studied as a whole so that attention is distributed uniformly throughout. Similarly, when an employee is learning to operate a machine or perform a job activity, seeing the overall operation promotes learning and retention. When isolated bits are learned separately, they must eventually be fitted into the appropriate slot; this requires additional learning even after the various parts have been mastered.

As a case in point, the operator of a bakery machine had difficulty remembering to activate the salting button at the right time. The resultant waste of dough was irritating to the supervisor and expensive to the company. In analyzing the situation, the supervisor discovered that the man had not been taught the operation as a whole; instead, several people had taught him specialized parts of the process. The supervisor decided to retrain the man, and this time the process was outlined, a checklist made, and the activation of the salting mechanism included at the proper point in the sequence. The job now became a logical series of activities, and the omission of one step was corrected.

In another instance, a department store in Boston decided to take a new approach to training salespeople in the techniques of completing sales. The normal procedure had been to spend about two days teaching new employees how to write out sales tickets, ring the cash register, and handle the other written and mechanical routines. When this had been completed, the salesperson then had to learn how to sell.

The new procedure was to set up a counter with merchandise and let one salesperson take the role of the customer and another the role of the clerk. Now the new employee learned the selling technique as a logical first step, and the completion of the sales transaction became more meaningful when it followed the customer's decision to buy. Learning improved, and the salespeople were able to handle the complete operation more efficiently when they finally arrived on the selling floor.

Sometimes, trying to learn too many unrelated activities at one time results in confusion and minimum learning. Most jobs involve many different skills and activities, but it is usually unwise to try to introduce them to a new employee all at once. Instead, all the steps of one activity should be learned thoroughly before going on to learning the next one. For instance, if all the steps in a bookkeeper's job

were presented to a new employee at once, the total operation would
seem so complex as to be impossible to understand. But if the procedure for receiving and verifying invoices is the new bookkeeper's introduction to the job, and if, after this step is mastered, the process
of posting to the proper department is well learned, and so on, quick
work can be made of training.

Most people seem to find that a certain amount of pressure speeds
up the learning process. The student who simply reads casually will
probably learn a minimum amount, but the more active approach of
outlining, writing down key points, repeating special passages, and
working with a degree of urgency will speed both learning and retention. The supervisor needs to recognize that learning can be substantially increased if he can bring in the more active factors—visual aids,
discussion, and participation by the learner—while at the same time
eliminating distractions of all types, which are the greatest deterrents
to learning.

LEARNING AND SUPERVISION

No one can have more interest in results than the person who is
delegated the responsibility for those results. In the case of a company, this is the supervisor. He is the company representative who
must train new people and improve the performance of the present
employees.

Work results will remain static unless knowledge is increased and
skills are improved. These are the direct result of learning. If the
supervisor is to discharge his responsibilities, he should keep the following facts in mind:

1. He needs to know the principles involved in learning.
2. He must be convinced of the importance of learning.
3. He should be aware of the reasons why learning does or does
   not occur.
4. He should be able to select the most efficient learning methods
   for his own people.
5. He should make adequate provision for interest and motivation.
6. He should evaluate progress and make appropriate adjustments along the way to insure that learning continues.

Training is the process by which the ability to perform specific jobs is acquired and increased.

12. Improving Knowledge and Skills Through Training

TRAINING IS AN EXPENSIVE ACTIVITY. One utility company has set the cost of executive training at $10,000 per man. The training of a single production, office, or sales employee usually costs at least several hundred dollars. Yet a company can justify the expense by comparing it with what an untrained employee wastes in payroll dollars, resources, lost customers, and jeopardized competitive position. The financial burden of an untrained worker can be far greater than the cost of training. Consider, for example, what an untrained shoe salesman can cost the company. He loses sales because he doesn't know how to fit shoes; he can't find the merchandise; he knows nothing about the unique properties of leather or the construction of shoes; and he doesn't know how to sell accessory items. His inefficiency so irritates some customers that they never come back. He makes extra work for the bookkeeping department by writing up transactions improperly. And because his fumbling and bumbling give him a sense of inadequacy and of failure, the likelihood that he will ever become a competent and productive employee is diminished.

A company is committed to paying each employee for every hour he spends on the job. In order to receive an appropriate return on its investment, it must make sure that each employee reaches and maintains a profitable level of production. This can be done only through an effective training program.

The financial burden of an untrained worker can be far greater than the cost of training.

OBJECTIVES OF TRAINING

The general objectives of training are to—
- Increase the quantity and quality of output by improving employee skills.
- Reduce accidents.
- Increase the return to the employee in personal rewards—that is, more pay, recognition, and other benefits which the employee wants from the job.
- Make the operation more profitable by reducing the amount of equipment and material required to produce or sell a given unit.
- Make it possible for the supervisor to spend less time in correcting mistakes and to spend more in planning.
- Minimize discharges because of inadequate skills.
- Improve morale and achieve a more satisfactory working environment.
- Enable new employees to meet the job requirements and enable experienced employees to accept transfers, operate new machines, adapt to new methods, increase efficiency, and adjust to changing needs.
- Encourage willingness, loyalty, interest, and desire to excel.

Training is a deliberate effort by the company to supply the employee with the skills and information which will enable him to perform the job satisfactorily. The starting point for this important management activity is the determination of need. The first step in determining training needs is to identify the skills required on the job; the second is to find out how much of those skills the employee already possesses; the third is to decide what he must learn to bridge the gap. The need for training is revealed in many ways: poor production results; incorrect or inefficient procedures; low merit ratings of job performance; adverse employee attitudes; poor quality; high wastage; antiquated work methods; or unachieved goals.

The supervisor has the primary responsibility for the training of his people. Some firms have a central training department; in others there is no formal training facility. In either case the ultimate responsibility for training rests with the supervisor. He knows the job better than anyone else, has the opportunity to conduct the training in a realistic rather than an artificial environment, has a more vital concern with the worker's adjustment and production, and is in the best position to observe, evaluate, and follow up.

Centralized training is especially useful for indoctrinating new employees—informing them about company history, policies, benefits—and for teaching general information that is necessary for all employees. For example, all department store salespeople must know how to make out a sales ticket and handle a cash register, no matter whether they will sell bath soap or bridge tables; so these procedures can be taught in a central training facility. In a well-equipped facility, an expert with a specialized training background can teach employees what they need to know without distraction and without interfering with the operations in any department.

But centralized training cannot altogether supplant the training each supervisor must provide for the employees in his department. Each department has special needs and special problems for which special adjustments must be made. And the social relationships within each department are unique and must be adapted to within the department. What is more, since the supervisor is himself rated on the basis of departmental accomplishment, his personal interest in results is often greater than that of a central training director. The final training and follow-up must therefore be done in the department by the supervisor.

It is evident that centralized and departmental training each have unique advantages; they complement each other in the well-planned program. The company, however, should not provide so much of the training that the supervisor feels he has no responsibilities in this area.

The preparation of a training program must be on the basis of the goals to be reached and the performance necessary to reach these goals. Planning should include the following considerations:
- Type of training needed.
- Most effective methods of presenting each type.
- Time and place for conducting the training.
- Preparation of the outlines, visual aids, props, and other material to be used.
- Selection and indoctrination of the instructors.
- Administration and scheduling of the program.
- Employee notification.
- Evaluation of the results.

One of the most serious challenges faced by the training function is the difficulty of measuring results. Many company activities can be measured and evaluated precisely, but not training. Perhaps, in a sense, training ought to be considered in the same light as advertising; although the exact value of one advertisement may be difficult to measure, the overall value of advertising is nonetheless clear.

An evaluation of training can be made by before-and-after comparisons of job performance and production through the use of questionnaires and rating forms to check results and through interviews with individual employees to determine their reactions. Or a more scientific method of evaluation may be used by dividing the employees into two groups before the program is begun; having one (the test group) take the training and the other (the control group) continue working as usual; and comparing the before-and-after performance of both groups. This method is especially useful in testing new training techniques—programed instruction, for example—to determine whether they are suitable for use throughout the company.

Special attention must be given to welcoming, inducting, and training new employees. Since the supervisor becomes the symbol of boss and management, what he does during the early stages can have a decisive effect on the employee's future work results and length of employment.

The new employee should be assisted in forming a favorable attitude toward the firm; his anxiety and uncertainty should be eliminated through exhibited friendliness and supplied information; he should understand fully his conditions of employment; and the supervisor should take time to become acquainted with him. The few minutes taken for a get-acquainted interview can set the stage for the employee's understanding of his new environment. Since the supervisor cannot cover adequately all the information the employee may want, the best thing he can do in lieu of this is to create an atmosphere in which the employee will feel free to talk with him.

The company receives no actual benefit from the employee's presence until he can make a profitable contribution on the job. Training is preparation, job performance is the harvest. The supervisor should have available a specific plan for teaching each job in order to insure that training will be accomplished as quickly and economically as possible. The four steps in this type of instruction normally include a complete introduction to the operation; a supervisor's or instructor's performance of the operation; the employee's performance of the operation; and correct practice to insure that the training is not forgotten.

EFFECTIVE TRAINING TECHNIQUES

An almost endless number of training techniques have been developed since World War II. The techniques discussed in this chapter are those found to be most effective in producing results and those which are practical for use by individual supervisors as well as by company training programs.

Individualized training is perhaps the most commonly used and is an effective technique. It consists of a supervisor training one man at a time through the process of explaining and showing how the job should be done. The first step in this technique is to recognize what the job requires, learn what knowledge the employee already possesses, and decide what he still needs to learn or master in order to meet the requirements of the job. This can be one of the most effective types of training, because it can be designed to meet specific individual needs.

Department meetings are ideally suited for communicating changes in work schedules or departmental operation and for uniformly disseminating other information to entire groups. These meetings should be announced in advance; the materials needed should be in readiness; the meeting should start on time; employees should have an opportunity to ask questions and to participate fully; appropriate visual aids should be used; the meeting should be stimulating and interesting; the employees should have a clear understanding of the purpose of the meeting and the action expected as a result; the meeting should end on an enthusiastic note; and it should end on time.

The real success of the group approach to training is dependent on the leader's ability to involve the entire group. It has been clearly established that employee involvement in the training process, whether through discussion or role playing, leads to greatly improved response. The extent to which the supervisor can involve the employees in the meeting determines the effectiveness of the training.

The incident technique uses one or more occurrences on which to center the discussion and to make specific points—without, however, singling out any one employee for criticism. Errors that are common to the group should be discussed, not one man's mistakes. After describing an incident, the supervisor asks for suggestions as to how it should be handled. Incidents can be drawn from the department, borrowed from other departments, or structured to emphasize the point that the supervisor wishes to cover. This technique is simple, doesn't require much time, is interesting, does an effective job of getting the point across, and involves employees in the discussion.

Role playing is one of the most flexible training techniques and almost always gains the employees' interest. As the name implies, one assumes the role of another person—supervisor, employee, or customer, for example. Each person playing a role is asked to improvise and use his own imagination in supplying the information necessary to move the interview to a successful conclusion. In order to make the situation more realistic, the two should have a specific job or job setting in mind. It is sometimes helpful if the individuals playing the roles get together ahead of time, compare notes, and decide how the situation should be handled. The entire incident should be read to the group before the two individuals begin role playing. Then, after 10 to 20 minutes of role playing, the entire group is asked to comment on what was covered that should not have been mentioned, what should have been brought out that wasn't, and how the matter could have been handled more effectively. Role playing gives the participants the feel of handling the problem, involves everyone in the discussion following the role playing, and can be one of the supervisor's most effective training techniques.

The case method is usually a longer and more involved version of the incident technique. It may cover a chapter in the life of the company and of the employees concerned with the case. Information on the case for discussion is given to the participants in advance to enable them to study it thoroughly. They are asked to list the things that went wrong, ways in which the problem could have been prevented, how the same sort of thing could be avoided in the future, and how the matter should be settled at this point.

When the employees assemble for the discussion, they should be seated around a table. The discussion leader's function is to get the ball rolling, keep the discussion on the subject, see that all essential points are covered, and act as a referee. The group should be led to develop ideas and solve the problems by recognizing the differences between problems which must be solved immediately and those which can be dealt with over a longer period—and by realizing that problems usually have several correct as well as several incorrect solutions and that each man's way of solving them reflects his own ability and personal characteristics.

To be effective, these discussions should involve everyone in the group and should express opposing points of view in order to insure a thorough analysis of the case. Sometimes, impromptu role playing is useful in clarifying the issues. When the case has been discussed thoroughly, the supervisor should pull together the thinking of the group and restate the conclusions. The case method is most commonly used for training supervisors and higher levels of management in the skill of problem solving.

The conference method generally has a leader or chairman, and one or more subjects may be discussed. There are no prescribed rules for this type of training meeting. The group usually functions in an informal way with almost complete freedom of discussion. The leader or chairman should exercise some direction or there is a danger that the group will stray too far afield and fail to cover the assigned task.

Demonstrations use visual aids or pieces of equipment to illustrate and supplement verbal instruction. Employees like demonstrations because they can actually see what is being done, thus making the training more interesting and easier to remember. Learning and retention are improved even more if the employee takes part in the demonstration. It is not only difficult but usually impossible to teach manual activity or machine operation to an employee without using the demonstration technique.

The following are visual aids commonly used in training: chalkboards, closed-circuit television, models, teaching machines, maps, manuals, film slides, movies, charts and graphs, actual objects, posters, opaque projectors, mock-ups of actual machines, specimens, bulletin boards, photographs, and film strips.

Apprentice training is still used for many jobs. A skilled worker performs an operation repeatedly and the trainee gradually learns through imitation. It was through this method that skilled craftsmen learned their trades in the past. Although the principles of imitation are still used, the techniques have been refined and made more sophisticated through the use of visual aids designed to speed up the learning process.

IMPORTANT TRAINING GUIDES

The trainer should review the training plan to make certain that he knows thoroughly every aspect of the job that is to be imparted to the learner. His ability commands the confidence of the learner and leads to fast and efficient mastery of the activity.

Determine how much the newcomer needs to learn. The supervisor should prepare a complete job description for training purposes, then compare the job requirements with the qualifications of the new employee. The job requirements minus what the employee already knows equal the training needed. The supervisor should not assume that because the employee performed a similar operation elsewhere, he is qualified to perform the job he is now required to do.

Prepare a training plan. This should include a breakdown of the job into its logical steps, with special notation of key points. In making the training plans, the supervisor should ask himself these questions:

- What do I want to teach?
- Why should the employee learn; what are the advantages of training for him?
- How can I show him these advantages?
- What does he already know that is similar?
- What method is best to use in teaching the unknown in terms of the known?
- What is the best follow-up, to be certain that the information is understood and used correctly?

Consider individual differences. Individuals come to the job with differing ability to learn and vastly different degrees of acquired skills. Some learn slowly at first; others learn fast. Insofar as practical, every person should be considered individually, and the training should be adapted to his special needs.

Most jobs cannot be learned in a day; mastery of the operation is delayed if too much is presented at one time, thus resulting in confusion instead of understanding. The wise supervisor knows how much the employee can absorb in one session.

Build in motivation and interest. The supervisor creates interest in training by showing the importance of the information and the skill and by showing the necessity for its mastery if the employee expects to meet the requirements of the job.

Maintain a sense of humor. A sense of humor creates a closer and friendlier relationship with the employee and lessens tension.

Insure clarity of expression and explanation. The presentation of information should be understandable. The supervisor should use only those terms and symbols with which the learner is familiar.

Build self-confidence in the learner. The learner needs to know how he is getting along. Recognition of progress gives him the confidence to move forward to additional learning.

Evaluate progress. Many companies have check sheets to gauge the amount of learning which has taken place. These sheets may be used at the end of the first day, at the end of the training program, or as a follow-up check after the employee has spent some time on the job. Evaluation of learning identifies incorrect habits and techniques and indicates what additional training is still needed. Remember that practice does not necessarily make perfect. For practice to contribute to improvement, a deliberate effort must be made to eliminate errors and to profit from each repetition.

SELECTING AND TRAINING AN ASSISTANT SUPERVISOR

In selecting an assistant, certain qualifications may appear to be of prime importance, such as seniority, production, ambition, interest in promotion, intelligence, aggressiveness, dependability, ability to get along with others, leadership qualities, and cooperation. Due consideration should be given to all these traits, but each must be evaluated in relation to the requirements for the position of department supervisor. The man finally selected must be the one who has demonstrated his leadership qualities more clearly than anyone else. He has maintained harmonious working relationships with others, yet he has also been an excellent producer. He has always been willing to assist others in the department even though this was not his assigned job. He has been looked to for leadership during the supervisor's absence, even though he did not have the title or responsibility.

The training program should bring the assistant from his present ability level to the point where he will be able to handle all the duties and responsibilities of the supervisor's job. Since the supervisor will in all probability be promoted or transferred, or will perhaps take another job or retire, he should regard the assistant as his eventual replacement.

Let him know everything that you do. Explain the responsibilities of the job and how it fits into the organizational structure of the company; in short, transfer your understanding of the job to him. Remember the effectiveness of coaching as a training technique. He is your understudy and his development is important to your future.

Ask his opinion. Before telling him how to do something, ask what he thinks. He will appreciate the opportunity to make his contribution, and it will give him an excellent opportunity to develop his judgment. Ask him to give reasons for his opinion. Rather than supplying answers yourself, encourage him to make decisions.

Build a feeling of responsibility and self-confidence. Make him responsible for part of the work and follow up to see that the work is done properly. Try to move gradually into the background, and let him move to the forefront. You must retain general responsibility and, if he makes a few mistakes, supply the needed support.

Support the assistant. Explain to the employees in the department that the assistant's instructions are to be followed in the same way as those issued directly by you. If an employee does something wrong because of the assistant's instructions, don't correct the employee. Instead, talk with the assistant and explain the correct procedure. Let him correct the employee. Never criticize the assistant in the presence of others. Public criticism is the surest way to destroy employee confidence in your assistant—and in you. Refrain from making remarks that show disapproval of your assistant's decision or handling of a situation.

Be straightforward and frank in dealing with the assistant. He usually needs plenty of constructive criticism as he learns and develops. He needs to know what mistakes he is making and how to correct them. Probably the most unfair thing you could do would be to keep him in the dark concerning his shortcomings. Your job is to train him; so give him training in a straightforward and constructive manner. He needs the benefit of your experienced judgment and direction—in a manner that will be of greatest benefit to his development.

Recognize and commend progress. If he makes a suggestion and it is adopted, give him credit for it. If he finds better ways of doing certain things, take it not as a reflection on the way things have been done but as an indication of the assistant's development and good judgment. Demonstrate that you appreciate the progress he is making.

Gradually put him on his own. The pilot-instructor teaches a student to fly by instructing, demonstrating, and letting the learner get the feel of things. Then the instructor rides along as a passenger, and the student handles the plane by himself. The last step is the solo, with the student in full control.

The supervisor-assistant relationship should be much the same. If the supervisor has done the proper job of training, he should gradually let the assistant get the feel of things until he is ready to solo. But even then, it is not enough to let him just get by; he must learn to refine and perfect his technique. The supervisor should keep in touch with the assistant in order to build his self-confidence, improve his skills, and give him the support he needs.

* * *

The primary end of training is the creation of a skill which in turn produces job results. But skill training is the simplest part; the necessity to train the employee's attitudes, loyalty, willingness, and desire to excel are the more difficult requirements. Before results are achieved the whole man must be trained—thus training which limits itself to skills falls far short of fulfilling its potential. As the supervisor approaches his training task, he should recognize the types of skills and traits necessary to produce the required results. He must also remember that training must be continual; so long as there is a need to learn new jobs, improve performance on the present job, learn new machines, and move to higher levels of responsibility, training will be a significant supervisory responsibility.

Knowledge forgotten is like the tide that has lapped on the beach and departed, leaving no trace; it must be acquired again from the beginning.

13. Improving Memory and Retention

No one associated with an activity can have more direct concern with the retention of information and training than the supervisor who is charged with getting results. An accurate measure of net gain is not what has been taught but what has been learned and retained. In fact, training that is forgotten may do more harm than good because knowledge and skill may be assumed and depended on when, in fact, they don't actually exist. The result is a waste of time and of the company's resources.

Training is costly; training that must be repeated is costlier still. It wastes time, money, equipment. Every effort must therefore be made to minimize waste by insuring maximum retention.

Memory is a wonderful instrument but, like all complex instruments, it must be used properly. Employees forget to wear safety equipment; they forget essential techniques of the job; they forget to be courteous to customers; they forget company policies. Many job failures are often summed up in the words, "I just forgot." Experts agree that memory can be significantly improved through deliberate effort. But first the individual must realize that a poor memory is not an inherited trait like the shape of his body; he has simply not been trained to remember. Actually, a normal brain has stored within it every impulse and experience to which it has been adequately exposed. The real challenge is to stimulate their conscious recall.

Memory is a wonderful instrument but, like all complex instruments, it must be used properly.

REASONS FOR POOR MEMORY

The first step to improving memory is to recognize the reasons for insufficient retention and to eliminate these stumbling blocks. Perhaps the most significant cause of poor memory is an inadequate original impression. Memory can be compared to a camera. The snap of the shutter stores "information" on the film. But this information will be no better than the exposure. Memory can also be compared to a computer. Vast amounts of information can be inserted, stored, and recalled by the machine. However, nothing can be reproduced which was not inserted, and correct answers will not be forthcoming if incorrect information is fed into the computer. The machine's capacity for retention and reproduction is based on the accuracy and adequacy of the original information.

Except for the adequacy of the initial impression, the most significant influence on the amount retained is motivation. People must have a reason for remembering; they must be able to see the benefit to themselves before they put forth the effort necessary for maximum retention.

Our civil laws operate on the basis that "ignorance of the law is no excuse." It is the citizen's responsibility to understand and follow the law; the penalties provide the motivation for remembering and obeying them. For the employee, the relationship between remembering and better pay should provide the motivation; the things he wants from the job are more likely to come his way if he remembers how to do his job properly, meets standards of job performance, and complies with company policy.

Many teenagers breeze along with a grade of A in driver education because he is approaching driving age and because the course is a prerequisite for a license. However, the motivation to make a good grade in Latin and other subjects is less if he doesn't understand the need for these courses and doesn't have as much interest in them. Accordingly, the employee must understand the need for the information he is being asked to master.

It is reputed that one famous political figure could call 20,000 people by name. This won him many friends and gained many votes for his side. Similarly, a well-known general of World War II was regarded as a walking file cabinet. While others were scurrying around to check the location of a division or the accuracy of a detail, he could produce the information from his seemingly limitless memory. To him, having the facts meant being able to make quick, correct decisions.

A department store saleslady who sold china on a commission basis could remember every customer who had ever bought a set of china from her. When customers walked in years later, she greeted them by name, asked how they had enjoyed the set, and told them what replacement pieces were available or suggested new patterns that would suit their taste.

In each of these examples, there were strong motives for remembering. In each case the retention of information served personal as well as professional interests. For the employee, remembering must be related to job security, satisfactory job performance, supervisory approval, and personal satisfaction if he is to be motivated to exert the effort not only to learn but to remember what he has learned.

In addition to an inadequate original impression and inadequate motivation, a cause of poor memory is lack of effort. Let's suppose that you go to a party and are introduced to 30 people. If you were to meet these same people the following night, how many names would you remember? Probably very few. But suppose you go to another party where 30 people are present and just before you enter the room someone tells you that you will be paid $1,000 for every name you remember for a 24-hour period. Now how many names will you remember the following night? Probably most of them, because you will now have an interest in listening carefully to each name, hearing it adequately, repeating it to fix it in your memory, and associating it so that it will be easier to recall. You are still working with the same memory and the same basic information; the difference is one of interest and motivation for remembering.

When a personnel department employee who was writing out records by hand remarked to her supervisor that she wished she could type, she was advised that typing courses were available. The same conversation was repeated six months later and then again a year after that. When she brought up the subject the fourth time, she was told: "You will never learn to type because you simply aren't willing to put forth the necessary effort." Few people are willing to put forth the effort required for efficient remembering.

John Kieran, famed memory expert, has said, "Everyone remembers what he is interested in. The more I learn about a person or subject, the more I become interested; and the more I become interested, the better I remember." It doesn't take much analysis of our own personal experience to realize that this is true. We remember vast amounts of information about our hobbies and special interests, but we sometimes have difficulty remembering elementary facts about our jobs.

If the supervisor is not to be disappointed in the amount of learning the employee retains, he must be as much concerned with the influence of interest and motivation as he is with the content of the training program. Unless these factors are embodied in the learning process, time and effort are largely wasted because the process has to be repeated.

HOW IDEAS AND EVENTS CAN BE RECALLED

It has been demonstrated that forgetting occurs very rapidly at first and then tends to level off with time. An activity can be learned completely and repeated without error, but a week later a certain amount will have been forgotten unless the activity has been repeated often enough. The supervisor who recognizes the initial rapid rate of forgetting does not assume that just because information has been learned one day it will be remembered the following day or at the end of 30 days. Instead, he spaces follow-up checks to determine the amount forgotten and plans additional training to refresh the memory.

Like learning, memory can be improved by applying the following four laws as the occasion demands:

1. The law of association. If different things are experienced or heard together frequently enough, the presence of one elicits the recall of the other. Just as we learn by association, so do we remember by association too. We recall the things that are easier to remember and then make the transfer to the more difficult. Things that are to be remembered and used together should therefore be learned together.

2. The law of succession. If two things are frequently experienced in immediate succession, the presence of the first one tends to produce the recall of the other. For instance, it is

sometimes difficult to remember offhand what letter comes before another in the alphabet—until they are recited in sequence. The advantage of learning in succession is that when you remember one item in a list, you recall the next, and so on.

3. The law of similarity. If two things are similar, the thought of one causes the recall of the other.

4. The law of contrast. Extremes or opposites serve as reminders of each other. When you think of the biggest person you have ever seen, you may also think of the smallest. If you think of the brightest room you ever saw, you also probably remember the dullest. The use of contrast improves the vividness of the impression and the ability to recall.

TECHNIQUES FOR REMEMBERING NAMES

It has been estimated that every time you call a person by name you have his undivided attention for the next eight seconds. We make friends and create business by remembering customers' names. Why? Simply because a person's own name is the sweetest and most important sound to him. If we expect to influence people, we need to master the technique of remembering both their names and the things that are of most interest to them. The first step in remembering names is to recognize that there is a technique involved and to follow a few simple steps. In fact, these steps apply with equal validity to remembering in general, not only to recalling names.

Be interested. You will not remember people's names if you are not interested in people. The first step, then, must be to develop or increase an interest in people. If we recognize the decisive role others play in our lives and the vital influence they have on our future success, it should be easy to stimulate this interest.

Pay attention—listen. If you don't hear or understand a name correctly to begin with, you certainly won't be able to remember it correctly. Concentrate on the name; give its enunciation your undivided attention; listen intently to the sound. If you did not understand it clearly, don't hesitate to ask that it be repeated. It flatters the person that you think him important enough to want to know his name.

Repeat the name. Repeat it immediately and often. As soon as you understand the name, say, "I'm glad to meet you, Mr. Berryhill," rather than just "I'm glad to meet you." When you speak a name you do two things: You get the feeling of the word and you hear it once again. This repetition—which is often possible during the conversation and when you take your leave—helps to fix the name in your memory.

Observe the person. You don't remember people by noting the shape of their feet; instead, notice distinguishing facial features, shape of face and color of hair, and other physical characteristics. These are trail blazers—special markings which will help you remember a man's name when you come his way again.

Associate the name. Some names can be associated with familiar objects or ideas or with famous persons. Names such as Black, Frost, and Forest offer natural associations. Hoover and Kennedy, Washington and Hamilton can be easily associated with historical figures. Other names can be associated with places, objects, or symbols which are comparatively easy to call to mind.

Think about the name and the person. Repeat the name and think about the person as you do. If you have observed the individual intently, you probably have a mental picture which you can associate with the name. Focus particular attention on the distinguishing features or on the famous person or on the idea with which you are associating the name. This intensive thought process will be of great assistance in fixing an image of the individual and his name in your mind.

Write the name down. Writing the name helps you to get the feel of it; of course, you must understand it correctly in order to be able to write it in the first place.

SUPERVISION AND MEMORY

The supervisor's job can be a frustrating headache if his employees are the forgetful type. His time and effort are wasted if they do not remember the company orientation and job training. Many unnecessary conflicts are created if they forget safety rules, company policies, and other requirements of the job. The supervisor needs to be concerned with retention and memory as they affect the employees in his department and as they affect the discharge of his own responsibilities. The basic principles are the same in both cases, but the supervisor must provide the methods and motivation for the employees as well as the stimulation for his own remembering.

Several points should be kept in mind about remembering: First, memory is not inherited; it is an acquired skill that can be improved. Second, memory is no better than the initial impression; the seeing, the hearing, and the understanding must be sufficient in the beginning. Third, interest is indispensable to good memory; we remember most about those things that interest us most. Fourth, there must be a reason for remembering; motivation is a reasonably accurate measure of the amount of information that will be retained. Fifth, memory can be compared to a muscle; the more it is used the more skillful it becomes. Sixth, exceptional retention is dependent on deliberate effort—not just once but continually.

Many people put up with unsatisfactory retention because they are not willing to exert the mental effort to master the techniques that lead to improved memories. Work, effort, interest, concentration, motivation, tenacity, and practice are necessary. A good memory is worth money, friends, influence, prestige, promotions, customers, and tremendous personal satisfaction and enjoyment. There are no secrets involved—merely the willingness to exert effort and practice effective techniques.

The secret of getting work done through women is the same as that of getting work done through men. It is the fundamental principle of discovering the special needs and interests of the individual and then adjusting the job environment to satisfy these needs.

14. Harmonious Results in Working with Women

MEN AND WOMEN are more alike than different with regard to the work environment. The same human relations rules should be used to supervise both. In supervising women, however, it is more important to follow the rules. Women are less interested in the job itself and more interested in the supervision and how it affects them. They are quicker to detect and resent unfairness than are men. The supervisor must build their self-respect and self-confidence, recognize good work, praise generously, criticize sparingly, and provide them with a sense of belonging.

An excellent starting point in working with women is to recognize that nothing should be expected of women which is not also expected of men. Therefore, they should not be expected to "mother" other employees, salve egos, or furnish feminine companionship. Women expect basically the same things from the job environment as men do and should not be expected to contribute more just because they are women.

Women are making more of an impact in the labor market if only through sheer numbers alone. Consider these statistics as reported by the U.S. Department of Labor:

In supervising women, it is important to follow the rules.

- Approximately 25 million women are now working.
- Almost 34 percent of the workforce—or one out of every three people employed—are women, and this percentage is expected to continue to increase.
- More than one-third of all women of working age are gainfully employed.
- More than one-half of all employed women are married and have husbands who are present in the household.
- Approximately 20 percent of working women have children over 17 years of age.
- The average age of working women is 41.
- Women are employed in every one of more than 400 job categories listed by the U.S. Census Bureau.

It is now customary for young women to enter the labor force after completing high school or college, for women to work who have school-age children, and for others to return to the labor force after an absence to rear families. They now return to the labor force at an earlier age than they used to because families tend to be smaller than they have been in years past. The number of women in the labor force will continue to increase, as will their total dollar earnings. The contribution which their work makes and the addition of their earnings to the general economy are essential parts of the nation's overall productive and economic wealth.

PLACEMENT OF WOMEN

Women's physical characteristics, abilities, social needs, and suitability for certain jobs are different from those of men. Every manager who expects the job environment to encourage productivity should consider these differences carefully when placing women. For example, women are not as strong as men. In recognition of this fact, most state labor laws restrict the amount a woman can be required to lift. Women also have physical and emotional cycles which may affect their attitudes and their relationships with other people. Women can, at the same time, withstand pain and extremes of temperature much better than men.

Not only can women do complex jobs and complete professional training programs as quickly as men, but they also excel at certain tasks—for instance, use of precision tools, inspection of products, assembly of small or intricate components, and color discrimination, such as pairing of colored items. They have more patience, make a better adjustment to routine work, and stay with it longer than men. They are willing to give more attention to small details and exacting work, an important consideration when placing women.

In surveys of worker interest and job needs, the majority of women have cited social or personal relationships as being among the most important aspects of the job, and a great many have also mentioned cooperation from others, friendliness, the fairness of the supervisor, and a pleasant working environment. Participation in a group on the job is often a primary interest. Women expect that their pay will enable them to support themselves or contribute to the support of their families, but many prefer the security and tranquility of a pleasant work situation to the uncertainties that may go with change. For this reason, women often refuse promotions.

Another placement factor is that a woman may stop working because of marriage, pregnancy, or family duties. If none of these takes her from the job, there still remains the possibility that a married woman will leave because her husband is being transferred. Obviously these points do not apply to all women, but because of them some firms hesitate to place a woman in a position that would require years of training and experience before the company could expect a return on its investment.

Most national companies that have plants and offices throughout the country find it advantageous to transfer people geographically, and in many businesses it is necessary for employees to travel occasionally. In both situations women tend to be less adaptable than men.

ASSISTING THE NEW EMPLOYEE

The initial adjustment to a job is often far greater for women than for men. More girls marry at 18 than at any other age, and almost one-half of married women were married by the age of 20. This means that a significant number of women marry and rear children before making their first application for employment at the age of 35 to 45. For these women especially, a first job requires that they make many drastic changes in their patterns of living. The restrictions of a time clock, the confinement to one place, the curtailment of conversation, the learning of new techniques, and the adaptation to new relationships sometimes require major adjustments. The woman who has never held a full-time job may be uncertain about her responsibilities, and she needs reassurance and encouragement from her supervisor. If she is not helped to develop self-confidence, she may become discouraged and leave. Furthermore, she may face an initial coolness from other women employees, since they are inclined to look on a newcomer with restraint and with questioning appraisal until they know how she will affect their relationships with the supervisor and with the social group.

For all these reasons the supervisor needs to display patience, understanding, and encouragement—especially in the beginning, when the newcomer meets the other employees, learns the details of the job and the physical layout of the workplace, and receives the training she needs in order to meet the requirements of the job.

CRITICIZING AND COUNSELING WOMEN

Women tend to think that criticism of their work reflects on them personally and that they therefore have a right to feel hurt. Thus any criticism should be linked with praise to avoid any suggestion that judgment of their work reflects on them as women. Recognize that women have a special sensitivity about certain subjects; so avoid them. For instance, don't call attention to their age or weight and be wary of expressing opinions that seem to imply disapproval of all women. Although it is seldom true today, resentment toward women as co-workers has been a bitter issue in years past.

Remember that a woman needs constant reassurance. To praise her once, to tell her once that her work is satisfactory, to reassure her once will not satisfy her for the rest of her working career.

Not only do women have a greater need for sympathy and understanding, they also have more personal and emotional problems. Such problems often require the assistance of a counselor if they are to be settled before they interfere seriously with the job—even though they may not have been initiated by a job situation. The husband and his habits, the children and their conflicts, the family financial situation, and a host of other outside factors can create problems requiring counseling. However, on-the-job personal conflicts with others account for many of the problems.

In handling off-the-job problems, the supervisor should be warned against becoming involved personally or giving too much advice. Whatever the relationship between husband and wife, it is their problem and they must solve it. It is fine to be sympathetic, but don't get involved or take sides.

IDENTIFIABLE FEMALE TYPES

In getting work done through women, it is important to understand why they are working. Almost 5 million women are at the head of families. Half of these family heads work. Women who are the sole support of their families work for the same reasons as men. Many women, however, don't have to work. They hold jobs to provide extras and improve their family's standard of living, to participate in interesting and challenging activity, or to meet "Mr. Right." When they work for such reasons, they can quit at any time without economic hardship or loss of prestige. In the supervisor's attempt to understand and work effectively with women, he needs to keep these reasons in mind. Since they are obviously different from the principal reasons most men have for working, the supervisor must supply a different type of job satisfaction if women are to be motivated to turn in a top job.

It is a very precarious procedure to try to classify women. However, their specialized interests and attitudes toward their work and toward other people justify the attempt.

The mature married woman constitutes the largest segment and most important group from the standpoint of numbers and production. Her tenure on the job may be uncertain, but while she works she exhibits a real sense of responsibility and mature judgment. She is less flighty and more stable than younger women. Remember, though, that she is doing two jobs. In work assignments, avoid unscheduled overtime for her. She probably has a family waiting for her at the end of the regular work period. Encourage her to suggest shortcuts and time-saving methods, because she is probably skilled at streamlining her own activities. The mature married woman can be one of the most profitable producers on the job. Because of her maturity, judgment, and objective thinking, let her make the full contribution that she is capable of making.

The dedicated career woman is willing to pay the price to get ahead on the job. She may be married, but her first allegiance is to the job. She is of the opinion that she can get ahead on her own, that she is at least as capable as any man, and that she is certainly not dependent on any man for her success. She is highly competitive, uses every reasonable means to win what she wants, and is unwilling to admit that there is anything she cannot do.

The career woman may give the impression that she can be dealt with on completely equal terms with men as far as the job is concerned. However, despite her display of hardheaded independence, she needs recognition and approval as a woman.

The career woman needs goals to work toward. As a result of her extra dedication, she may make very few errors; but she will certainly make some. When she does, correction should be gentle, not a stinging rebuke. Since she wants to do the job correctly, merely pointing out the proper procedure is probably all that is necessary.

It is sometimes necessary to restrain the career-minded woman, lest she run roughshod over others: She may be impatient with people who do not have her drive and dedication, and she may be intolerant of their shortcomings because she considers job accomplishment more important than the niceties of accommodation to the pressures of the social group.

The younger woman may or may not be married, but her chief characteristic is immaturity of behavior and judgment. If this is her first job experience, it takes her some time to settle down. She is usually responsive to supervision, since she is used to home authority —though if she resented supervision from her teachers and parents, she may resent it on the job too.

Her first few weeks on the job are the most important ones. She can be an ideal trainee if she has a quick mind and wants to learn. The main problem is to get her to understand the ways of business. Be firm with her; she has probably been used to influencing her father and will try the same thing on the supervisor. The youngster can be a star on the team or one of the chief headaches, depending largely on the type of leadership she receives early in the job. She has ability, energy, and enthusiasm, but it will take attention and firmness to help her settle down and develop good work habits.

The marriage hopeful. Incentives and stimulation have little effect on the woman whose eyes are on the altar. She isn't looking for promotions and is not too greatly concerned with pay increases. She may be completely wrapped up in how she looks and in whether she can be seen at the right places by the right people. She is especially difficult to motivate because the supervisor is not able to supply what she wants most from the job.

The best bet is to give her a sense of purpose and to appeal to her pride. She should want a good recommendation when she leaves, and she certainly doesn't want to leave a record of failure. If all else fails, the next step is discipline. Be firm with her before she loses all interest in the work and affects the morale of the others in the group.

There is danger in trying to stereotype people, and it is obvious that an individual can fall into more than one of these groups—the married woman may not be mature; the altar-bound girl may be steady and responsible.

SOME COMMON MISCONCEPTIONS

"Women talk too much." Do women talk more than men? Experts generally agree that they do, and their need to communicate creates some special problems for the supervisor. He must deal with lengthy periods spent in the washroom and with continual conversations that can interfere with the job. But if women are isolated, they are unhappy. The satisfying conversational group on the job can be used to advantage if the work being performed is not hindered by conversation.

"Women rely on intuition instead of thought." Do women really have insight which men do not possess? Psychologists say they do and explain that feminine intuition stems from sensitivity to the feelings and reactions of others. Many little things—tone of voice, gesture, way of walking—go completely unnoticed by a man, but a woman notices and reacts to them.

"Women are nonconforming conformists." No woman wants to deviate so far from the norms of behavior and dress that she will be considered different or strange. Yet at the same time, she wants to be different. This desire to be an individual and still conform can be a definite advantage to the supervisor. The best way to influence the

group is through the one person who sets the style in dress and behavior. Whether the rest period is to be changed, or new standards are to be set, or discipline is to be tightened, instituting the change can be done more effectively through the one who sets the pace.

"*Women need to win.*" Some women are born competitors and play the game to win. They are poorer losers than men, and the job environment should therefore provide an opportunity to win. A woman can win in many ways—by gaining acceptance and approval on the job, by receiving recognition for having done an outstanding job, and by getting pay raises and increased responsibility as she progresses on the job.

"*Their presence creates problems.*" If a romance develops on the job it can be distracting and affect job results. However, if it becomes serious, the two people involved will probably continue to be serious about their work so as not to jeopardize their jobs.

The Don Juan of the business set who tries to prove that he is irresistible to women introduces a different problem. Though he is usually harmless and rarely fools anyone except himself, his activities can waste his time and that of others. A firm approach with such a man is often all that is needed.

With regard to off-color stories and profanity, women like to think they are able to take care of themselves; if a man offends, they can subtly and effectively put him in his place. However, women have a right to be protected from the habitual offender. The supervisor has the responsibility for the conditions under which his people work, and this is one area he must control.

Men should not expect social partners on the job, and women should not expect the same consideration they receive on social occasions. Both men and women must be able to distinguish between patterns of behavior on and off the job. Excessive carry-over from one to the other is likely to create problems.

"*Women have a higher rate of absenteeism.*" Perhaps the most serious problem in the employment of women is their high rate of absenteeism. They are out more often and for longer periods of time. They collect, per individual, almost twice as much from hospitalization insurance, thus increasing the rate the company has to pay. One government unit noted that they claimed three times as much sick leave. Since this can be a primary consideration in placing women in certain jobs, it is important to analyze the absentee picture. Why are women out more? Surprisingly, much of their absenteeism is not their own fault but that of other members of their families. But women also have more personal illness and require more absences for surgery. Further, they must usually suit their vacation plans to those of their husbands. If a woman worker cannot arrange to take her vacation at the same time, she is likely to take time off anyway.

The difficulty in dealing with absenteeism among women employees is that they have sentiment as well as need on their side. But even though many of the absences are justified, it doesn't mean that the company can do nothing about the situation. The problem can be handled in this manner. First, the reasons for the absences must be analyzed to determine if they can be reduced. If they cannot, it must be ascertained how seriously the work is affected and what the prospects are for a correction. If the situation warrants it, the supervisor should talk with the woman whose absences are excessive, explain that the company simply cannot justify keeping her on the job, tell her that it will be necessary to replace her, and suggest that when she can work on a regular schedule she will be welcomed back and that every effort will then be made to place her in the same or a comparable job.

Because absenteeism can be particularly disrupting on certain jobs, some companies do not employ women who have children under the age of six; a few prefer not to employ women with as many as three school-age children.

"*Women create more problem situations.*" Either separately or in combination, on-the-job and personal problems create moments of crisis in the lives of women. Men are better able to leave personal problems at home and plunge fully into their work. But a mother's anxiety can be a gnawing concern which causes irritability in dealing with co-workers on the job.

Most supervisors who work with women will sooner or later be exposed to a baptism of tears. When this does occur, don't lose your head. Give the tearful one plenty of time to recover with the least amount of attention or embarrassment. Make every effort to get her mind off the problem that has provoked the tears and demonstrate through your composed and sympathetic manner that the world will probably survive.

Try to get her to examine the facts objectively. Give her every opportunity to discuss the situation, but don't pry. A chance to talk about what is troubling her will relieve much of the emotional pressure. Let the tears flow if they must but continue talking about the situation; gradually the conversation can be shifted, and the tears will cease. Although not too common, tears can be used deliberately to gain an advantage. When this happens, they should not be ignored; but they should not be allowed to unnerve the supervisor or cause a major change in work patterns.

EVALUATING WOMEN AS SUPERVISORS

There are many who state emphatically that women do not make effective supervisors. However, the facts show that they can and do make very successful supervisors. Numerically, they are coming into their own at the supervisory level and in top executive jobs despite certain handicaps.

The woman supervisor faces a formidable prospect. Most men would rather be supervised by a man; they feel it lowers their dignity and status to have a woman tell them what to do. But it is actually female reluctance to accept the leadership of a woman that constitutes the most serious deterrent to greater use of women as supervisors. It is revealing to examine the complaints often lodged against them: They do not give sufficient credit to those who work with them. They are too personal. They put emphasis on loyalty to themselves rather than loyalty to the organization. They can't render objective decisions because they're too emotional. They are fussy, pry too much, and are too hard to please. They don't have enough confidence in others to delegate responsibility. They don't trust other women.

Further, some women contend that working for a woman is not interesting and exciting; having men around adds spice to even an otherwise dull job. And women are said to be too emotional and sensitive to stand the pressure of management and render objective decisions.

Certainly the best advice that can be offered about these complaints is this: If the shoe pinches, take it off. Any woman who recognizes that she is at fault on one or more of these points should make every effort to correct them. In spite of the reluctance of some people to accept female supervision, women still perform as topnotch executives. The physically strong, aggressive leader has been replaced by the teacher, the persuader, the sensitive leader. The very human traits which are sometimes the subject of criticism can also be a woman's chief assets if they are used appropriately.

OPPORTUNITIES FOR WOMEN AS SUPERVISORS

In a comparatively short time, women have entered the labor force in fantastic numbers, and they have taken over many supervisory and executive positions. Although much of the prejudice against women as managers is gone, some still remains. Because of this, women may have to work a little harder to win the respect and approval of others. Although no woman can be expected to think and act like a man, the woman manager must meet the standards that have been set by men if she is to be a successful leader in the business world.

Men are readily accepted as supervisors, but when a woman accepts a position of leadership her work is really cut out for her. She has to overcome the reluctance of the people she will supervise as well as people at other levels in the company, and she has to convince them that she is serious about wanting to get the job done and achieve results.

Women make excellent employees and they have earned the right to executive responsibility. The business world would be a far less interesting and exciting place without them. It is to the everlasting credit of women that, despite the handicaps they have faced, they have emerged by the thousands in the ranks of management at all levels. Today they hold many top management jobs because they have demonstrated that they can measure up in every respect to the requirements of executive leadership. Many men are awed by the way women are able to meet home responsibilities and job demands. Women have demonstrated their ability to combine the two by being excellent managers both on and off the job.

If women are treated fairly, recognized as important individuals, shown gratitude for their contributions, and given reasonable consideration, they will reward the supervisor with their cooperation and maximum job effort. Could anything more be asked of a man?

SPECIAL NOTE

Two special government regulations deal with the employment and job consideration which must be given women employees. The first is concerned with equal pay for equal work regardless of sex. This law, an amendment to the Fair Labor Standards Act which became effective June 10, 1964, provides that where men and women are doing substantially the same job they must be paid on the same basis. The second law deals with the rights and considerations which must be given to women. This regulation, contained in Title VII of the Civil Rights Act, forbids discrimination because of sex regarding employment, basis of pay, promotions, job assignment, discharges, and other job-related considerations.

Every supervisor concerned with the employment or supervision of women should be familiar with these two pieces of legislation and with what the company expects in the way of compliance. The supervisor acts as an agent for the company and therefore, from a legal standpoint, his activities regarding these laws are important to the company and to the individual concerned.

There are moments in the life of every individual when his greatest need is for a friend. The supervisor who gives sympathetic friendship through counseling renders a genuine service and earns the employee's eternal appreciation.

15. Counseling: Helpful Understanding

COUNSELING ALLOWS THE EMPLOYEE to talk about emotional problems and to find a satisfactory solution. It requires listening as the individual discusses what is troubling him in order to help him better understand and solve his problem. Most companies have found that counseling is good business as well as good human relations. The employee with personal or job-related problems may be inefficient and unproductive, and he may create problems for other employees, for his supervisors, and for the company. Both the supervisor and the company have an interest in correcting this job interference. A most important aim of counseling is to help a man develop the ability to solve his own problems by examining them in a new perspective and by selecting the best of available alternate solutions. When the employee is relieved of his worries and frustrations, he is in a position to make a more harmonious and productive job contribution.

Physical proximity and the organizational relationship of supervisor and employee thrust the role of counselor on the supervisor. Since he must handle counseling as the need arises, he should familiarize himself with this highly specialized technique. In his relationships with people, especially in the counseling area, the supervisor must be constantly aware that people want to be understood more than they want to understand.

A need for counseling may be indicated when an employee exhibits radical changes in behavior, attitude, or job performance. Sometimes it is the employee who recognizes that he has a problem which he has not been able to solve to his own satisfaction. When this is the case, he may take the initiative and seek the supervisor's assistance. Sometimes, on the other hand, it is the supervisor who recognizes the employee's need for counseling to help him solve a problem. In such a case it is the supervisor who takes the initiative and suggests a counseling interview. In any case the approach to a solution is basically the same. A need for counseling may be indicated by any of the following situations.

- The employee's mood and manner change.
- The employee's job performance changes from satisfactory to unsatisfactory.
- The employee becomes irritable and is at odds with everyone.
- The employee's energy level takes a sharp dip.
- There is a sudden rash of seemingly unjustified accidents.
- There is an increase in careless mistakes.
- The employee resents suggestions and correction.
- The employee becomes a trouble-maker.

These are only a few of the symptoms of problems that affect job performance or harmony in the department and require that the supervisor take action. Situations that require counseling are difficult to handle because they are usually of a personal or emotional nature. Some are job-related, but a significant number concern family and other off-the-job matters. Even when the root of a problem lies in areas over which the supervisor has little or no influence, it can still be as damaging to job achievement as the factors which he can control. He must therefore handle these situations with patient understanding.

THE GOAL OF COUNSELING

The goal of counseling is to minimize or eliminate any problem that interferes with workforce morale, productivity, acceptance of change, or harmony. This goal can be reached through several channels.

Communication. Inadequate or inaccurate communication can create problems and build barriers between the supervisor and the employee. The counselor has the opportunity to uncover and correct

As a counselor, the supervisor must play the difficult role of impartial observer, willing listener, and sounding board.

areas of poor communication which may be causing misunderstandings. And the knowledge that he is free to communicate with the supervisor often helps to lessen the pressure of the employee's problem as it relates to his job.

Guidance. Although the counselor must serve in an advisory capacity, he should not give advice which he is not qualified to give or try to force advice when it is not wanted. Indeed, he should refer employees to specialists in or outside the company who are qualified to give advice about special problems. Or he may suggest the possibility of seeking guidance from a minister or professional counseling agency in the community.

Release of emotional tension. A problem often reaches an almost explosive stage before the individual is willing to discuss a subject that may be a source of personal embarrassment. Yet talking with someone about it tends to release some of the pent-up tension—a step in the right direction. The elimination of emotional pressure often makes the problem less overwhelming and frightening, and the employee is then able to follow through to a satisfactory solution.

Reassurance. Many emotional problems are created by a sense of insecurity. For instance, rumors may lead a man to think that his job is about to be eliminated. As his feeling of insecurity grows, he begins to resent authority, loses interest in his work, and becomes an unsatisfactory employee. Counseling gives the supervisor an opportunity to reassure the man that there is no truth to the rumor, thus restoring his sense of security.

Reorientation. An employee may be disturbed because he has failed to achieve certain promotions even though he does not now have the qualifications to achieve these goals. Perhaps he needs additional formal education or specialized training programs. Counseling can help him reorient his thinking so that he will be more realistic in terms of the total situation.

THE COUNSELING TECHNIQUE

Counseling is distinctly different from other types of interviews. If it is not conducted skillfully, the result can be to destroy the employee's confidence in his supervisor and make the problem worse. There are five basic guides for the counseling interview:

1. Method. In the correction interview, the supervisor directs the course of the conversation. The counseling interview, how-

ever, is nondirective, and almost the entire course of the interview is left to the discretion of the employee. The supervisor must resist the temptation to take charge, express his own opinion, and give advice.

2. Responsibility. The employee must be made aware that he is responsible for solving his own problem. The supervisor may help him work toward a solution, but he must not take the responsibility for making the decision.

3. Status. The employee is equal to the supervisor in authority and function during the counseling interview.

4. Role. The employee must be allowed the independence to choose his own solution. The employee and supervisor have special roles in the counseling interview and should not assume each other's function.

5. Emphasis. The emphasis in counseling is on feelings and problems deeper than those that appear on the surface. The supervisor should encourage the employee to discuss hidden feelings and emotions and to focus on self-expression, insight, and recognition of the potential solutions.

Many supervisors do not have the temperament and patience required for counseling. When this is the case, the employee should be referred to someone better qualified to counsel him. However, the supervisor who is not willing to handle simple counseling problems is denying his employees one of the things they have a right to expect from him—sympathetic understanding. The chance to talk out a problem is itself of considerable therapeutic value. In order to put his thoughts into words the employee is compelled to think his problem through completely, perhaps for the first time. And sometimes, by the end of the discussion, he will have arrived at a satisfactory solution.

The supervisor should conduct the counseling interview in private. No employee should be expected to discuss his problems in the presence of others. Uninterrupted privacy is essential for counseling interviews. As the employee is likely to be in a state of emotional anxiety, he should be put at ease. The supervisor's ability to do this and to minimize barriers to free and frank discussion have a decisive influence on the success of the interview.

Communicate a feeling of interest and understanding. Convince the person that you are interested in him as an individual. As his trust and confidence are bolstered, he becomes more willing to discuss his problem. At the beginning of the interview, the employee is often reluctant to discuss his difficulties. When this happens, the supervisor should open the conversation, but he must always remember that his role is that of listener and not talker. Some ways to break the ice are to comment on the length of time the employee has been with the company, compliment him on favorable job performance, or talk about other neutral subjects. The employee can then turn the conversation in any direction he wishes. If he still avoids the issue, the supervisor can probe gently into pertinent areas.

The employee should be encouraged to talk, and the supervisor should listen in a friendly, patient, and sympathetic manner. Listening is an active process that requires more than merely being in the presence of someone who is talking. This is especially true of the counseling interview, since the primary role of the supervisor is that of serious and understanding listener. Thus do not disagree or argue with what the employee says. He has a right to call the shots as he sees them. Disagreement almost invariably jeopardizes the chances of resolving the issue successfully. The supervisor should avoid surprise, amazement, or critical response to what the employee says. If the employee feels that he has startled the supervisor, he may back off completely.

It will at times be evident what the employee is trying to say and what he is trying to avoid. But the supervisor should not try to put words in his mouth. Let him choose his own way of revealing the problem. Encourage the employee to keep talking until the complete story has been told. Often he gets halfway through what he wants to say and stops. It is then up to the supervisor to keep the conversation going without seeming to force the issue. Try to grasp what the employee is omitting from the conversation. Often what he avoids talking about is the focal point of the problem.

Whether the employee needs to know where he can get special courses or whether he needs the help of a professional counselor, the supervisor should be able to supply, when necessary, the special information required.

AREAS OF EMPLOYEE COUNSELING

Employees' personal problems, whether job-related or not, fall into several categories.

Vocational and educational. Many employees, especially younger ones, have problems concerning vocational goals. If they do not receive guidance, they often become frustrated and disgruntled with their present jobs and exhibit many of the symptoms which signal the need for counseling. If an employee does not have a realistic approach to his goals, the supervisor should help him examine his goals objectively and adopt a planned and practical approach to them.

Relationships with other employees. The source of many problems is human relations on the job—personality conflicts, jealousies, resentment of authority, and conflict of job interest among employees. Counseling can help resolve such conflicts.

Family. These problems are the most difficult because they are beyond the control of the supervisor. Yet the opportunity to talk about them may make such problems more tolerable. Or the supervisor may be able to refer the employee to a family counseling agency in the community for help.

Health. Many people worry about their health. Their symptoms, real or imagined, often cause feelings of anxiety. If this nagging worry continues because the employee has neglected to seek expert medical attention, the supervisor can encourage him to see a doctor. And if the employee is worried about the expense of medical care, the supervisor should tell him where to seek financial help.

Financial. Worry over money or inability to meet the family's financial obligations can keep an employee from doing a satisfactory day's work. There is a limit to what the supervisor can or should do in this area. But he can certainly tell the employee about any financial assistance—such as a credit union—available through the company. Or he might refer the employee to someone who can help him to plan a family budget.

Job-related situations. An employee may feel that his progress is too slow or that he has no chance for further advancement. Another may expect a transfer and feel threatened by the unknown new job. A third may have been offered a higher-paying job elsewhere but can't decide whether to accept it. Whatever the problem, the supervisor can use the counseling session to offer reassurance where reassurance is in order and to help the employee work out the best way for him to deal with the situation that is troubling him.

One day an employee came into the personnel office to resign, stating that he planned to work elsewhere because he was not making enough money to pay his bills. Further questioning revealed that he had not yet looked for another job because he thought that it would be unfair to do so while he was still employed. During the conversation, the personnel director pointed out that because of the man's limited skill he would probably be paid at about the same rate by other companies, that he would certainly lose his seniority and accumulated employee benefits, and he might lose income between jobs. After due consideration, the employee was able to see that he was not likely to make any more money elsewhere and that his real problem was one of better financial management rather than more pay.

This list indicates some of the general categories in which opportunities exist for the supervisor to be of service to the employee. The supervisor needs to be alert to situations which may call for counseling because personal and emotional problems are as damaging to job productivity and harmony as any of the more overt difficulties considered to be a normal part of the work routine.

DEVELOPING COUNSELING SKILLS

Certain counseling techniques and skills are very helpful to the supervisor. The supervisor should be familiar with personnel policies and procedures, educational and financial resources, promotion policy, grievance procedure, specialized counseling, and other information which may help the employee to resolve his problem. The supervisor should also be familiar with services available through community- or government-sponsored agencies and ways in which the employee can obtain this assistance. If the employee recognizes his need for such assistance but is reluctant to make the initial contact, the supervisor should consult with the personnel department. In some special situations he may be advised to arrange an appointment between the employee and an outside agency if the employee asks him to do so.

The most important counseling skills are those of interviewing and listening. The supervisor must gain and keep the confidence of the employee. He should be able to conduct an interview in such a manner as to encourage the employee to discuss his problems and make plans to deal with them. To do this he must learn to stay in the background, yet encourage the employee to talk about his problem, recognize the possible solutions, and make his own decision.

Emotional maturity and stability are marks of the well-adjusted counselor. He should be interested in understanding all types of people and problems; he should respect the rights and dignity of the individual; he should be objective, trustworthy, and sufficiently flexible to adjust to all types of people and problems without undue strain.

The employee never loses sight of the fact that the supervisor is important to his future, and he wants his approval and respect. He is therefore often reluctant to discuss anything which may reflect unfavorably on his ability to handle his own problems.

The supervisor must work hard at developing a permissive atmosphere in which the employee feels free to talk, knowing that the information he reveals will not affect him adversely and will be kept confidential. This reassurance is communicated by the relationship which the supervisor maintains with the employee on a day-to-day basis, by the way he conveys his concern and sympathy, and by his constant availability.

Many large companies today have professional counselors as full-time staff members. These counselors are professionally trained, have no line authority, cannot influence the future of the employee's job, and do not reveal the nature of the counseling interviews. In this environment the employee knows that he will obtain professional assistance without discredit. Since it is almost impossible for the supervisor to remain completely neutral about factors which can influence the work in the department, he should refer employees to these qualified counselors whenever he is confronted with problems he cannot handle himself.

*   *   *

When an employee who has a problem seeks the supervisor's help in finding a solution, his expression of confidence is a sincere compliment. But the supervisor must not yield to the temptation to play the role of big brother or try to take charge and solve the problem. Instead, he must play the more difficult role of impartial observer, willing listener, and sounding board. He must not pry; he must not get involved in the employee's personal affairs; he must be discreet; he must keep confidences. Above all, he must respect the employee's right to make his own decisions. Skillfully handled, counseling can establish a bond of mutual trust and confidence between employee and supervisor.

A critical test of the supervisor's leadership is his ability to make an accurate appraisal of each employee's contribution to the company. This appraisal provides the basis for recognition and job improvement.

16. Evaluating and Improving Job Performance

THE SURVIVAL AND GROWTH of a business enterprise depend on evaluation—evaluation of the raw materials it buys, of the finished products it sells, of its production standards, of its marketing techniques, of its manufacturing methods, and of a host of other factors that affect its profitability. Since payroll expenses constitute more than half the expense dollar in most companies, the efficient management of the employee's time on the job is essential. Evaluation of employee job performance is the tool with which to gauge whether employee time is being managed efficiently. It is the basis for determining how to improve performance on each job in every department. It keeps the supervisor informed about how each employee is doing. And it provides the employee with the opportunity to learn how well he is doing and how he can do his job better.

The armed forces pioneered in the development of evaluation procedures as a means of making a systematic comparison of large numbers of officers. Since there was frequently the need to promote one man out of ten candidates, and since the ten were often scattered around the world, a technique had to be devised for determining each man's qualifications so that promotions could be made on merit. The solution was to rate each man regularly, thus providing a running

195

If job evaluation is an informal and unreliable process, it is often unfair to both the employee and the company.

record of each man's qualifications and the way he discharged his duties and responsibilities. Today, performance rating programs are used widely not only in the military and in government but also in business and industry.

Evaluation of job performance is a constant process. If a rating is informal and unreliable, it is often unfair to both the employee and the company because it does not identify the performance areas deserving commendation or those requiring correction. Until these are identified, the supervisor cannot construct a specific improvement program.

The real value of evaluating job contribution becomes clear when it is recognized that the company pays more to buy the time of its employees than for all other expenses combined. This time is purchased for one reason—in order that it can make a productive contribution to the goals of the company. Job performance evaluation is an attempt to measure how much contribution is being made, its value, and where it can be improved.

Every company has some basis for determining who gets a promotion, who is to be granted a raise, who is to be released in the event of a general layoff, and who is to be given additional training. If the measuring instrument is unreliable or inadequate, the results can be no better.

A job performance evaluation program is the company's best method of assuming a responsibility for helping the employee to do a better job. The evaluation program aids the employee in reaching his maximum potential and aids the company in making profitable use of the employee's time. If there is no company-sponsored evaluation program, the supervisor is still responsible for determining the contribution made by each of his employees. The information that follows should enable the supervisor to do a more reliable and objective job of evaluation regardless of the type of program in use.

PURPOSE OF A RATING PROGRAM

Most employees are conscientious and want to do a good job. If they have the ability and receive proper training, they usually do pretty well. Each employee, however, should be told how he is getting along and should receive constructive coaching for improvement. The purpose of a rating program is to analyze the strong and weak elements of the employee's job performance in order to—

- Set performance standards for everyone in the department.
- Improve the efficiency of the individual and the total work group.
- Recommend pay increases, promotions, transfers, or dismissals.
- Identify serious deficiencies so that they can be corrected.
- Determine individual and group training needs.
- Determine the relative value of each employee's service to the company.
- Avoid overlooking employees who merit increases as well as those who are slipping in their performance.
- Meet the employee's right to know how he is getting along and how the company regards his work.

An evaluation program helps the supervisor to spot problems in his department and to identify specific areas where employees need assistance. It opens pipelines of communication, thus enabling the supervisor to get the ideas and suggestions of his people. It also presents the supervisor with an opportunity to make suggestions to employees regarding work improvement as well as to talk with them about employee benefits, future company plans, and continuing company goals. It develops leadership and supervisory qualities and reduces bias in evaluating others.

ADVANTAGES TO THE COMPANY AND THE DEPARTMENT

Some of the benefits of job performance evaluation are these:
- It provides criteria for measuring performance and determining the assets and liabilities of each employee.
- It assists the supervisor in setting standards and quotas for each individual in relation to the overall department goals.
- It gives the supervisor an opportunity to evaluate the effects of training and supervisory leadership.
- It should result in increased individual and collective achievement.
- It should result in better employee and supervisory morale,

because it demonstrates the company's interest in its employees and their development. It also assures that if any aspect of an employee's performance is unsatisfactory, he will be given an opportunity to improve.

- It should reduce employee turnover, because it assures recognition of outstanding performance and provides a systematic way for improving the productivity of those who might otherwise have to be discharged.
- It should reduce payroll cost through better utilization of every employee's potential. If every employee learns to work more efficiently, a more profitable operation results. The program also motivates the employee to work harder in order to receive a favorable rating.
- It facilitates long-range personnel planning, since the promising younger man can be spotted and given special attention. The program also provides an inventory of the individual's potential and qualifications for promotion.
- It has the major advantage of indicating how well a department is being operated. It reveals what kind of relationship exists between supervisor and employees, whether employees have had appropriate training, whether leadership or motivation is lacking, what procedures and arrangements in the department need to be reappraised, and what areas need improvement.

A performance appraisal program, however, is not intended to be a panacea. It should not be expected to correct problems that crop up every day, although many of these might eventually be eliminated through the improvement of overall performance and attitude. The correction of these problems should not be delayed until a job performance review. The rating should not be used as the sole determinant in making decisions on promotions, discharges, transfers, and pay increases. Since it may represent only a part of the employee's value to the company, it should be used in conjunction with all other relevant information. Although it can serve as an effective means of individual training, it should not replace any other training presently in use, and it cannot and should not be expected to substitute for top quality day-to-day leadership and supervision. A rating program can, however, make the use of all other leadership tools more successful.

METHODS OF RATING

Personal opinion is the best-known rating method. This serves a purpose, but certainly in a very unsystematic way. The lack of effective results reflects the unreliability of this method.

The checklist method consists of rating various characteristics on a scale from zero to five. The higher the number, the better the rating. The sum of the weighted points is the employee's score.

The profile method rates a number of traits which are itemized and described. When the employee is assigned a rating from excellent to unsatisfactory on each of the traits, a line can be drawn between the marks to produce a "profile" of the individual's job performance.

The cluster method groups related traits into categories. The number of traits rated is thus reduced to such areas as leadership, ability to plan and organize, emotional stability, and judgment. The employee is then rated from superior to unsatisfactory in each category.

The descriptive method consists of a written description of general characteristics and job performance. Certain crucial areas such as human relations, initiative, and judgment are always covered; but more attention is given to whatever characteristics are most meaningful to the evaluation of one particular person. This method has the advantage of comparing the person's performance with a pre-established standard. Its main disadvantage is that it is difficult for a new supervisor or one without writing skill to do an adequate job of rating.

The fitness report is used by the Navy for its officer group. It consists of a rating of certain factors at given intervals of time or when an officer or his commanding officer is transferred. The rating ranks each individual on a scale as compared with others in the group.

The group rating method is used in a few instances. This requires that a group of people, possibly several supervisors who are familiar with the employee's job performance, make the rating. Sometimes *seniority* becomes a prime factor, and in rare instances the need of the individual is considered in placing a value on his job performance.

Most large companies need several types of rating forms, each of which reflects those elements considered to be of greatest importance on each individual job. For instance, the form used for a production employee should be different from that for a salesman, who represents the company to the public.

Regardless of the methods used, the supervisor plays the key role in any rating program. In the absence of any type of company-initiated program, the supervisor may wish to install and follow through with his own informal program as a means of assisting his employees and improving the results in the department.

SUCCESSFUL PERFORMANCE APPRAISAL

The top executive must believe in the program and actively support it. The supervisor should understand and approve the plan to be used, since he is the critical middle man. His job is not an easy one, and unless he is sold on the program, he will not put enough into it to guarantee its success. If his role is mishandled, no amount of care and doctoring of the results can make the program effective.

The rating form must include provisions for rating all the factors important on each job. The form should include the seven standards which are important on practically every job: quality of work, volume of work, knowledge of the job, initiative, work attitude, dependability, and cooperation with others.

Clear, specific, and detailed instruction should be given to the raters. Many experts feel that the supervisors should play an important part in writing the descriptions of the various characteristics. They will then be in terms which will be understood by other supervistors and employees, and the standards will be more realistic and specific.

THE SUPERVISOR'S ROLE

The rating must be done by the immediate supervisor who assigns work, reviews it, knows the attitudes and feelings of the employee, and is familiar with the employee's job performance. He has the following duties in the rating program:

- Communicating information about the program to the employees.
- Completing the rating forms.

- Conducting rating interviews.
- Engaging in follow-up action.

TRAINING OF RATERS

Rating is not an easy task. To do it accurately requires the supervisor's best effort. Most companies recognize the importance of the rating program and train supervisors to rate accurately and fairly. The supervisor is told why the program is being used, its advantages and disadvantages, and what it can do for him, his department, and his people. The rating forms are thoroughly explained, and appraisal factors are defined and explained. Common rating errors and ways to minimize them are brought to his attention. The technique of the interview is emphasized and perhaps demonstrated by having supervisors act out the roles of participants in an interview. The supervisor is encouraged to consult with his own supervisor or the person responsible for the rating program in order to check his judgment and thus benefit by another's experience.

During training the following guides for effective and reliable ratings should be emphasized:
- The rater must be familiar with the behavior and job performance of the employee.
- An adequate amount of time must be spent on the rating.
- The rater must be able to evaluate objectively and make use of factual information.
- The rater should be willing to seek and follow advice in connection with the rating.

COMMON RATING ERRORS

When one phase of an employee's work is outstanding, or when he has some personality trait or characteristic that impresses his supervisor favorably, the rating on *all* characteristics may be higher than it should be because the supervisor's judgment on all points is colored by his reaction to this one factor. This is known as the "halo effect."

The most common cause for a negative halo is the occasional run-in between an employee and the supervisor. If the employee has done something to cause the supervisor to be criticized, for example, this may influence the level of the whole rating.

The error of low tolerance occurs when everyone in a department is rated low as compared with other departments. This generally results when the supervisor is particularly demanding of his employees and when his standards are excessively high.

The central tendency is probably the most common error. The novice rater who is not certain of his facts and who has difficulty in making decisions may follow the line of least resistance. The average or central rating is a way of avoiding conflict with the employee or the company.

Another error is the high or lenient tendency. This results when the supervisor avoids the hard decisions of rating according to merit, or doesn't want to hurt anyone's feelings, or wants all his employees to be happy or to like him; so all are rated high.

An additional error is the "no fault in friend—no virtue in enemy" evaluation. Other common errors include inadequate observation of work performance, failure to evaluate facts properly, and lumping together traits which are not similar.

To avoid such errors, the rater should be familiar with each trait being rated. He should know the definition of each trait and how it differs from other traits, its relative importance to the job, and how it can best be evaluated. He should grade every employee on the same trait at the same time. This makes the rater focus on the trait and its relationship to the job rather than on his feeling toward the individual.

The rater should make maximum use of production records, statistical information, and other objective data which are not based on personal opinion, and he should rate as though his own future as well as that of the employee and the company depends on the accuracy of the rating.

One further caution is in order in evaluating employee performance: The standards against which performance is to be judged must be realistic. For example, when an employee's production record is low, his work would ordinarily be classified as less than satisfactory. If the fault is his, the classification is justified. But if the employee works at a machine that is old and slow and subject to frequent breakdowns, the cause of the poor production record is beyond the employee's control. In such a case, judging performance against a stand-

ard that can be met only with new, fast machines is unrealistic and
unfair.

CHARACTERISTICS OF A GOOD RATER

There can be little doubt that job performance evaluation is greatly
influenced by each rater's own characteristics. His physical condition
influences his observation of and reaction to other people. His skill,
past experience, and education are also reflected. There are, however,
general characteristics which are common to all efficient raters.

Sincere interest in the rating. The supervisor should believe that
performance evaluation is a useful tool which serves the best interests
of the employee, the department, and the company. He should also
be willing to participate in training in the rating procedure.

Willingness to make the necessary time available. Most rating programs stipulate that evaluations must be completed by a certain
date. If the supervisor waits until the last possible moment and then
completes the form in great haste, it has little value. He must recognize that it takes time, study, and careful consideration to fill out the
rating form properly.

Well-adjusted personality. Quirks of personality may show up in
the rating and cause distortion. If, for example, the supervisor who is
over-enthusiastic about certain things demands the same response
from others, he may underrate qualified employees who do not share
his enthusiasm.

Sympathy and understanding. The rater should not expect perfec-
tion; he must instead be understanding of the weaknesses as well as
the strengths of those whose work he evaluates.

Flexibility and objectivity. An employee may deserve "excellent"
on dependability and "unsatisfactory" on quantity of production.
This demands flexibility on the part of the rater so that he can go up
and down the scale objectively in accordance with the actual job performance and call a spade a spade.

Willingness to recognize his own limitations. Self-examination often
reveals many traits in the supervisor which may influence his evaluation of the performance of his employees. These should be identified
and every effort made to counteract any tendency to let them influence judgment. The rater should recognize the wisdom of seeking assistance from others when it will result in a more accurate rating.

THE RATING PROCEDURE

When evaluating job performance, the rater should:

- Read carefully all instructions and information about the rating and ask for assistance if there is anything he does not understand completely.
- Base the rating on the employee's actual performance, not on his potential ability. It is often difficult to separate what a man has done on the job from what the rater thinks the man is capable of doing.
- Avoid letting temporary ups and downs in performance alter the rating. The employee may engage in spurt improvement in order to improve the rating. By the same token, temporary illness or problems on the job may throw him off his normal level of productivity. Performance for the entire period should therefore be considered in determining the rating.
- Keep isolated instances in perspective. One customer complaint or letter of praise should not in itself make for a good or bad rating. Think of isolated instances as part of the overall picture.
- Never discuss the rating of one employee with other employees.
- Remember that the employee should be rated unsatisfactory only if his performance is below the standard established for the department. If he is rated excellent or exceptional, he should be making a contribution above and beyond the department standard. Each rating should be a reflection of actual performance in comparison with the measuring criteria, and the collective rating of the employees in a department should be reflected in overall department results. For instance, if all the department's employees are rated high on productivity but the department's production has dropped below standard, something is obviously wrong with the individual ratings.

THE EVALUATION INTERVIEW

A major goal of evaluation is the improvement of job performance. If the rating form is completed and then hidden in a file, nothing has been done to reach this goal. It is during the evaluation interview that the supervisor has an opportunity to give recognition for good work and make effective use of the rating as a basis for performance improvement.

The supervisor who comes to a performance appraisal interview unprepared may be letting himself in for a hard time. If he considers the work of an employee unsatisfactory he should be ready to back up his opinion with evidence. If, for example, a salesman's tactlessness and brusque manner have antagonized several customers, the supervisor should have the details of these incidents so that his comments can be specific. Generalizations may be rejected by the employee in such a situation; and if he is an aggressive individual, he may cause a furor that could damage morale throughout the department.

No one likes to be reminded of the shortcomings of his job performance, but the employee who really wants to get ahead recognizes the need to know where he stands. The degree of acceptance of the rating depends largely on the manner in which the interview is handled. The interview must therefore be planned so that the employee receives recognition for his outstanding work and guidance for improving his job performance and for building a closer relationship with the supervisor. The employee should leave the interview self-confident, in high spirits, and determined to improve. In preparing for the interview the rater should:

- Review the factors that affected the evaluation.
- Have on hand records and other pertinent information.
- Organize a simple, straightforward plan for conducting the interview.
- Review possible problem areas or uncertain ratings with other key persons before the interview.
- Arrange a time when neither he nor the employee is under pressure or short of time.

CONDUCTING THE INTERVIEW

Put the employee at ease. This is not difficult if the relationship is already cordial. In any case, the supervisor should make a point of being friendly, sincere, and solicitous.

Restate the purpose of the interview. Stress the benefit to the employee.

Go over the evaluation. Explain the reasons for your rating of each factor, starting and ending with the favorable factors. Remember throughout the interview that you are discussing not the man but his performance on the job and that it is easier for the employee to accept criticism about his job than about himself. Keep in mind that some of his shortcomings may have resulted from your failure to guide, instruct, and motivate him.

Encourage the employee to speak freely. Let him ask questions, make suggestions, and offer ways to improve his own performance as well as the operations in the department.

Avoid putting the employee on the defensive. The supervisor should not conduct the interview as though it were a trial, with himself as prosecuting attorney and the employee as defendant. The objective is to reach agreement on past job performance as compared with a satisfactory standard and on the opportunities for improvement.

Be specific. Whether you are complimentary or critical, refer to specific instances. And clear up any misconceptions or misunderstanding that the employee may express about any phase of the job.

Give credit where credit is due, and set goals for job improvement. Remember that once good work has been adequately recognized, the most important responsibility of the supervisor is to offer—and ask for—constructive suggestions for job improvement.

Let the employee explain the obstacles he considers detrimental to better job performance. He may bring out some very real problems which prevent him from performing at his maximum level. If he reveals a situation which needs correction, the supervisor should investigate the matter and talk with the employee again in the near future about what has been done to improve it. If the employee's points are not valid, the supervisor should explain why they are not sufficient justification for poor job performance.

Welcome objections from the employee. The most difficult interview is with the employee who says nothing. It's like trying to make a sale to a man who shows no response. You don't know whether he agrees or disagrees with what you say. You don't know his reasons for not buying; so you have no opportunity to answer any objections. It is much easier to conduct an effective interview if the employee is willing to talk freely about any objections he has to the rating. This gives the supervisor something to work with and is an indication of the employee's interest.

CONCLUDING THE INTERVIEW

In the job performance evaluation interview the supervisor and employee may talk about many things. The employee has probably felt both good and bad during the interview. But when it is all over and the employee goes back to his job, what is his frame of mind? Is he enthusiastic? Does he feel that the company and the supervisor have been fair to him? Will this be reflected in better job performance? To insure that the interview achieves its purpose the supervisor should do the following.

Work out a definite plan as to time and method for achieving improvement. Don't be content to talk in generalities. Identify specific areas for improvement; consider each one separately, and work out a program.

Make a record of the key points for follow-up and see that the employee also has a record of the program which has been agreed on. This should make clear to the employee what specific action he will be expected to take to improve his work.

Bring the employee back to a high level of self-confidence before ending the interview. Communicate your full confidence in his ability to make the changes that have been agreed on.

End the interview on the highest possible note. Again thank the employee for his job contribution and his good work. If there is to be a follow-up interview, give him the approximate date. Thank him for his suggestions. Assure him of your continuing interest in him and your availability at all times to answer his questions and to assist him.

UTILIZATION OF EVALUATION RESULTS

After the rating and interview have been completed, the supervisor and the company can use the individual and collective results of the rating program as guides for management decisions and follow-up action. Many companies use the ratings for the following purposes:

- As a measurement of improvement in individual job performance. It is useful to compare the most recent rating with previous ratings to determine what changes have been made.
- As a basis for determining training needs. If the ratings reflect

a lack of information or skills in some area, management can provide corrective training.

- As a basis for promotions, pay increases, and transfers. Decisions concerning these factors are more objective if they are based on a merit rating program.
- As a follow-up check on company employment and placement procedures.
- As a help in standardizing the evaluation between departments. It insures that the same duties, responsibilities, and overall job contribution receive the same compensation throughout the company.

FOLLOW-UP

If the rating has identified some areas which need immediate attention and if the supervisor has worked out with the employee what corrective action should be made within a specified period of time, a follow-up interview should be arranged to check progress. In addition, the supervisor should follow through promptly on any action he has committed himself to take and talk with the employee about the results of this action without undue delay.

The follow-up interview should be recorded and made a part of the employee's personnel file. This is especially true if the interview is a warning. Because of current wage-hour laws and other government regulations, this recording is necessary in order to protect the company in the event of a later discharge.

*   *   *

No supervisor should feel that the absence of a formal evaluation program relieves him of responsibility for evaluating employee performance.

Performance appraisal and appraisal interviewing offer both a critical challenge and a unique opportunity to the supervisor's leadership and supervisory skills. To develop the high degree of critical judgment and finesse required, he should obtain as much training and assistance as possible. The supervisor who handles a rating program successfully is well on his way to effective leadership.

The improvement of work methods offers management its greatest opportunity to increase productivity at less cost in employee time and effort.

17. Techniques for Improved Work Methods

Willa Cather once remarked that "man is the only animal that fights to stay in a rut." Today, however, growing numbers of companies want to get their employees out of the rut of obsolete work methods and procedures. Company survival is dependent on improvement—on finding a better way, on speeding up the process of change, on leading the field with the changes that mean a competitive advantage. The emphasis today is on work simplification, operation improvement, job enlargement—all aimed at increasing the operating efficiency of the organization by improving its working methods and procedures.

Many large companies use the services of specialists, such as time and motion study experts, to improve methods and procedures. But these efforts are doomed if the supervisor is not involved in the development and application of the new improvements. Too often the analysis and improvement of work methods are considered to be the responsibility solely of the time and motion specialist. The supervisor, however, should recognize that this is and always has been an important part of his job. The specialist brings a scientific and systematic approach to the problem and has specialized training and experience, but he lacks the supervisor's daily exposure to employees and work methods. The supervisor must guard against the natural tendency of letting closeness to the job and the habits of years blind him to possible improvements. Instead, he should cultivate an objective approach, question everything, and recognize that no one method is the only or best one just because it is the one now in use.

210

In its simplest form, improvement consists of examining how a job is being done; eliminating any step, movement, or phase of the operation which is not essential; and developing improved procedures for doing the job. However, the idea that there is one best method should be approached cautiously, because today's most efficient technique may be obsolete tomorrow. It is essential to remember that the improvement of work methods is not a one-shot effort but should be a part of the supervisor's everyday responsibility.

APPROACHES TO METHODS IMPROVEMENT

Scientific investigation. The supervisor who seeks to bring about improvement in work methods can profit from the techniques used by the scientist in tackling a problem. As a matter of course the scientist goes through the process of—

- Stating the problem to be solved.
- Recognizing the materials and resources with which he has to work.
- Being thorough and systematic.
- Investigating previous work in the same field.
- Discussing the problem with others and learning from them.
- Assuming that the problem has at least one and possibly several solutions.
- Remaining objective and being guided only by facts and results.
- Recording every activity. As much may be learned from failure as from success.
- Testing every theory, principle, and conclusion.
- Looking for similarities with other problems and studying their solutions.

Like the scientist, the supervisor should never consider that he has found *the* solution to a problem; instead he should continue to look for improvements and refinements.

Improvement of equipment. Many companies have made dramatic changes and improvements in the design and function of tools and equipment, thus enabling employees to produce more with less effort. Yet many others still use the wrong size and type of screw driver or other basic tool, thus slowing down production.

Many improvements that should be made are so simple that they

Company survival is dependent on improvement—on finding a better way.

are overlooked. For example, in one firm large cardboard cartons were opened by tearing up the flaps. Some were glued; others were secured with sharp staples that were dangerous when they were pulled loose. Yet inexpensive knives with safety guards had been in existence for many years especially for this purpose; when they were finally obtained, the job of opening cartons was done faster and more safely.

Alert supervisors have made significant improvements in their operations by introducing more appropriate tools or by altering the equipment being used. It is the supervisor's responsibility to detect instances where equipment can be changed or improved, even when procedures appear to be going smoothly.

Improving the training program. Most of the methods and procedures used by employees are those they have been trained to use. Perhaps the quickest and easiest way to bring about an improvement in work procedure is to retrain present employees and change the program for new employees.

One department store had had difficulty in getting employees to engage in suggestion selling. Both initial and follow-up training stressed that whenever a sale was made, the salesperson should suggest an additional item in order to increase total sales. This program, however, was only about 15 percent effective. The situation was analyzed and the training procedure changed. The new program incorporated the complete process of selling from the time the customer was approached until she was handed her package, thanked, and invited to return. There was only one important change; after the customer said, "I'll take it," the next step was to show her a second item. This was always a companion item or one which was appropriate to the customer's needs or to the season. The salesclerk now learned this step in logical sequence, and the selling procedure was incomplete without it. As a result of this change in training which made suggestion selling an integral part of the procedure rather than an incidental addition, the number of salespeople engaging in suggestion selling increased to 60 percent.

ANALYSIS OF WORK METHODS

Performance of the operation. The best way for the supervisor to learn the details of an operation is by actually doing it. In this way he will get the feel of each step—its difficulty, exactly how it is being done, and how it can be improved.

Observation of the worker. By observing the employee who does the work, the discerning supervisor will detect areas of difficulty and should be able to devise ways in which the procedure can be improved.

Employee questionnaires. Having employees answer questions about their work obliges them to think about the routine they follow and may result in constructive suggestions for improvement. When the questionnaires are considered collectively, overall patterns of improvement are often evident.

Employee interview. Talking with the employee about how his job is being done and how it could be improved should encourage him to present his ideas and to look for ways to perform his job more easily and more efficiently.

Charts and manuals. A great many industrial operations and business procedures have been studied minutely by industrial engineers and efficiency specialists. Their findings have been published in book, chart, and manual form and are available to the supervisor who seeks to improve the operation in his own department.

Work flow charts. The highway engineer determines the location of two cities on his map and then lays out a route and specifies a road surface best suited for carrying traffic between these two cities. As he plans this road, he considers ways to eliminate curves, fill in valleys, grade down peaks, bridge rivers, avoid dangerous intersections, and place essential signs along the way. Each of these steps is considered with one end in view—a smooth, quick, safe, and economical trip for the motorist who will travel over the road.

When the plan has been spelled out, the highway engineer develops a chart to establish the sequence of steps that must be taken to build the road according to plan and to assure that both men and materials will be where they are needed when they are needed. This is a flow chart—a detailed record of every step that must be followed to complete an operation, showing not only what must be done but also when and in what sequence.

The supervisor too can use the flow chart to advantage. By detailing the steps in each operation performed in his department, he can portray visually which steps are done simultaneously and which are done in sequence from initiation to completion of an operation; and he can determine whether greater efficiency can be achieved by rearranging the order of the steps or adjusting the flow of materials needed for specific steps.

Study of unrelated activities. Many dramatic improvements have been made in industrial work procedures by alert supervisors whose observations of seemingly unrelated activity have offered clues to more effective ways of working in their own departments. Remember that it was the smooth coordination of a line of chorus girls that gave Knute Rockne the idea for the four-horsemen shift for the backfield of his football team at Notre Dame. And it was a random apple falling from a tree that led Sir Isaac Newton to develop the law of gravity.

Progress in related areas. Business and industry have continued to benefit from advances in education by applying these advances to company training. The competitive pressures of free enterprise force the constant search for better and more efficient methods. This search leads to any area which offers possibilities for improved operation.

GUIDES FOR IMPROVING WORK PROCEDURES

The first step in improving work procedures is to describe completely how the job is now being done. This should be a complete audit—a word picture of the work flow process and a diagram showing the step-by-step procedure and the overall picture. Identify the necessary action. The description must be complete enough to show each step of the operation clearly. For example, a list of the steps in answering the telephone might read something like this: (1) Reach for the receiver with left hand; (2) lift receiver; (3) bring receiver in contact with ear; (4) talk into mouthpiece; (5) reach for pencil and message pad with right hand; (6) write message; (7) finish talking; (8) replace receiver with left hand; (9) replace pencil and message pad with right hand.

When the steps in an operation have been itemized, the next requirement is to study every step, movement, and detail. Ask questions: Why is the job being done this way? Is what it accomplishes necessary? Are we trying to improve an operation that is not necessary in the first place? Can what is now being achieved be accomplished better some other way? Is the work being done in the right

Principles of Motion Economy

E Eliminate idleness. Never use the hands as a holding device.

A Avoid unnecessary motions.

S Smallest body member should move the shortest distance.

} FOR THE HANDS

I Improve workplace with bins, lip trays, and workplace appliances. Pre-position tools and materials.

E Employ fixtures, clamps, and guides for productive work.

R Relieve hands with foot controls, ejectors, chutes, and drop delivery.

} FOR THE WORKPLACE

location? Why is it being done where it is now? Could it fit better into the work flow at some other point? Who should do this part of the job? Is the job being done by the person best suited to do it? Is a worker's skill being wasted on too simple tasks?

What follows is a *motion economy checklist* for a manual operation developed by a well-known company to train supervisors and employees in improved manual work methods.

1. Does each element *begin* simultaneously with both hands?
2. Does each element *end* simultaneously with both hands?
3. Are simultaneous arm motions in opposite and symmetrical direction used?
4. Are hand motions of the lowest classification for satisfactory operations?
5. Does motion path stay within the normal working area?
6. Can sharp changes of direction be avoided by using a continuous curved motion path?
7. Are small objects slid instead of being picked up and carried?
8. Are materials and tools located in proper sequence at definite work stations?
9. Is maximum use made of rhythm and automaticity?
10. Can pieces be pre-positioned for the next operation?
11. Is proper-height chair with comfortable seat and back rest provided?

Remember that any changes which make the job easier, faster, more accurate, or less expensive should be made. These principles can be applied to the job of the secretary, the bank teller, or the assembly line worker. The goal is always the same—the reduction of unnecessary activity and effort.

When the questions have been asked, the answers have been found, and a direction for improvement has been determined, the next step is to develop a new plan incorporating all the desired changes and improvements. The best plan is one which eliminates the greatest amount of nonessential motion, effort, and waste.

When the plan has been developed and management approval has been obtained, it's time to explain the details to the employees, let them know about impending changes that will affect them, emphasize the advantages of the plan, and answer their questions. Then, once the plan has been put into operation, all that remains to be done is to keep a close check on it so that adjustments can be made as needed

—and it's time to start looking for ways to make further improvement.

Dr. James L. Williams, former director of industrial relations for Burlington Industries, said: "The most important factor in production is 'man' in industry. Two factories can be just alike in layout and manufacturing, yet one will succeed while the other may go out of business. Two retail stores can have the same sales advantages, yet customers flock to one and avoid the other." The difference lies in the willingness of people to increase their own skills and the methods by which they work. The improvement of people's skills through training means improvement in overall results. Many companies seek to upgrade job techniques through better placement, maximum utilization of employee skills, proper allocation of the workload through delegation, and individual attention to employees who need assistance with these improvements.

Appropriate delegation is a means to growth, to expanded influence, and to increased results through people. It is doubtful if any other leadership approach exerts as quick or as significant an influence on the supervisor's capacity for managing a larger responsibility.

18. Effective Delegation of Responsibility

STATED SIMPLY, delegation is sharing the load. A single employee working by himself carries the full burden. When the workload increases beyond his capacity, a second employee must be hired. Eventually someone is needed to supervise the group; and as the burden of leadership increases beyond one man's capacity, the supervisor must share a portion of the load in order to get work done quickly and allow time for decision making. The following statements are symptoms of a need for delegation:

- "I wish someone else around here would start worrying about getting the work done."
- "I know I have too much to do, but no one else wants any responsibility."
- "That delegation stuff sounds good, but it takes longer to tell someone else what to do and then have to check on him all the time than it does to do it myself."
- "I don't want any more responsibility. There aren't enough hours in the day to do everything I've got to do now."

One of the most important ways for increasing results is to give more people a measure of responsibility for achieving those results.

The only business that can be successful without delegation is the one-man operation.

By sharing a portion of the supervision with an assistant and a portion of the responsibility with each employee, overall results can be improved; the supervisor can devote more of his time to work which cannot be delegated; and this in turn leads to still further departmental improvement.

The only business which can be successful without delegation is the one-man operation. Wise executives learn early in their careers that in order to grow, they must expand their leadership by means of delegation. They recognize that failure to delegate stifles the growth of the business, and this in turn limits the opportunities for personal growth.

A study of the great business leaders of America reveals a significant relationship between successful delegation of responsibility, the growth of the company, and the growth of the executive. One of this country's greatest magnets was prouder of having delegated responsibility than he was of the size of his mills. He said, "Take away our factories, but leave me my organization and in four years I will have re-established myself."

A chain of department stores in the Midwest failed because the president insisted on personally approving the purchase of every cash register and office machine, on deciding which lines of merchandise should be dropped or added and how much money should be spent on advertising—in short, on making both major and minor decisions regarding the operation of the more than 50 stores. Failure was inevitable because the job was too big for one man.

The need for delegation of responsibility began a long time before the increased complexities and demands of modern business. One of the earliest references to delegation occurs in *Genesis*, where Jethro tells Moses, "Choose able men from all the people . . . and place such men over the people as rulers of thousands, of hundreds, of fifties, and of tens. And let them judge the people at all times; every great matter they shall bring to you, but any small matter they shall decide themselves; so it will be easier for you, and they will bear the burden with you." It is noteworthy that "Moses gave heed to the voice of his father-in-law and did all that he had said."

No manager can keep track of every detail of every job for which he is responsible. The more nearly he tries to do this, the more he limits his span of leadership, stifles the growth of the enterprise, and defers the development of leadership in his people. Too little delega-

tion is typical of the man who believes that to get a thing done right
he must do it himself and of the energetic man who often piles one
responsibility on another until he succumbs to the pressure of "executive overload." At the opposite extreme is the man who delegates
responsibility but forgets that he must also delegate authority before
results can be achieved.

Responsibility is a duty or obligation to act. With it must go the
right to act—that is, the authority. And to insure that the responsibility has been fulfilled a third ingredient, accountability, must be
included; that is, the person who has been given a job to do must
account to his supervisor for his actions in carrying out the assignment. For example, when a supervisor delegates responsibility for the
department's stock of supplies, he must also delegate the authority to
reorder and he must hold the employee accountable for keeping
enough stock on hand. If the supervisor were to withhold the authority to reorder, then the delegation of responsibility for stock maintenance would in fact be meaningless.

HOW WELL DO YOU DELEGATE?

Most supervisors think they do a pretty fair job of delegating.
They realize that it is a reflection on their overall leadership and
faith in other people if they fail to delegate—so many cover up,
even to themselves. Delegation actually begins with the ability to
analyze and categorize problems, to break big problems down into
manageable units, to size up capabilities of subordinates, to communicate clearly, to develop controls, and to follow up on the activities
of the group. These are the building blocks for realistic delegation.

What would happen if you were suddenly taken out of circulation?
How well would the work go on without you? Are you constantly tied
up with giving employees instructions? Are you spending too much
time checking on details that could just as well be left to their good
judgment?

Are you up to date with your work? Is your desk loaded with reports, forms, and other memos which must have your personal
approval? How much has the work of other people been delayed
because you haven't had time to approve these things? Do they really
need your approval, or could someone else handle the details? How

much work do you have to carry home? How much of this work can be channeled to someone else?

Are your employees afraid to make decisions because of past reprimands or because you have asked them not to decide things on their own? Do you lack confidence in other people's ability to follow through successfully on their own? Are you afraid to risk letting them do a few things on their own initiative—even to the point of making an occasional mistake?

Are you willing to seek the advice of others, especially the employee group, or are you afraid that to ask for their suggestions would be an admission that you don't know all the answers? Are you reluctant to admit to the employee group that you need help to get the job done?

If your answer to these questions is too often "yes," then you need to give serious attention to improving your delegation practices.

THE NEED TO DELEGATE

In order for a business to grow, people must grow with it and be able to accept greater responsibility. Delegation is one of the best ways to assure this essential growth. The failure to delegate can be damaging in many ways. It causes a shortage of men who are trained and ready to assume greater responsibility. It causes key supervisors to be so overburdened with routine that the planning, supervising, and other important leadership responsibilities are not met properly. It limits decision making to only a few and fails to develop the capability in others.

Failure to delegate makes it necessary to promote a man before he has had adequate training—or go outside the company to obtain the skills and leadership needed for executive jobs. It drives many young men to resign because they are getting nowhere. And it results in a general apathy among the employee group.

Each individual executive certainly has much to gain from the delegation of some of his responsibilities. But more than that, he should never lose sight of the fact that it is expected of him—not only for his own development but for the long-range benefit of the organization as a whole.

A reasonable first step in delegation is to analyze and categorize activities which must take place in a department. Big problems

is necessary if he is to develop into a mature and responsible adult. Likewise, the employee develops a sense of enrichment when the supervisor is willing to trust him with additional responsibility. It is doubtful if anything else will develop his potential as quickly as the challenge to live up to a new responsibility. The supervisor should be cautioned against delegating too much too fast, however; too great a challenge may leave the employee feeling overburdened and unable to cope with his new responsibility.

When a supervisor shares his work, his department will grow faster because more of the people are given the opportunity to develop and use their full potential. At the same time, the employees who have the qualities of leadership can be trained to replace the supervisor so that he can be freed for further promotion.

SELECTIVE DELEGATION OF AUTHORITY

Not all authority can be delegated. In some instances it would not be legal to do so; in others, the supervisor is specifically required to make certain decisions. Some matters that cannot be delegated are the power to discipline, long-range planning, and policy making. When authority is delegated, the nature and bounds of the authority and the effective date upon which it is expected to begin should be spelled out, and a notice should be given to all interested parties to insure cooperation. Further, those who are to assume the authority should be given freedom of action. But sufficient controls must be set up to check the results and the effectiveness of the delegation. Accountability must be a part of the picture.

An appropriate time to delegate or change responsibility is when other changes are occurring—personnel changes, for example, or changes in the machines or the layout of the work area. But whenever the change is made the delegation of authority must be as clear and precise as possible. Fuzzy bounds of authority can cause conflict and frustration for the individual who is trying to fulfill his responsibility and can create resentment and confusion throughout the department. If the supervisor expects the affairs of the department to proceed smoothly and efficiently, the authority of each person must be clearly understood by everyone in the department.

Avoid delegating authority until there has been an opportunity to make certain that the recipient knows how to use it. The delegation of authority should not be a matter of taking indiscriminate shots in the dark at an unknown target. Rather, the supervisor should be sufficiently acquainted with his people to know what each man is able to accept and discharge successfully. The delegation of authority to a man who cannot handle it can be damaging to both the individual's job performance and the department's goals.

If practical, start delegating authority on a gradual basis and check with the employee frequently to answer his questions and give him the self-confidence he needs. And above all, be tolerant of his mistakes. He should not be expected to assume the authority you delegate to him without making any errors. When mistakes are made they should be corrected, but the supervisor must avoid sarcastic criticism. Instead, coaching is in order to help him understand what corrections are necessary and to be sure the best interests of the department are being served.

MASTERING THE SKILL OF DELEGATING

Every supervisor can profit from an occasional objective look at the degree of success he is having in delegating work and responsibility. There can be no better way of doing this than by actually checking the results in the department or by an appraisal of the supervisor's job performance. It will also help, in pinpointing results and needs, if the supervisor asks himself: Are my people properly challenged and do they have sufficient goals to work toward? Are they constantly growing in their willingness and ability to accept additional responsibility? What additional work or responsibility can be delegated to them? Am I doing work that others could be doing just as well? Do I have the time to do the things that cannot be assigned to others? Is there sufficient evidence of growth in all areas because of the steadily increased delegation?

Ability and willingness to delegate are trademarks of the growing executive. The executive who delegates demonstrates that he is mature, is confident of his position and ability, has confidence in other people, and is willing to build leadership in his subordinates. The failure to delegate stifles the growth of the business and of every individual associated with it.

The goals of a business enterprise are shaped, clarified, and coordinated through effective communication. Without understanding, the enterprise is doomed to failure—understanding is both the aim and the by-product of communication.

19. Goal Achievement Through Two-Way Communication

THE STORY IS TOLD of a visual signal sent from a hilltop immediately following the battle of Waterloo. "British defeated. . . ." This news spread throughout England, and the country went into mourning. Not until later was the full message received: "British defeated Napoleon at Waterloo."

Communication breaks down when the message that is sent and the message that is received do not jibe. Not all breakdowns in communications are as spectacular as that about the defeat at Waterloo, but they can have serious and widespread repercussions. Remarks made in jest but taken seriously can lead to major grievances. Chance comments by an executive can result in a change in company policy; instructions that are misunderstood can cause a whole department to fall behind in its production schedule.

Effective communication is the key to successful group dynamics. To succeed as a leader a man must be able to communicate—to express his ideas accurately and precisely—since this is the first step in the process of getting things done through people. The following statements are symptomatic of the communication gap:

- "I didn't know you wanted me to check every item."
- "Nobody told me it was a dismissal offense not to put a receipt in packages."

- "Why is it that the employees in your department never seem to get the word?"
- "You can't trust management to give you the facts around here."
- "I heard the company is losing money and may close at the end of the year."

It has been said that nine-tenths of the people don't know what the other tenth are talking about. People in general and companies specifically fail to develop a common language of words, symbols, and methods for understanding.

Neither our complex business structure nor in fact our very culture could exist without reliable systems of communication. In *Exploring the Ways of Mankind* Dr. Walter Goldschmidt refers to language as man's peculiar gift and adds, "Without the human capacity to communicate intricate patterns of thought—to re-create experience in words—culture could not exist. . . . Language, then, is an elaborate structure of vocal symbolization, capable of infinite variation, through which ideas, understanding, and feelings are communicated and through which we tend to perceive the events of the world." In animals, the knowledge one generation acquires cannot be passed on to the next generation. Each generation must learn from the beginning everything it needs to know. It is language that enables man to both store and transfer his knowledge from generation to generation and from person to person. Within the company framework this is precisely the job of communication—the transferring of knowledge, skills, and understanding in order to influence the employee group.

Words are the supervisor's tool for selling himself, expressing his ideas, explaining his plans. But he must also recognize that communication goes beyond verbal expression—it includes action, example, and attitude. The supervisor communicates with a look, a changed voice tone, a shrug of the shoulder, silence, and many other means. He communicates when he doesn't intend to as well as when he does. When he storms into the office Monday morning after a bad weekend, he is communicating. When he snaps out orders like a tyrannical overlord, he is communicating much more than just the words he speaks. And what he communicates by his action, example, and attitude, as well as his words, influences his employees' total pattern of job performance.

Communication activates. As a management tool its purpose is

To succeed as a leader, a man must be able to communicate.

not only to inform employees of plans and goals but also to show that the movement from plan to achievement is beneficial to both employees and management. It is equally important that management understand the employee's problems and needs. The belief that major company decisions are not an appropriate concern of the employee has been abandoned, and management now recognizes its essential need for favorable employee reaction and opinion. Management is serving its own best interest when it maintains effective two-way communication with its total personnel group.

UNDERLYING CONCEPTS

Communication is the free exchange of information, ideas, and even attitudes among employees and between employees and management. Failure to communicate can lead to administrative errors, lowered production, increased costs, excessive turnover, negative public relations, and blighted individual development—in short, to a less efficient operation. Communication involves two distinct processes—sending and receiving. But the mere fact of sending a message does not insure that it will be received—understood—as the sender intended it should be. So the person initiating a communication must be concerned not only with the organization and effectiveness of the presentation but also with the condition and receptiveness of those to whom the message is directed.

The too limited concept of communication is that it consists of capsule doses of information—letters to the employees, memos on the bulletin board, a company newspaper, a department meeting. In reality, these are but the veneer of the communication process. The real job of communication is an accurate two-way conveyance of understanding and objective facts; the influencing of thinking, feelings, and attitudes; and the active mental involvement of both employee and management.

If six men were separated from their supervisor by a soundproof wall, he could not influence the group, and it would in effect function without leadership. If the members of the work group were also isolated from each other, each would be limited still further. When the walls are removed, the situation is completely changed. The supervisor now shares his experience, knowledge, skills, and enthusiasm with the group. He learns from them and they learn from each other. As a team, the group can accomplish far more than it did when the walls were up and each man worked alone. But the removal of walls is not in itself enough; for maximum benefit, word barriers must also come down. Communication must take place actively.

THE SUPERVISOR'S COMMUNICATION ROLE

The supervisor is the most decisive link in the communication lifeline. He is the bridge between top management and employees. He is the only person who is in constant contact with these two groups that must understand each other if the purposes of both are to be realized.

The importance of the supervisor in the communication mainstream cannot be overemphasized. The best-laid management plans are shortcircuited unless he assumes his full responsibility. He is not only the principal instrument of communication but, even more decisively, the interpreter of messages. By his past relationship and attitudes, he determines to a large extent the receptiveness of the employees. He also influences management's action and reaction toward the employee group by his interpretation of their responses. For instance, whether he reports that employees are bitter and hostile toward a proposed change in policy or whether he says they feel they need additional information and requests assistance in making a more effective presentation will certainly affect the company's attitude toward employees as well as its method of handling a change.

Although the supervisor is by no means solely responsible for communication, his role is nonetheless critical. A problem department is often a problem because of faulty understanding. Unsatisfactory work is often traceable to inadequate understanding—or misunderstanding—of how to do the job. Most grievances, too, stem from a lack of understanding. And failure to understand is the result of failure to communicate effectively.

WHAT TO COMMUNICATE

Every employee should receive all the information necessary to maintain his job interest and to increase his job contribution. The specific types of information conveyed vary among companies and among units and levels in each company. There are, however, areas of communication common to virtually all businesses and situations:

- Company rules, policies, and benefits, including changes.
- Production schedules and quotas.
- Health and safety information.
- Product changes, sales campaigns, special promotions, and contests which will affect the employee or in which he is expected to participate.
- Information designed to build favorable attitudes and improve cooperation.
- Recognition of outstanding service and accomplishment.

COMMUNICATIONS MEDIA

In *Personnel Policies and Practices Report,* Prentice-Hall lists the most common communication tools as employee handbooks; contests; bulletin boards; information and reading racks; meetings, conferences, and individual interviews; company magazines and newspapers; letters, leaflets, and pamphlets; movies, film strips, and slide presentations; visual aids and posters, such as safety and production charts; company reports to employees; telephones; suggestion systems; and public address systems.

The variety of communications media is almost unlimited. Many firms use only a few of these because of their limited size or need. Others, usually larger firms which are engaged in a variety of activities, utilize most of them. There is no hard and fast rule for using different media; the choice should be dictated by the needs of the particular situation.

IMPROVING THE DOWNWARD FLOW OF INFORMATION

The downward flow of communication enables management to tell its side of the story—the "why" and "why not" of company activity. It presents essential information about instructions, policies, and plans; and it also helps the employee understand, accept, and cooperate with management's decisions and proposed changes. An adequate flow of information downward tends to diminish fears and suspicions which may result from misinformation or no information; make available the company's side of the story; provide a pipeline for conveying instructions, policy, and plans; build pride in employees and *esprit de corps* in the company; improve morale and team feeling; and help the employee to understand, accept, and cooperate in moving toward company goals.

When a specific department—personnel, public relations, or communications, for example—is charged with the communications responsibility, much of the downward communication is planned, prepared, and initiated by this department. But regardless of the method used, the supervisor cannot depend on others at higher levels to furnish him with all the information the employees in his department need. He must remember that from such sources he receives general information which is prepared for all other departments. He must follow up with meetings within the department and personal contact in order to make the information more relevant and specific.

INCREASING THE UPWARD FLOW

By opening the channels of communication upward, management can increase employee acceptance of its communications. Despite this, the upward flow of communication is one of the most neglected areas in management. The need for downward communication is readily apparent—as are the attendant problems—but the potential and advantages of upward communication are less obvious.

An upward flow of information reveals the attitudes and feelings of employees and their reactions to downward communication. Knowing that management will listen encourages employees to use their minds as well as their muscles toward job results and improvement; they are more likely to make suggestions for improving the efficiency and economy of the operation if they are encouraged to express their ideas. Of equal importance, if they have the "ear" of management, employees are more likely to report potentially troublesome problem situations that could get out of hand. A textile worker once remarked, "It says in the employee handbook that this company has an open-door policy. But just try getting into the boss's office. It might as well be in China for all the good it does me; either he isn't in, or he's too busy, or he's hurrying to a meeting. I've given up; I'll never try to see him again." Unfortunately, this situation is all too common.

What can management do to eliminate barriers to the upward

flow of information? What steps can be taken to make the open-door policy a reality? Every company must answer these questions with appropriate action. The employee must feel that what he has to say will be welcomed and will be given consideration. The supervisor should not display disinterest or impatience with what the employee is saying. Often the physical distance separating the employee and supervisor is itself a barrier. In large organizations the office of the supervisor may not be be easily accessible to the employees. Though the supervisor is not always able to change the location of his place of work, he can compensate for physical separation through written communications and more effective personal contact.

If an employee's suggestion is not responded to promptly—or remains unanswered—he may well be discouraged from making any further suggestions And one of the strongest deterrents to upward communication is failure to act on undesirable conditions; when management fails to act, the employee loses faith in its sincerity. If there is good reason for leaving things as they are, then this information should be given. To the employee, the strongest communication is not management's words but its actions.

The supervisor often fails to keep his ear to the ground and assumes that no news is good news. His failure to adopt a posture of interest and deliberately seek out employee opinion discourages the employee from seeking him out. Yet upward communication is a most important leadership tool and source for work improvement. Through it a clearer picture of the work, accomplishments, problems, plans, attitudes, and feelings of employees can be gained; and the individuals, policies, actions, or assignments which are likely to cause trouble can be spotted. By welcoming upward communication, management taps a fertile resource of ideas: its employees. Let your employees know that they can depend on you—that they will get the correct information from you as soon as it is available. Let them know by your intent and follow-up behavior that you are their best source of information. The better you keep them informed, the better they will keep you informed.

SUGGESTION SYSTEMS

Many companies use suggestion systems to encourage upward communication. The technique contains many desirable features: an opportunity to get a message to someone who can take action; assistance in making suggestions; a specific form on which to make them; acknowledgment of all suggestions; rewards for those that are usable; a specified time limit within which the employee can expect action; and the knowledge that management welcomes and encourages this type of communication. A suggestion system is effective because it offers benefits to both the employee and the company. It is a creative outlet for the employee, since it affords an opportunity to contribute his ideas and opinions. It may also increase his job security, improve his chances for promotion, and be a source of financial reward for worthwhile suggestions.

The role of the supervisor in the suggestion system is an important one, and what he does can make or break the entire project. A favorable and cooperative attitude on his part is essential in promoting suggestions from the employee. He should acquire thorough knowledge of the system's rules and policies so that he will be able to answer questions about the process. Many of the suggestions will pertain to his own department; when he is asked to investigate their value, he should do so promptly and fairly. He should actively promote regular use of the suggestion system by encouraging the employees to submit their ideas.

Messages that come down from management to employee are prepared carefully, often by people with special skill in the use of words. But employees often are less skillful at expressing themselves and may be reluctant to submit ideas or suggestions for this reason alone. When this is the case, the supervisor is the essential link in the chain of communication upward; by helping the employee translate a roughly conceived idea into a clearly written suggestion he performs a service important to both employee and management.

DEVELOPING THE SKILL OF LISTENING

Most people are not good listeners because they do not stop talking long enough to listen or because they do not know how to listen. Most managers spend the major part of each working day trying to communicate with others; a good deal of this time should be spent in listening. Failure to listen—and learn from what the other person has to say—wastes valuable time.

Father Theodore V. Purcell of Loyola University conducted an 18-month study of employee attitudes at Swift and Company and reported in the *Harvard Business Review* "that of all the sources of information a foreman has by which he can come to know and accurately 'size up' the personalities of the people in his department, listening to the individual is the most important."

But listening is not simply a passive waiting for the other man to stop talking so that you can begin. It is instead an active process that requires that the listener be receptive and interested, give his undivided attention, and ask questions or take appropriate notes. And once the message has been received, it is important that the supervisor give full credit for suggestions and information rather than claim the ideas as his own. To do otherwise would eliminate a source of future information and antagonize the employee at the same time.

There can be no doubt that listening oils the wheels of achievement and understanding. But it also enriches the individual's personal life as well. The skilled listener develops a sensitivity which enables him to share the experience and emotions of others.

GUIDES TO MORE EFFECTIVE COMMUNICATION

We all admire the person who is able to say the right thing at the right time. This is not simply a matter of intuition; it is the practice of skills developed through experience. No two people communicate in exactly the same way, and each has to adapt the techniques to his own particular personality and ability. But a sincere effort to apply the guides that follow and to work at sharpening communicative skills will result in improved human relations which should be ample evidence of success.

Plan your communications. Build communication planning on facts, straight thinking, valid conclusions, and mature judgment. Develop a clear concept of what you want to communicate. Keep your immediate and long-range objectives in perspective. Know the man who is to receive the communication—what type of individual he is, how receptive he will be, what he is most interested in, what his personal values are, what approach will be most effective with him.

Know your own abilities and limitations and compensate for them in determining your most effective approach. Plan your approach as carefully as you would plan any other aspects of your job. Make notes. Don't leave important details to chance. Aim for lasting results. A response is no proof of understanding, and without understanding nothing has really been accomplished.

Clarify your ideas before trying to communicate them to others. Clarence Randall has said, "I don't advise you to start talking until you have begun thinking. It's no good opening the tap if there is nothing in the tank."

Consult with others. If your communications could affect others outside your department, it would be wise to seek advice before proceeding.

Communicate for tomorrow as well as today. Although it is necessary to meet today's goals and needs, the supervisor should not ignore long-range goals, nor should he delay unduly in communicating disagreeable information, since delay only makes it more difficult and distasteful.

Be consistent with follow-up action. How much you convince people of your sincerity depends more on what you do than on what you say you will do. This means that clear assignment of responsibility, adequate delegation of authority, fair reward for effort, and consistency in policy enforcement are more important than expressed good intentions.

Communicate the right information in the right amount. Saying too much serves to confuse the receiver. Saying too little fails to supply all the needed information.

Make it original, colorful, and interesting. Use the most effective tone, words, media, time, and occasion to insure the most effective reception.

Gain attention and interest first. Remember that before you can communicate you must have both the attention and the interest of the receiver.

Execute thoroughly. Plan and execute communication with great care in order to convince and to elicit response. Communication is not an end in itself; it is only an instrument. If it does not achieve the desired result, it has served no useful purpose.

Communicating is like eating in the sense that today's intake will not satisfy tomorrow's hunger. Communication must be an everyday affair to be successful. It should not be something the supervisor concentrates on at intervals when he has time. Employees must believe that they can depend on the supervisor and on management to furnish correct information. Management states its intent through its communications but demonstrates it through follow-up action. The better employees are kept informed, the better they will keep management informed.

If the policies and philosophy of management filter all the way down to every employee in the company and through them to the public, and if everyone who gets the message has a full understanding of what is going on and how he fits into the picture, then communication has in fact been successful. The final test is favorable response.

Vast treasures lay hidden below the barren deserts of the Middle East until they were tapped and the wasteland flourished. The human mind too contains reservoirs of vast power and potential which can enrich both the individual and the company.

20. Creativity: Pearl of Great Price

A PHILOSOPHER ONCE SAID, "Man is the greatest thing on earth, and the greatest thing in man is his mind." Another called an idea "the pearl of great price." Both were saying that man's mental capacity is a vast resource of priceless ideas and creativity.

In 1935, at the age of 29, Chester Carlson set out to invent a push-button copying machine. During the years that followed, he worked almost day and night, used his own meager earnings to buy materials, developed a machine that worked, and approached more than 20 companies that turned him down because they saw no practical use for his crude and toylike process of copying. He received his first royalty payment in 1947—the start of the millions which were to come his way because of this one invention. In 1964 alone, the office copier industry's rentals and sales amounted to more than $480 million. This was made possible because a man had an idea; he believed in it; and he exhibited remarkable persistence in working it out and eventually selling it to others. This is but one example of what can be accomplished through the creativity, belief, and persistence of just one mind at work.

Business and industry today hunger for ideas and are ready to reward the people who can supply them. Ideas form the foundation of progress; without an infusion of new thinking, no business enterprise can succeed for very long. Idea men are rare, not because ideas are so difficult to conceive but because, if they are to be developed, hard work is usually involved. An idea can originate in a flash of inspiration, but before it benefits anyone, it has to be developed, sold, and applied. It is at this point that too many bright ideas lose their luster.

A young advertising executive stood before a group of California orange growers in 1918 and said, "I have an idea. Let's teach people to drink oranges." Consider for a moment the thousands of growers, shippers, and processors and the millions of consumers who have benefited from this one idea.

A man spent some time during one summer in an area where the ground remained frozen. He observed that when scraps of food were thrown out the back door they lay preserved and didn't rot. The man's name was Birdseye. A whole new industry was created because his observation was followed up.

Within each person ideas lie dormant, capable of bursting forth into a rich harvest of progress. Ideas are not the exclusive property of mystical men. The talent for creating them exists in every individual, but the use of certain techniques is necessary in order to insure a fuller development of this potential.

IDEAS DON'T JUST HAPPEN

Creative and constructive thinking, like any other skill, can be developed to a high degree of proficiency. The key to the creative process is the individual. No group or committee ever had an idea. Generally speaking, though, most of us are more creative when working with one or more other persons, at least part of the time.

Ideation and creativity are important to every company; to firms such as advertising agencies they are the very lifeblood of the business. This critical dependence on new ideas and creative thinking has prompted many firms to conduct training sessions in the creative process. Because of the success of these deliberate attempts to be creative, businesses of all types are now making the techniques of creativity a part of their management training programs. Although

Ideas are not the exclusive property of mystical men.

these techniques are highly variable according to specific needs, the following guides will provide a reasonable approach to individual ideation.

What is the problem to be solved? The first step is to identify and write down the problem that needs to be solved, the product that needs to be altered, the process that needs to be improved.

Make a start. With the problem before you, bombard it with ideas. Don't let your mind drift—keep it directed to the problem. Use your mind like the laser beam, whose tremendous power stems from the concentration of rays on one small area.

Write down the ideas as they occur. It has been said that a pencil can serve as a crowbar to move our minds. Write down the ideas immediately. Don't stop to analyze or evaluate them. Continue looking for more ideas.

Use a checklist. Jot down all the changes that can be made in a proposal. How many different ways can the product be used? What additional groups can use it? Saturate yourself with background and knowledge about the problem so that your checklist will be meaningful.

Choose a time. Set aside some time each day for thinking—then stick to the plan. Make thinking a part of the daily routine. If you wait until you have time for creative thinking, you will never get around to it. If you want to develop new ideas badly enough, you will provide the time.

Pick a place. Ideas can and do occur everywhere—in the midst of busy activity, while traveling, while working on an unrelated subject. But experience indicates that certain surroundings can be more conducive to ideation than others. Find the place that is best for you and spend some time there.

Ask yourself questions. A curious mind opens many doors. Repeat the who, what, when, where, how, and why every step of the way. Use these questions regarding every product, use, and technique. Can it be made bigger or smaller? Can it be divided or combined? Can it be reversed or changed? Ask yourself questions to stimulate your thinking.

Set a goal. If new ideas are important, set a quantitative idea goal. Set an ambitious but realistic goal. The very fact that you have a target will help to stimulate ideas.

Give yourself a deadline. For too long, the creative process has been relegated to a corner of the mind. Utilize the pressure of a time schedule to force bombarding of the problem in order to produce ideas.

For the mind to produce, it must be put into forward gear. It must
be challenged, stimulated, exercised, strained, and forced to act. But
ideas have to come from someplace—they cannot be produced from
complete vacuums. Ideas will have a much better chance of birth if
certain stimulators are applied to the process. These include travel,
personal contact, creative hobbies, reading, and writing. Borrowing
ideas and improving them. Combining two or more ideas. Changing
ideas. Associating new facts. Trying to apply techniques and ideas
from different fields. Being a Sherlock Holmes for ideas. Talking with
people. Asking what they are doing and why they are doing it that
way. Think of ideas as thousand-dollar bills—then you'll search high
and low, and you'll be persistent.

The employee group can be a rich source of ideas and creativity.
Use of a suggestion system and promoting upward communication
will be helpful in tapping this reservoir of creativity. If the supervisor
is willing to recognize the tremendous potential of employee ideas, he
will make every effort to utilize this potential for the benefit of his
department. He should at all times remember to give appropriate
credit for employee contributions.

Employees will communicate their ideas to the supervisor only
after he has demonstrated that he is receptive to their ideas, is willing
to give serious consideration to them, and makes every effort to share
the benefits of the ideas with the employees who present them. He
must communicate his receptiveness in his daily relationship, keeping
in mind that an employee idea can be killed by a sneer or a yawn, by
a quip, or by a frown on the supervisor's brow.

BRAINSTORMING: GROUP IDEATION

One popular method for developing ideas is called brainstorming.
It is basically a technique for discovering and developing new ideas
through the group approach. Several days prior to the session, an idea
or cluster of ideas will be given to each participant. He will be told
certain things about the problem—enough that he will know the
rules which will be observed during the session. He will be told to
think about the subject ahead of time, to write down any advance
ideas, and to apply the various approaches to the problem which were

listed earlier in this chapter. He will probably be given the following four rules:

1. Judicial judgment will be ruled out. No attempt will be made during the session to evaluate the merits of ideas.
2. Freewheeling will be recommended. Go as far afield and be as wild as you like so long as you keep to the subject.
3. The more ideas the better. The need is for quantity. The greater the number, the greater the likelihood that good ideas will be presented.
4. Combine one idea with others. Improve on the ideas of other people. Attach one idea to another.

Participants are usually asked to come to the session prepared to enjoy the fun. The ideas presented during the session are usually written down or tape-recorded. It is the leader's responsibility to keep ideas flowing. He should prevent criticism or evaluation of ideas and should attempt to keep the ideas centered around the announced subject.

Experiments have proved that ten men brainstorming an idea together usually produce more and better ideas than the same ten men will produce working individually. Brainstorming has the advantages of enabling participants to alter one another's ideas, of triggering new ideas based on what someone else has said, and of producing a beneficial atmosphere from the mental stimulation of association with others.

If it is not feasible to get a group to brainstorm an idea, it can be done individually by following the same basic rules. The object is to produce a quantity of ideas and worry about their evaluation at a later time.

Usually, in the case of group brainstorming, some person who is familiar with the subject will evaluate the ideas suggested and bring the best ones before the appropriate individual or group for possible action.

SELLING IDEAS

A company does not benefit simply because it has manufactured a product. Customers must be sold on the product to the point of purchase before the seller can benefit. Similarly, an idea that is not sold or used has no value. The supervisor who has originated ideas should also know how to sell those ideas. Getting the acceptance of others is the critical problem for most people. Their ideas too often wither and die for lack of customers. The following guides should be helpful in selling ideas to others.

Prepare the idea. Before you leap from the diving board, know that you can swim and that the pool is filled with water; know the height of the diving board, the depth of the water, the distance to shore, the temperature of the water; decide whether it is a good idea to jump in the first place and the consequences of the jump.

Apply the same advance preparation to your ideas. Countless excellent ideas have died a sudden death because they were exposed to critical examination before they were strong enough to endure. Whatever their possibilities, they were unacceptable because they were presented prematurely, before they were quite jelled. Thus the potential of the ideas was lost and the originators were discourged from future attempts.

To a great extent, the future of an idea depends on the thoroughness of its development. Have all angles been considered? Has the idea been used before? Is the idea good but impractical because the cost or consequences are too great to make it acceptable? Is the idea well organized? Are you prepared to communicate everything about the idea that is necessary in order to sell it to your supervisor? Are your facts accurate?

Present the idea. Gain the attention of the individual you want to sell. Make an effective presentation. Know more about the idea than you will have to present. Be prepared to answer all pertinent questions. Don't be put in the embarrassing position of having to say, "I'm sorry, I can't answer that; I didn't think of it from that angle." Be able to prove the advantages and to present adequate ways for overcoming the disadvantages.

If practical, try to obtain authorization to test the idea. You may need an opportunity to prove what the idea can accomplish.

If the idea is a good one, don't give up. Some of the most significant ideas to come from men's fertile minds have been turned down cold, many times. "The thing will never fly." "The world is flat." "Television will never work. It just isn't practical." If you believe sufficiently in an idea, stick with it. But never be ashamed to admit that your idea was wrong. It was Santayana who said that "a fanatic is a man who redoubles his efforts after he has lost sight of his objectives."

FLY HIGH ON JET-PROPELLED IDEAS

Ideas are based on facts—facts accumulated through years of experience, work, and study. Since facts are available to everyone, so are ideas. Edison was a prolific inventor; yet the wonders he developed were not the result of sudden flashes of insight. He created from vast resources of information. He assembled and reassembled facts available to all the scientists of his day.

Form the thinking, searching, and writing habit. Many executives who are convinced of the importance of ideas keep a pencil and notepad handy at all times—when they travel, or read, or attend lectures or business conferences—lest they lose or forget an idea or the germ of an idea.

If you will make time available, you can start on the idea trail. The sky is the limit. You can be as creative as you are willing to be. You will find no greater source of growth and improvement than what can be created from your own fertile mind. The real idea man is rare; small wonder then that he commands so much respect, prestige, and salary. Remember that an important responsibility of leadership is to think up ideas to solve problems, to make your department and company more successful, to get more done, and to make your own job easier. Work for ideas so that they can work for you.

Einstein did not convince the world of his genius by saying he was a genius; his public image was created by what he did, not by what he said he did. And so it is with a company's public image; in the eyes of the world a company is what it does, not what it says it does.

21. Guides to Favorable Public Relations

WHO IN YOUR COMPANY is responsible for public relations? You are— and it doesn't matter who you are or what your position. Every employee is the molder of the company's public image. Public relations is what people think and say about your company because of the impression it has made on them.

You may have read of high-powered word magicians who sit in Madison Avenue offices and work miracles of public relations. The fact is, though, that a company image is not created artificially; it is based on what people experience about a company for themselves.

Kinsey M. Robinson, chairman of the Washington Water Power Company, has said, "We may talk in print until we are exhausted; our lawyers and publicity men can make the most logical statements on earth. But unless our employees are enthusiastic about what we do, they can neutralize our motives by the single comment—'bolony.'"

The supervisor has a special interest in good public relations as well as a prime responsibility for its success. A good reputation enables the company to attract and retain a better workforce. People like to work for the firm that has the best reputation; morale remains higher, good employees stay longer, because they can take pride in the place where they work. Productivity is greater and the quality of the product is higher when employees are proud of their company.

A good public image helps open doors for the company's salesmen, doors that otherwise might be closed to them. This means that it is easier to make sales, and this in turn improves the job opportunities for everyone in the organization. And if the company sells a product or service directly to the consuming public, good public relations can influence the public's decision to buy.

Good community relations assures the business a fair shake. Municipal governing bodies, such as the city council and county commissioners, make decisions which vitally concern the company, including tax evaluations and assessments, zoning, the routing of streets and highways, and the authorization of railroad sidings. These decisions are more likely to be favorable to the company if it maintains good relationships with community and employee groups.

During times of crisis, misfortune, or emergency the community's reaction often determines whether the company can remain in that community. Goodwill and a good public image are like insurance during such times when the company needs community friends.

The company's ability to stay in business depends to a considerable extent on its public image. Public preference is the purest form of democracy. It is the public's feelings toward a company, as reflected in the cash registers, that ultimately determine the success or failure of the business.

CREATING A FAVORABLE CORPORATE IMAGE

The increasingly competitive nature of most business and industry, the greater mobility of customers, the speed of transportation, and the ease of communication mean that every company is competing with every other in the field regardless of location. It is not always the best product or service but often the ones which are most effectively linked with public relations and advertising programs that receive the greatest acceptance.

It is for this reason that many businesses are now giving the same careful, systematic, and thorough attention to the total area of favorable public relations as was formerly applied only to production and sales. This new emphasis has led them to employ experts, spend large sums of money, and engage in elaborate training programs for supervisors in order to promote a favorable image. At the same time, in-

A company image is not created artificially; it is based on what people experience about a company for themselves.

creased attention is being given to employee benefits, employee activities, company publications, and other considerations that affect what the employees and the public believe and say about the company.

It is because of this concentrated effort and the important role of management in this area that supervisors must be concerned with creating favorable public relations.

The first step should be to determine the current status of the company's reputation or image; then a program must be planned and implemented to bring about the desired improvement. The following are recommended steps for creating and maintaining a favorable corporate image.

Favorably influence the people who shape your company's image. It has been estimated that every employee influences approximately 50 people outside the company. What will the employees in your department tell their neighbors and friends about the company? Remember that outsiders will believe what employees say because they work for the company. If each employee influences 50 people, you as a supervisor should influence twice that number. In addition, you represent the company to the employee. If you are fair and understanding, so is the company; if you are unreasonable and unreliable, so is the company.

Get your house in order. Public relations has been called doing a good job and getting credit for it. What type of job are you doing in your department? Is your house in order? What treatment do your employees receive? Do you set an example of loyalty and pride, and do you continually sell the employees on the fact that they are working in a fine department and for the best company around? Do you encourage employees to keep their gripes and complaints inside the firm rather than airing them on the outside? Do you urge your employees to speak well of the company because they are part of it? Remember that the foundation for good public relations is good internal relations.

Be a good housekeeper. Hosts like to be proud of the appearance of their homes; so get your employees interested in making a good impression on customers and company visitors. Many companies consider their spotless plant one of their most important advertisements. Create in each employee a sense of pride in the appearance of the department.

Promote safety, courtesy, helpfulness, and friendliness. The potential customer's only contact with the company may be through one employee. Will that contact improve or harm the firm's reputation?

Maintain favorable relations with community groups. This includes news media, law enforcement agencies, governmental units, and civic associations. Every community has scores of civic groups which need a place to meet, speakers on special subjects, and experienced leadership guidance. Opportunities to win their goodwill are tailor-made for the alert and responsive company. Warm relations with these community groups can foster the image of an organization which is concerned with people and with community welfare.

Practice good communication. Keep your employees informed so that they can keep the public informed. The community has a concern for the welfare of the company and an interest in what it is doing. Press releases can be instrumental in supplying this information, but perhaps the most effective way is through the employees.

Protect the company's reputation. If the company claims to maintain top quality, its quality control program should insure this in every item that leaves its factory. If it advertises a liberal return policy, every employee should conscientiously strive to carry out this policy. If it stresses service, it must give service in full measure. One major food producer considers its most valuable asset to be its reputation for the quality and freshness of its products. In order to protect this reputation, the route salesmen are instructed to pick up leftover products which have reached a certain age. These items are not sold at reduced prices or given to employees; they are cut open and destroyed so that the company label can be protected and its reputation guaranteed.

If a company claims a liberal employee benefit program, then the program must be available and it must be administered fairly. If the company prides itself on its concern for its employees, then it should demonstrate this concern during illnesses, personal emergencies, discharges, and retirements as well as in its employee activity programs.

GO THE EXTRA MILE

Perhaps in no other area of activity can a firm get by with so little or accomplish so much. It may be possible for a business to survive even if it does virtually nothing in the area of public relations. However, if it goes all out because of a genuine concern for people, for the community, and for its own best interests, the sky is the limit. The following are steps along that extra mile in public relations.

Corporate community citizenship. Community citizenship means the support of community projects; the beautifying and care of company property; the maintenance of favorable employee and public relations; and the active support of business, cultural, educational, and religious activities. No business can function as an island unto itself, completely isolated from the interests of the community. The company is in the community boat, and as that boat goes, so go the fortunes of the business.

One large electrical utility company maintained a number of substations throughout the city, consisting of unattractive cold gray masses of transistors and transformers surrounded by steel link fences. By planting rosebushes around the fences and putting up attractive circular signs bearing the words "Citizenship and Service," the company not only improved the appearance of its substations but also improved its corporate image.

Promote mutual friendship. Every organization should take the initiative to make certain that all its employees, but most especially its management team, know the community, its people, its facilities, and its needs. Greater stress should be placed on this when a company is new to a community or when some of the management group has been transferred into the area.

It is also up to the company to let the community get acquainted with it. This can be accomplished to some extent through written communications, booklets, and talks by company personnel, but the best method is to hold open house and plant tours. Businesses are often surprised at how little the community knows about their operations and how much the feeling toward the company improves after people have had an opportunity to look for themselves. Even such businesses as banks and department stores have many interesting behind-the-scenes activities which are largely unknown to the public.

Provide community leadership and talent. The purpose of a business is to operate successfully and make a profit, but it should never lose sight of the fact that it should also help its employees to more satisfying and constructive lives. One of the best ways for accomplishing this is through individual participation in community groups and activities. Business executives have already proved their leadership and organizational ability; civic groups have need of this special type of talent. A real service can be rendered by the company leader who is also willing to be a community leader.

The company should both permit and encourage its key people to participate in community affairs, within the limits set by their work. Before a man accepts community responsibility, especially if it requires time during working hours, he should clear it with his supervisor—and he should be careful not to commit the company in any way without prior authorization.

Executive participation in community activities not only benefits the community, but it also benefits the company and the man. Many executives have refined their management skills, learned to work more effectively through people, improved their public-speaking ability, and increased their value to the organization as a result of their community activity.

A word of caution is in order at this point. It should be remembered that each man is a representative of the company and cannot divest himself of this identification. The good that he does benefits the company. But if by the same token he doesn't do a good job, is uncooperative, fails to follow through, seeks positions of leadership but does no work, or makes enemies, the company suffers. If he is to participate, he should do the best job possible.

Public relations consists not of major promotions but of a steady building, brick by brick. The result is influenced more by action than by stated intentions. The very nature of the free enterprise system leads each company to promote its own best interests with its employees, its customers, and the general public. This activity deserves the same management attention as do other vital factors affecting the success of the company's operation.

Every man is the architect of his own achievement, but only the successful are willing to admit that the result is of their own design.

22. Moving up the Executive Ladder

THE CASUAL OBSERVER is often puzzled to know why promotions don't always go to brilliant men but are often won by those considered less likely to succeed. The answer is simple: The successful ones know what they want and go after it. They have a plan of action; they have determination and drive; they compensate for their deficiencies with purpose and tenacity that leave behind their more talented but less dedicated competitors.

As much care and planning go into building a successful career as go into designing and erecting an outstanding building. The successful executive recognized that the odds are against accidental success, decided what he wanted, and committed himself to paying the price. He put first things first. He developed a sense of values. He decided how his time could be spent most profitably—both on and off the job. He set his sights on ultimate goals rather than settling for momentary pleasures.

The keys to accomplishment and success are conviction and follow-through. Many people have small success, and exert small influence, because they think, plan, and act small.

One brilliant newspaper reporter was distressed when a less talented staff member was promoted to assistant city editor. The man who was promoted wasn't especially gifted or even well liked, but he had done something the brilliant reporter had failed to do: He had planned a course of action that would make him the logical choice for promotion when an opening occurred. Every free moment

Are you satisfied with your present position, pay, influence, and authority? Are you content to stay where you are for the remainder of your working career? Will the company be willing to let you stay where you are and go on making the same contribution even though the company as a whole must improve or go out of business?

If the answer to these questions is "no," then time is short. A personal plan of action is needed which will qualify you for promotion. The first step in drawing up a plan is to decide what you want to accomplish. What are your assets and shortcomings in relation to your goal? How have others achieved the same goal? What action will move you toward the goal?

KEYS TO EXECUTIVE PROGRESS

Management experts generally agree that the pendulum of specialization has swung too far and is beginning to swing back. The specialist can perform within the confines of his limited concept, but he has difficulty in managing activities which require judgment beyond his specialization. The supervisor who rises in management in the future will have to be concerned not only with the technical aspects of the job but also with management organization, salesmanship, personnel, public relations, and a host of other areas. This requires broad general knowledge about many things. The man who expects to be part of a highly complex and smoothly functioning management must be versatile. The following factors should receive the attention of the supervisor who seeks to move to higher levels of responsibility.

Develop an executive personality. This factor will play a vital role in your success or failure as an executive. It will shape your attitude toward other people and theirs toward you. A poor personality can cause the best plan of action to fail; it can doom the most carefully worked-out scheme, because you must create a good impression if you expect to move ahead. From the start you should learn to look, think, and act like an executive. Naturally, you won't try to take on executive authority before you have the job; but you can be management-minded, you can be interested in seeing that the company is successful, you can be concerned with eliminating waste and increasing profit, and you can demonstrate that you have the mental capacity and attitude that qualify you for the management team.

To determine the traits of a good executive, the University of Chicago's Committee on Human Development studied the personalities of 300 executives. From the results, Dr. William E. Henry has drawn this composite picture of the best executive:

- He has a strong desire for personal achievement. He gets as much kick out of achievement on the job as some men get out of winning at golf or football. He is never satisfied with what he has already accomplished but feels compelled to move relentlessly on.
- He must constantly move upward. He is not content to stand still. If his present job does not offer him the opportunity to move up, he will seek it elsewhere. He needs proof of progress in the form of pay increases, new titles, greater responsibility.
- He must advance socially. His ambition extends beyond his job to his personal life. He seeks symbols of success—a fine home, a big car, a place in the prestige social circles of the community.
- He respects authority. He is a good follower because he looks to those in positions of influence as a source of help for his own advancement. He realizes that to run afoul of the power structure is to jeopardize his own future.
- He is decisive. He knows how to make decisions and is not afraid to do so, even though some of them may be wrong.
- He is assertive. He has the courage of his convictions. He isn't afraid to stand up and be counted, even if his opinion isn't popular.
- He constantly fights failures. He knows that yesterday's home run will not win today's ball game. He never assumes that success will be automatic. He fights to do a satisfactory job and to keep the respect of his superiors. He knows that the company has a right to expect constant improvement. He is realistic about what he must do to achieve success and critical of his own accomplishments.
- He is mentally and emotionally mature. He stands on his own two feet and accepts responsibility for his own actions.

Be knowledgeable on a wide front. Even the first-line supervisor must possess a wide variety of information and skills in order to carry out his duties and responsibilities. He must know about the company, its products, its manufacturing and marketing processes, and he must know about the economic and labor conditions in the community and how to get results through other people.

A prominent businessman once told a meeting of training directors: "Most executives are receptive to new ideas if they're good. But men who have the final decision in management are cautious. They have to be. They can't afford to go off half-cocked. Therefore, when you make recommendations to them, you must be sure they are well thought out and are useful to the company as a whole. Perhaps it is not management that is rigid in its views. Perhaps we make no special effort to learn the other functions of management. If we had a comprehensive understanding of all the problems of a company, maybe we would be better training men."

The specialist has a place in business and industry, but that place is not in top management—at least not until he acquires a diversity of knowledge and skills. He serves a vital function, but his specialization often limits his interest as well as his knowledge to such a narrow field that he is unable to grasp the overall management picture.

Recognize that learning should never cease. The executive who expects to grow must make education a constant pursuit. The humanities should be given an appropriate place in his continuing acquisition of knowledge. General cultural enrichment gives a man knowledge that he may be able to utilize in unforeseen ways; in addition to direct benefit on the job, it can enrich his personal life. As a case in point, an advertising man who spent two hours on the commuter train daily always carried paperback books to read while he traveled. When an associate in the company commented on this "waste of time," a fellow employee replied, "Well, I don't think it's a waste of time; he writes the best and most original copy of anyone in the agency."

Remain young in spirit and eager for new experience. The mark of a truly great mind is that it never grows old. It remains young in spirit, eager to learn and to enjoy new experiences. The habit of study will keep a man identified with the mainstream of dynamic activity. If he becomes too set in his ways and too conservative in his thinking, he is buying a one-way ticket to oblivion. Companies need the active and inquiring mental posture that is constantly looking for new and fresh ideas. Learning and vitality are a matter of attitude, not of chronological age.

Make time available for what is important to you. It seems reasonable that a man ought to spend his free time doing the things he enjoys. After all, it's his own time. He works hard on the job and is therefore justified in devoting his off-the-job time to off-the-job activities.

One university professor has said, "Any man who is willing to devote 15 minutes a day to the acquisition of knowledge can secure for himself a cultural background that is superior to that given by any college in the country." Time is one of our most precious and perishable resources. Each of us has as much each day as those who seem to accomplish twice as much as we do. One of the most common supervisory complaints is, "I'm too busy, I haven't enough time." Yet it is not so much a matter of amount as of organized use. The proper use of time should be approached in this way: First, make a complete record or audit of how your time is spent for at least a week, and identify the amount of time spent in each area. Next, decide what can be eliminated. You will no doubt discover that considerable time is spent on unnecessary things. If these are dropped, more time will be available for essentials.

An analysis of what remains will reveal that some of the things you now do can be done by someone else. Letting others who are qualified make some of the decisions and do some of the things you have been doing will release more of your time for other activities. Establish a priority system for the use of your time. List the things which must receive attention and arrange them in order of importance. Now that your plan of action is complete, discipline yourself to follow it. Intelligence and ability vary with individuals, but every man has the same number of hours in his day. Whether you fritter away your time or use it to improve your executive stature and enrich your personal life is a choice only you can make. There is a direct relationship between the profitable use of time and career accomplishment.

RESOURCES FOR SELF-DEVELOPMENT

An almost unlimited reservoir of resources and assistance is available for self-development, much of it at no cost. Some firms offer courses during working hours or pay tuition for certain courses that are given at schools and colleges. Many national organizations conduct training and development programs designed to meet their specific needs. If a man is really serious about wanting to get ahead, he will be willing to spend his own time in order to increase his value to himself and the company.

Learn from your own supervisor. He will probably be able to offer many suggestions for increasing your qualifications for executive growth. Ask him what courses he would suggest. Study the duties and responsibilities of his job in order to determine what additional skills you must acquire before you will be qualified to move up. His advice will be authoritative because it will be based on experience, and his thinking is important in your future.

Learn from top management. Most executives are quite willing to talk about how they got where they are today. Not everything they say will apply to you, but their decisions and philosophy on company operation and management will indicate what you must do to gain their approval. Let them know of your interest in getting ahead and what you are doing to prepare yourself for a bigger job. If you can also back up your expressed ambition with results, you will be tagged for special attention and promotional consideration.

Take advantage of all training offered by the company. Many company programs are planned and conducted by the best trainers in the field and are often superior to those available in colleges and graduate schools. Most businesses recognize that appropriately qualified supervisors and executives cannot be hired from the outside; often they must be developed and promoted from within. How eager are you to take advantage of training when it is available? Do you have to be forced to take courses which have been designed to help you move closer to a promotion? The most competent managers are always Johnny-on-the-spot at company courses—ample proof that success goes hand in hand with the acquisition of new knowledge and skills.

Modern communication and transportation have brought most of us within reach of vast resources for self-improvement. Among those usually available are organizations of personnel and training directors, executives, foremen, and purchasing men and many other special-interest groups whose primary function is to keep their members abreast of developments in their own specialized areas, improve their qualifications, and enhance their professional standing. Also available in most communities are evening colleges, industrial schools, trade courses, or other adult education programs. Fees are usually reasonable, and in many instances employers will pay all or part of the tuition. These courses offer opportunities for professional as well as cultural and special development. Many trade associations, such as the American Institute of Banking, have professional development programs which may be conducted locally or through correspondence. In addition, many large universities and a number of national companies offer correspondence courses.

Books, magazines, and training aids are to be found at public libraries on every subject from Aardvark to Zymurgy. The executive who is not utilizing his local library is missing a rich resource of professional and cultural assistance. Successful executives also subscribe to technical magazines pertaining to their special field of interest, and some companies have a policy of paying for them. A large volume of valuable printed material is also availabe through trade associations such as the American Management Association and the National Foreman's Institute.

EXECUTIVE DEVELOPMENT: WHOSE RESPONSIBILITY?

Make no mistake; your company is interested in more than just your present ability. Management development is one of the fastest-growing areas in industrial training, for there is an increasing realization that an efficient management team is more important to the survival and growth of the organization than any tangible item on the balance sheet. As a part of the management team, you can depend on the firm to take an interest in your development and to plan formal programs to accomplish this purpose. But the fact remains that development is up to each individual. If you expect to rise faster and go further, you will have to go the extra mile on your own initiative.

Don't depend on the company to manage your own personal and professional development. Remember that you have more at stake in your future than it has. If you falter and fail, you can be replaced; you, not the company, will suffer most if you fail to seize the opportunities afforded by the company environment. All you have to offer is your knowledge, skills, and leadership contribution. How much is it worth today? How much will it be worth next year? If you don't make a more valuable contribution next year, you won't deserve more pay or responsibility.

A business engages deliberately in a program of research to determine what products or services it should offer to the public. It then develops the products as efficiently and quickly as possible. But before the company can benefit, someone must be willing to pay for these goods or services. Similarly, each executive should research his strengths and weaknesses, discover his potential, seek to develop it to the fullest extent, and then utilize his skills in the organizational environment that has the greatest need for his contribution and is willing to pay for it.

Individual growth in management is a step-by-step response to opportunities with total resources. The person who advances furthest and fastest is the one who makes the greatest response to these opportunities for executive success.

23. A Program for Executive Growth

THE THOUSANDS OF EXECUTIVES who have gained the top rung in their companies, and the thousands of others who are on the way up, have a wealth of information to share. How they achieved their positions and how they say they could have reached them even faster if they had it all to do over are most revealing.

No executive or management expert can develop an infallible guide that will guarantee success. There is too much of individual personality and varying circumstances for any one set of rules to be infallible. However, a look at the characteristics and behavior patterns which usually lead to success will be beneficial to the ambitious executive who is seeking to blueprint his own success. It is a smart man who learns all he can from both the success and the failure of others.

BUILDING BLOCKS FOR EXECUTIVE GROWTH

Executive success is fashioned of many things which must all be integrated and coordinated into a smoothly functioning whole. Some guides for the ambitious individual who seeks to become a dynamic executive who can move rapidly upward are these.

Plan a specific program for self-improvement. Include adequate

The smart man learns all he can from both the success and the failure of others.

provision for budgeting time; developing good work habits; planning and scheduling things that must be done; evaluating and improving your own performance; working at being liked by others; acquiring more poise; becoming a more effective speaker; improving leadership attitudes; developing the characteristics of integrity and habits of mental alertness; and adjusting present and future plans in order to keep your sights aimed high.

Your specific program for growth should be infused with daily improvement. Miracles can be accomplished by the supervisor who each day does the job a little better and accomplishes slightly more than he did the day before.

Improve your relations with your own boss. Outside of yourself, the most important person in your business future is your boss. Who he is, the type of executive he proves to be, and what he thinks of you are vital factors in your future.

On first consideration, the suggestion that you pick the right boss may seem a little ridiculous, but on deeper analysis the idea has merit and is not so farfetched. Not only does a company select the man for the job; the applicant also analyzes the company to determine whether it can offer him the opportunity he is seeking. For the same reason, the ambitious executive should try to pick the right boss within the organization. It is certainly true that a man doesn't always have the prerogative of choosing his boss; but in many instances his requests and his desires will influence his placement or transfer within the firm.

What type of boss is the right boss? He is the manager you would like to become. He is the trainer who will guide you to more skillful performance. He is the executive who has confidence in other people, who is willing to delegate responsibility, who is constantly seeking improvement, and who is willing to enlarge on your executive potential. He is a man who likes to see people get ahead, doesn't stand in their way, and is the first to say, "This man is ready for promotion." Aside from your own attitude and application, this type of leadership will have the most decisive influence on your executive progress.

Be the type of executive you would want working with you. Every executive must be three people: supervisor of his department, associate of those on the same organizational level, and an implementer of the programs of his own supervisor. Every man has a boss, whether it be a manager at a higher level, stockholders, or customers. The loyalty and support you give your boss will be an indication of your qualification to move up the ladder. How can you be an effective and valuable contributor to your supervisor's needs? Consider these possibilities:

- Give him the information he needs and has a right to expect from you. Don't embarrass him by not letting him know what is taking place.
- Exercise initiative. Don't wait to be told—demonstrate that you can see what needs to be done and follow through to get it done.
- Don't try to win arguments with him in front of others. You don't gain by trapping him into admitting a mistake. Nor do you enhance you own opportunity by belittling him or showing how much better you could have done the job.
- Be quick to support his programs. He probably knows more about company plans than you do. Give him the benefit of the doubt—ask discreet questions, seek information, but always lean in the direction of support rather than away from it.
- Think before you speak. The damage that an impulsive blurter can do to carefully calculated plans is tremendous.
- Don't try to grab or hog the limelight. Your recognition will come from the help you give him. If you try to outshine him, you can expect to be cut down to size. He appreciates your support, but he does not want to be overshadowed.

An announcement in the paper was headlined: "Assistant Credit Manager Named Operating Manager." A few weeks later, the executive vice president of the company that made the announcement was having lunch with several of his business friends, and the conversation got around to the promotion. One man remarked, "I knew you planned to fill the position, but I was very surprised that Frank got the promotion—which in essence makes him your assistant. I know you have several key executives who've been with the company longer and who had higher positions than Frank's. I imagine that a couple of these men were expecting to receive the promotion. What gives?"

The executive vice president replied, "I can understand why it may seem surprising to you, but let me explain. I've never asked Frank to do anything that he didn't do well. I've never had to go back to check whether he had carried through on a job. When I've asked him to accept a responsibility, he has always been available. Frankly, he has made my job a lot easier for the past several years. As you know, we've had several projects in the company that I got credit for, but Frank did a lot of the spade work on them and pushed them forward. He has been of tremendous assistance to me in helping get things done. I felt that I needed this sort of man to help me more of the time, and I can assure you that he deserved the promotion. Truthfully, he has helped me more than any of the others even though he had less opportunity because of his limited authority."

Your boss wants the type of support and cooperation that will make his job more effective and successful. The man who makes the greatest contribution to this end is likely to be considered best qualified for promotion.

Build friendships. There is a tremendous difference between what other people must do for you and what they are willing to do if they like you and want to be of help. The man who has friends, not just associates, in the company and the community at large can be a far more effective executive. An executive cannot function in a vacuum, but he can accomplish almost anything when he has a team of loyal supporters who want to see him succeed. Personal friendships with people in the community can have a decisive effect on the operation of a business. But it is even more important that a manager have employees on the job who cooperate willingly and work with him toward mutually beneficial goals.

Building friendships is the result of having genuine concern for others. It means giving them confidence in themselves and encouragement to face tomorrow. It is building people up instead of tearing them down. It means making them feel comfortable around you and giving them confidence in your integrity. It stems from good manners and a clear conscience.

Maintain an inquiring mental posture. It's true that we learn most of what we know from others, but tremendous untapped opportunity still exists for original thinking and for the man who questions traditional theories and seeks better ways. Progress is made by those who question general assumptions, who don't resist new theories, and who don't dislike new ideas. Thought has become so standardized that the reaction of friends and competitors to any given proposition can be anticipated. This gives the original thinker the edge in anything he wants to do. It is for this reason that one business fails while another moves forward—the failure is so set in its ways that the competitor can anticipate every move and counteract them. Then, with some original thinking of its own, it moves rapidly out in front.

Robert McNamara, U.S. Secretary of Defense, uses an effective technique in meeting his awesome responsibility as manager of the largest enterprise in the world. He asks: Why? Why is it done this way? Why isn't it done a different way? Why is it necessary to follow this procedure? Why can't a better way be found? Often the only reason a thing is done in a particular way is just that it has always been done that way. Startling changes and improvements can be made by using the questioning technique. The purpose of a questioning attitude is to produce a man who can step back and look objectively at the total activity. The executive who develops an inquiring mind is the one who makes the greatest contribution and the one who deserves to move upward.

Expand your influence. As the executive moves up in management he increases his sphere of influence. First he influences only himself, then a department, then several departments. He must recognize that people change and so do their needs, and he must constantly adjust to these changing needs if employees are to continue to look to him for their goal realization.

The wise supervisor does not stop trying to influence an employee's behavior simply because he has failed to respond. Instead, the supervisor must take the position that although the employee may feel he can get along without the supervisor, the supervisor cannot get along without the goodwill and support of the employee.

The supervisor can expand his area of influence through sympathetic counseling, effective resolving of complaints, development of people, and realistic service to others. Executives who cannot influence people cannot supervise them. And if the breadth and depth of this influence are not enlarged, they do not deserve to move up the management ladder.

Maintain perspective. To be effective, an executive must have the duties and responsibilities of his own job well organized and he must be able to function effectively in relation to other company activities. The best starting point and the best permanent reference point for doing this are a perspective on the job itself and a realistic overall view of the entire company.

Know what your job really covers and the results expected from your department. Analyze the potential of the position and what constitutes ideal performance. It may well be that the scope of your job is larger than the job description. Jobs have a way of changing with time—nothing official, just a shifting with the talents of the individual occupying the position. Don't be satisfied with merely meeting the minimum requirements. Instead, develop your own listing of the key results expected and then exceed them. Be systematic in analyzing what is now being produced and plot long-range plans which will improve results.

Maintaining perspective means keeping the various aspects of the position in proper balance. Most executives have likes and dislikes with relation to their duties and responsibilities. Some like the mechanical or statistical part of the job, which can be measured precisely, and prefer to ignore the less precise areas—those pertaining to training and personnel, for instance. Yet to disregard any significant aspect is to lose essential perspective. The effective executive must keep the whole job in view as well as its individual parts. This perspective allows him to keep all parts of the job moving forward and to guarantee that an effective relationship is maintained with other company activities.

This problem of job balance has been of concern for years in planning middle-management development programs and in moving men to higher levels of management. At beginning levels, supervisors deal with only one department and with restricted responsibility. But take a look at the position of a top manager. He has to be concerned with at least seven major areas of responsibility: purchasing, production, finance, personnel, sales promotion, expense control, and community and customer relations. If he neglects any one of these or fails to do an effective job in any one, the entire operation will be affected adversely. If he expects to grow in management, he must make up his mind to be both knowledgeable and effective in all these areas. The higher he advances in management, the truer this becomes. This is the job perspective that will be necessary if he is to grow into the full responsibility of top management.

MOVE FORWARD AND UPWARD

How does the executive keep moving forward and upward? The answer to this vital question is not complex: What is required is simply a recognition that growth in responsibility and compensation is dependent on increased value to the organization. This value can only be the result of improved ability and the capacity to carry a bigger load of responsibility.

No company president or chief executive has ever been known to complain of having too many good men; rather, the question is: Where do we find enough talented men? For the supervisor who seeks to move upward in management, the following steps deserve attention.

Appraise and improve your own job performance. If your position and the position above yours do not have realistic descriptions of duties, responsibilities, and expected results, the first important step is to develop them. When this has been done with your supervisor and others in the company, you will have a reasonable picture of what you are expected to do and how well you are expected to do it.

After standards have been developed, evaluate and appraise your job performance in relation to these standards. Be realistic and not short-sighted in your own self-evaluation. Whatever advantage there may seem to be in trying to fool other people, there is none in trying the same thing on yourself. Be your own severest critic. Deal harshly with areas where you are not meeting expectations. Discipline yourself to bring about the improvement which the evaluation indicates is needed.

Ask your supervisor to evaluate your performance and assist you with a plan for improvement. Remember that his appraisal is important to your future. If he feels that you are not meeting requirements and that you need to improve in some areas, this is the most important information you can receive. And when he indicates that a change is in order, respond in full measure. No good purpose is served in discovering where improvement is needed unless the improvement is made.

Be guided by facts. Questions are usually more effective than orders. Many people resent being told what to do. However, when asked their opinion and how they think a job can best be handled, they are eager to cooperate. The supervisor can get across his own program through the effective technique of asking questions to get it accepted. Certain pitfalls should be avoided, though—prying, asking embarrassing questions or questions the individual may not be able to answer, cross-examining, and implying that you know something the other person doesn't.

Improve your ability to accomplish results through others. The supervisor's responsibility is to weld a group of ordinary people into a capable and enthusiastic team. When he succeeds, they will give more service, get more pay, and derive more pleasure from the job. He must be able to see possibilities in a person who is just on the edge of failure, to search for and discover the thing that is holding him back—lack of courage, inadequate knowledge, a need for better direction of energies—and guide him skillfully from failure to success.

A technique for getting results through people was expressed in the following way by Charles H. Brower, then president of Batten, Barton, Durstine & Osborn, Inc.:

> What you and I have to do, patiently, and day by day, is to teach those over whom we are given supervision that work can be fun— that the only real reward that life offers is the thrill of achievement, and that the place where achievement amounts to most is on the job. A hole in one isn't half as thrilling as landing a big order—a piece of furniture built in your basement workshop will never be as thrilling as a sales plan that works—a sailfish mounted on your wall will never be quite as exciting as a well-earned promotion.*

Increase your contribution through better decision making. Decision making is the critical test of management—the ability and the courage to reach the right conclusions and take the right course of action, skill in persuading others to cooperate with total dedication, and then follow-through to a successful conclusion.

Decisions must be based on factual information, not hearsay or personal opinion. When factual information is not available, the validity of the decision must depend on the judgment and intuition of the person making the decision. To the casual observer, many decisions experienced executives make may seem to be snap judgments because there has not been time to gather and evaluate the facts. Yet what is snap judgment to the inexperienced can be utilization of experience, superior knowledge, and the skill necessary to coordinate both experience and knowledge into a decision that successfully meets the needs of the occasion.

How do you rate when it comes to the acid test of decision making?

---

* Speech before the National Sales Executives Association Convention, Washington, D. C., May 20, 1958.

Several negative choices are available: Do nothing, do nothing right, let someone else decide, appoint a committee, delay, check the decision with others so if it is unpopular or doesn't work out there will be someone else to blame. On the other hand, you can take the firm and positive approach: accept the responsibility; recognize what needs to be done; make the decision when it needs to be made, without undue delay; and once it has been made, set in motion the action necessary to insure its success.

Fortune magazine has listed business executives, politicians, and military officers as the principal decision makers of the world. A specific technique for decision making was first developed by the military. A former colonel in the Air Force has described the military method as consisting of these five steps:

1. Determine the mission. What is the goal? What is the objective to be accomplished?
2. Describe the situation and courses of action. What supplies, men, and resources are available? What are the possible courses of action?
3. Analyze the various courses of action. What would each require? What consequences and probable results can be anticipated?
4. Estimate how the opposition will probably react. (Napoleon's generals had all gone to the same military schools and their decisions could always be anticipated by the opposition.)
5. Make the best decision. At this point a decision is not a snap judgment but a calculated decision based on experienced judgment, evaluation, and analysis.

Many executives cannot describe their technique for decision making. Some even say that when they think about a problem too much they are likely to make the wrong decision. It is certainly true that the athlete and the military leader do not always have time to stop and ponder every move. Their reactions result from training, drills, and practice. Then, when a situation calls for an almost automatic reaction, the ability to react is there.

The business executive can learn to make decisions by the same techniques. Undue dependence on stereotypes or rigid molds is inadvisable, but the supervisory training technique of role playing and the case method of problem solving provide practice in decision making.

Make your leadership more positive. If a department head has difficulty in getting the people in his department to follow instructions, it may be his own fault. The very manner in which he gives instructions, supervises, and communicates his decisions may suggest he lacks confidence in his own ability to lead. To be successful, leadership must be positive. Requests should be made and instructions should be given with the full expectation that there will be a definite response. An apologetic approach to leadership is doomed to failure.

The executive needs to be confident in order to instill confidence in others. The very nature of his communication and association with his people should justify the confident response of his people. This can be accomplished only through forceful leadership.

Learn to manage yourself. The successful manager of others begins by managing himself. The man who leads must obviously have some general knowledge of what the position requires. But the test of his growth is whether he practices sufficient self-management to bring his fullest potential to bear on the duties and responsibilities of the position. Not lack of ability or knowledge but lack of self-management accounts for the failure of many men to reach the top rungs of leadership. The man who can discipline and manage himself can usually manage others. Further, if a man can channel his own time and energies in a positive direction, it is a reasonable assumption that he will do the same with the resources of the company.

Be the uncommon man. Herbert Hoover had this to say about the common man:

> Among the delusions offered us by fuzzy-minded people is that imaginary creature, the common man. This idea is a cousin of the Soviet proletariat. The uncommon man is to be whittled down to size. This is the negation of individual dignity and a slogan of mediocrity and uniformity.

> The common man dogma may be of use as a vote-getting apparatus. But the greatest strides of human progress have come from uncommon men and women. You have perhaps heard of George Washington, Abraham Lincoln, and Thomas Edison. They were humble in origin, but that was not their greatness.

> The humor of it is that when we get sick, we want an uncommon doctor. When we go to war, we yearn for an uncommon general or

admiral. When we choose the president of a university, we want an uncommon educator.

The imperative need of this nation at all times is the leadership of uncommon men or women. We need men and women who cannot be intimidated, who are not concerned with applause meters, not those who sell tomorrow for cheers today.

Much can be said for the organization man, the man who fits nicely into the stereotyped mold of the executive. But it must also be said that opportunities for such men are extremely limited, because there are so many of them. The higher positions in management are filled by uncommon men who are willing to apply uncommon devotion and effort to their jobs. No company president can draw straws to decide which of five average supervisors to promote; rather, he must find the one who has demonstrated the potential for making an uncommon contribution.

Dare to be uncommon. Be willing to work harder, plan better, think clearer, and achieve greater results. Recognition, prestige, and compensation await the man who rises to uncommon accomplishment.

If the individual is dedicated to climbing the executive ladder, he must not be lured into the fatal sleep of averages. Remember that the average executive is the worst of the best and only the best of the worst. Statistically speaking, the man who has one foot on a hot stove and the other on a block of ice should by the law of averages be comfortable. The ambitious executive remains constantly aware that promotions do not beckon those who are just average.

Executive leadership can be most exciting, challenging, and rewarding to the man who is willing to fulfill the requirements of his position in an uncommon way.

24. Conclusions Worth Applying

EMPHASIS HAS BEEN PLACED on the supervisor's responsibility for results. There can be no real compromise with this obligation—it is his primary function; it is what the company expects in return for his salary. This approach may seem to treat the supervisor's job as one of cold calculation, with little regard for human feeling and with people considered only as cogs in the production machinery. But the fact is that the leader who approaches his job in this way is overlooking his most important responsibility—to be interested in the people he works with, to share their joys and accomplishments, to help them find in their jobs a source of fulfillment. If a supervisor is to achieve results through people, he must remember that people must find satisfaction in their work if they are to give their best efforts to the job and meet its requirements.

The supervisor who misses this point is missing one of the most significant aspects of his job. It is this factor which adds the final dimension to leadership. Few other positions offer the same opportunity for helping people in their personal and professional growth and for sharing in their achievements.

No supervisor should ever assume that his leadership is for his benefit alone. The team of supervisor and supervised should form a partnership. Appropriate leadership benefits the employee; employee performance benefits the supervisor. Each should understand that the achievement of departmental objectives is of mutual benefit. The supervisor who can establish the concept of partnership with his

A supervisor should never assume that his leadership is for his benefit alone.

employee group will be gratified with the overall accomplishment of his partners for progress.

THE MORAL RESPONSIBILITIES OF LEADERSHIP

The most important obligation of leadership is that of teaching by example. Just as the parent cannot escape the responsibility of personal example, neither can the business leader. The attitudes, the work habits, and the very spirit of the supervisor often set the pattern for the employees.

Both doctors and lawyers have a professional code of ethics, and so should the professional executive. He must not disregard the feelings and rights of others. He should be constantly aware that he holds in his hands and under his control the livelihood and an important segment of the life of each employee. Just as the minister treats information given to him as confidential, so must the supervisor. His code of ethics must include keeping promises. He should not make promises lightly, and once he has made them, he is ethically obligated to keep them.

The ethical code of the manager also means accepting responsibility for his decisions and actions. He should welcome this opportunity and not attempt to shun it or shunt it off on his own supervisor or his employees. His position has assigned to it certain duties and responsibilities, and he should meet these to the limit of his ability.

As Americans we recognize that people are entitled to dignity and consideration, deserving of an opportunity for full development, and not to be trifled with or downgraded. People want to be remembered, to be spoken to, to be recognized, and to be considered in such a way that their importance and status are clear. Most people enjoy conversation, especially the opportunity to talk about their accomplishments as well as the accomplishments of those who are close to them. This need affords the supervisor the opportunity to keep in touch with his people—not just with the details of their work, but with other aspects of their personal lives.

Casual conversation and free exchange of information can make both supervisor and employee seem more human; keeping in touch in this manner not only serves individual needs but certainly enhances each person's goal achievement. The supervisor should welcome every opportunity to talk with the employee and to both receive and communicate information of mutual interest.

THE GOAL OF INVOLVEMENT AND PARTICIPATION

Employee participation is one of the most overworked phrases and most underdeveloped activities in the area of leadership. There is little doubt that when employees feel an involvement and are allowed to participate fully, they are better satisfied and put forth greater effort. Yet supervisors excuse their failure to involve employees by saying that it takes too much time, or that it's easier just to make decisions and then give orders. This practice reveals that supervisors often misunderstand or misinterpret the real meaning of individual involvement which encourages participation in establishing and achieving group goals and a sharing of responsibility. Involvement and participation are not limited to physical activity. They include the whole man—his personality, his need to be heard, and his desire to participate in those decisions which affect his life.

Management's concern with employee participation is not solely one of meeting human needs; there is ample evidence that it results in improved job performance. Training sessions are more effective when employees become personally involved. Safety campaigns are more successful when employees feel that they are participating in the planning and decisions.

There is no implication here that all decisions can be made by employee vote. But the supervisor can take the time to sound out employee feeling. He can encourage participation in training. He can take advantage of countless opportunities to encourage employees to satisfy their innate desire to be creative and to function as full-fledged members of the team.

UNLOCKING THE DOORS TO FUTURE GROWTH

The only valid claim to growth an executive has must be that of rendering a genuine service and producing results in the areas of his responsibility. Whatever other factors enter the picture, the solid foundation on which to base an executive career remains the twin bulwarks of quality and quantity of performance. The following keys can unlock the doors to the resources which are essential for executive growth.

The master plan. No structure can be any more attractive or functional than it was designed to be in the blueprint used for its construction. A master plan deserves the careful, systematic, and thorough attention of the ambitious manager. It should be in sufficient detail and of sufficient scope to afford a view of the finished product and to furnish detailed specifications so as to insure that work can move steadily toward the ultimate goal.

The formulation of this plan should be coordinated with those managers who have functional responsibility for its overall results. It should be ambitious enough to assure improvement and growth, but at the same time it should be realistic enough to be within reach.

The tools and techniques of achievement. The builder first views the task before him as a whole, but he then separates it into specific activities, each to be used at the right time and with the tools best suited to each situation.

The supervisor too is a builder in a sense; his task is to structure a productive team. It can be said of his job that the identification and mastery of the tools and techniques of leadership constitute the decisive factors in success or failure. If the leader is to be successful, he must use the right combination of leadership tools and techniques.

Understanding and influencing people. Understanding others begins with an understanding of ourselves; it continues with a recognition of the basic needs and desires of people. Only when there is an understanding of human relationships can the supervisor be effective in his daily job of influencing people toward specific goals.

The factor of human leadership. Every team needs a captain. The direction and distance traveled by any one group are determined by its leader. Top management recognizes that departmental leadership is the most decisive single factor affecting the accomplishments of the department.

Leadership is many things: It is what the leader is and what he does; it is the traits he possesses and exhibits to others; it is the stepping stones he provides for others; it is the enthusiasm and inspiration which he is able to infuse in others; it is the confident and willing support he is able to elicit from others. Expansion of this leadership is the most reliable test of executive growth.

Prescription for job-related problems. Unresolved problems can be as damaging to the goals of a department as a hole in the bow is to a ship's safety and progress. The factors of attitude, causation, motivation, correction, complaints, and change confront the supervisor with potential problems. Once these arise, resolving them requires constant watchfulness, early diagnosis, and skillful handling.

Although their influence can be negative, problems can also be used by the supervisor to exert a positive influence on job performance. As in the case of every other job influence and resource, the supervisor has the responsibility of turning these problems to the most favorable advantage. But the best way to deal with problems is to prevent them.

Growth through the development of people. The installation of new machinery often necessitates the expenditure of large sums of money, and the overhaul of procedures may require major and often complex changes. However, the daily, gradual development of people involves no major outlay of cash or disruption of routine. Rather, it can increase results, perhaps not dramatically but steadily and continually. Everything the employee learns, each training activity, and every improvement in skill should result in improved performance. This can be one of the most dependable and economical keys to departmental progress.

Enlarging the span of leadership. Not every supervisory job can offer growth in the amounts and at the rate of speed which will satisfy the ambitious executive. Perhaps his growth needs can be realized only through transfer to a larger department, the supervision of two or more departments, or promotion to a higher level of responsibility. In preparation for promotions of this type the supervisor should pay particular attention to delegating responsibility to others, training an assistant, and improving communication. To disregard these vital areas of growth is to squander the opportunity to continue up the executive ladder.

The executive in the mirror. It is common knowledge that "it's not what you know but whom you know" that determines whether you get ahead in business. But the "who" is the man in the mirror. This man more than any other will determine the future growth and progress of the executive. Every man must shape, control, and determine his own job performance and his own executive growth. Get to know yourself, recognize your strengths, identify those traits and handicaps which will interfere with your executive growth. Discipline yourself in accordance with your own needs. And develop self-confidence in order to keep moving forward. You hold the keys to your own success; don't be satisfied until your goal has been reached.

The future. Time is the clay with which the future is molded. The present is the time when the executive must improve his skills and acquire new ones; now is his opportunity to show proof of his executive ability. Time cannot be borrowed, stored, or stopped, but it can be ignored and squandered. Time cannot be reclaimed in order to change what is to what might have been. Time ought not to be laurels on which to rest or failures over which to weep. Time offers benefits, through experience gained, for those wise enough to be guided by its message. The future is opportunity itself. If each individual thought of time in terms of the present being chopped off hour by hour and day by day, and forever lost, he might have a more realistic appreciation of the value of time. Each day wasted is one less in which to make of his future what he wishes it to be.

BUILDING THE STEPS TO SUCCESS

The great wall of China was built thick and high to keep invaders out. Those who built it considered it insurmountable. But invaders had only to build steps in strategic places and they could quickly scale the wall that took thousands of men countless years to build.

Similarly, from some points of view the problems of leadership appear insurmountable. From others, these problems are only obstructing walls which must be scaled. One man comes to such a wall, stops, sits, and contemplates his cruel fate; another builds steps. It is the man who scales the walls who is discharging the responsibility of leadership. To the capable executive *problems have a way of becoming goals and opportunities.*

Success is not available at discount prices. More people could be successful if they were willing to pay the high price in painstaking preparation, long days of hard work, and perhaps even sleepless nights of problem solving. Creative genius and leadership success seldom result from strokes of luck; they are more often built on the solid rock of effort, tenacity, and determination.

Admiral "Bull" Halsey is supposed to have said about heroes,

"There are no great men, only great challenges that ordinary men are forced by circumstances to meet." It is opportunity which enables ordinary men to rise to greatness. There can be no better proving ground of greatness than a position of leadership in business and industry.

*   *   *

Much of what is related here might properly be tagged "Mistakes I Have Made." This book has been an attempt to share both failures and successes which have revealed a surer route toward the goal of results through people. It is hoped that you will use them to move more effectively and rapidly toward your own goal.

One final reminder: Be open-minded. Seek better ways. Move forward. The future holds a potential of unlimited success for you—if you are willing to bear the cost in order to reap the rewards.

The ultimate goal of executive leadership is its overall contribution to the employee, the company, and the whole of human society in which it functions.

About the Author

RAY A. KILLIAN is vice president and director of personnel and public relations for the group of 400 Belk stores. He received his undergraduate degree at Lenoir Rhyne College and did graduate and special study at the University of North Carolina, George Washington University, and Harvard University Graduate School of Business Administration.

Mr. Killian was associated with the Committee on Scientific Research and Development, Washington, D.C., and he was personnel director for the North Carolina Department of Revenue and later for Belk Brothers Company before assuming his present position. He has taught at Queens College and the Graduate School of the University of Virginia system. He has conducted many training programs and seminars for managers and supervisory personnel. He is a frequent speaker before local and national audiences regarding management leadership subjects and has written numerous articles for national publication. He has been chapter president and national director of the Society for Advancement of Management and has served as president of the Personnel Directors Association and on the Board of Directors for the National Retail Merchants Association.